Psychoanalysis

and Literary Process

Edited by

FREDERICK CREWS

Winthrop Publishers, Inc.

Cambridge, Massachusetts

© **1970 by Winthrop Publishers, Inc.,** *17 Dunster Street*
Cambridge, Massachusetts 02138

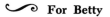 For Betty

↪ PREFACE

The following essays grew out of a graduate seminar in psycho-analytic criticism which I first offered at Berkeley in 1967. This book is not, however, intended as a monument to my course. The authors represented here all brought a prior psychoanalytic interest to their work with me, and their talents were such as to make any teacher imagine that he had happened upon a magic educational formula. As I explain in my own essay, psychoanalytic theory does not constitute such a formula. Yet remarkable things do occur when people who have provisionally agreed to share psychoanalytic as-sumptions look at a literary text together. The seminar gave each of us an ongoing corroboration of the reality behind psychoanalytic concepts—a corroboration which, for good Freudian reasons, seems perennially necessary even to the most committed mind. But the present essays resulted from solitary effort, and their value derives substantially from long and deep acquaintance with the texts under discussion. The last thing we would claim is that Freudianism can become a shortcut to such knowledge.

Our book has two purposes, to demonstrate the range and po-tential usefulness of psychoanalytic criticism and to assist readers who are disposed to practice it themselves. My introductory essay deals with some of the more common academic resistances to Freud-ian discourse and touches on some of its pitfalls, but the other

essays, which are highly detailed, have spared me the task of prov-
ing that psychoanalytic criticism is feasible. The theoretical grounding of such criticism cannot be covered in any single book. We
have, however, compiled a short bibliographical guide (page 284)
that could serve as a more efficient and graduated introduction to
psychoanalytic problems than we ourselves received. Recalling that
theory only becomes meaningful when it explains something experienced, we think the case for psychoanalytic criticism can best
be made through successful instances of its use. Readers are invited
to follow these essays closely and ask whether their sense of the
books being discussed is not significantly enriched in the process.
The essays are arranged, not chronologically or by merit, but in a
very approximate order of accessibility, with the more complex
and technical arguments coming toward the end of the volume.
None of the essays, including my own, is meant to speak for the
views of the contributors as a group.

Many kindnesses, public and private, have facilitated the making
of this book. All of us feel indebted to the other members of our
seminar, several of whose papers were omitted solely for reasons
of space. My own work has been especially encouraged by Dr. Jose
Barchilon and Dr. Edward M. Weinshel and by Leonard Manheim,
Simon O. Lesser, and Norman N. Holland, and my essay has bene-
fited from advice offered by C. L. Barber, Noam Chomsky, Dr. Alex
Comfort, Dr. Bernard C. Meyer, Norman Rabkin, Mark Shechner,
Michael Shriber, Henry Nash Smith, Lee Sterrenburg, Gardner
Stout, and Dr. Robert S. Wallerstein—none of whom is at all responsible for the essay's deficiencies. Since my essay departs somewhat from the path established by Professor Holland's *The Dynamics of Literary Response,* I should like to emphasize that book's
unmatched clarity and rigor.

A year at the Center for Advanced Study in the Behavioral Sciences, Stanford, financed partly by the Center and partly by the
American Council of Learned Societies, spurred my interest in
psychoanalytic matters. I am also grateful to the Regents of the
University of California for a Faculty Research Fellowship and a
salary supplement during a sabbatical leave. David Leverenz wishes
to thank the Maybelle McLeod Lewis Memorial Fund for support
of his work.

Frederick Crews

Berkeley, California
December 1969

~ CONTENTS

ONE ꙮ ANAESTHETIC CRITICISM

FREDERICK CREWS

L'homme s'affirme
par l'infirmité.—Victor Hugo

I.

The critical essays in this book have in common an overt reference
to hypotheses and rules of procedure that were neither derived from
literature nor primarily meant to apply to literature. Such criticism
can go wrong in several ways: by using weak hypotheses, by using
strong and pertinent ones in too mechanical a fashion, or by warping
literary evidence to meet presuppositions. The recourse to "extraliterary" theory is not in itself, however, a methodological error.
The simple fact that literature is made and enjoyed by human minds
guarantees its accessibility to study in terms of broad principles of
psychic and social functioning.

This point would seem too obvious to dwell on, but it is widely
resisted among the very group to whom it should be most axiomatic,
professional students of literature. Most literary scholars observe an
informal taboo on methods that would plainly reveal literary determinants. Such methods are considered intrinsically antihumanistic, and criticism systematically employing them is regarded as

ipso facto shortsighted. Academic critics often circumvent the taboo by disguising or compromising their explanatory inclination, thus earning a hearing at the expense of some consistency and clarity. But the prohibition itself deserves scrutiny, not only because it is intellectually indefensible but also because its operation has grave consequences for the teaching of literature.

The majority view of deterministic schemes was aptly conveyed by Northrop Frye, one of the most influential of living critics, as he gave assurance that his own theory of literature would not borrow its conceptual framework from sources outside literature itself. Any extrinsic system, he said,

> gives us, in criticism, the fallacy of what in history is called determinism, where a scholar with a special interest in geography or economics expresses that interest by the rhetorical device of putting his favorite study into a causal relationship with whatever interests him less. Such a method gives one the illusion of explaining one's subject while studying it, thus wasting no time. It would be easy to compile a long list of such determinisms in criticism, all of them, whether Marxist, Thomist, liberal-humanist, neo-Classical, Freudian, Jungian, or existentialist, substituting a critical attitude for criticism, all proposing, not to find a conceptual framework for criticism within literature, but to attach criticism to one of a miscellany of frameworks outside it. The axioms and postulates of criticism, however, have to grow out of the art it deals with. The first thing the literary critic has to do is to read literature, to make an inductive survey of his own field and let his critical principles shape themselves solely out of his knowledge of that field.[1]

Insofar as this statement pleads against replacing sensitive criticism with a crude ransacking of literature to illustrate hypotheses about other matters, it is beyond dispute. More is meant, however. Frye is asserting that the critic, if he is to retain his objectivity, must derive his principles "solely" from his inductive survey of literary works. The point recurs insistently in *Anatomy of Criticism* and is

1. *Anatomy of Criticism: Four Essays* (Princeton, 1957), pp. 6–7; copyright © 1957 by Princeton University Press; reprinted by permission of Princeton University Press.

extended into a cautionary view of *all* "axioms and postulates," whatever their source:

> There are no definite positions to be taken in chemistry or philology, and if there are any to be taken in criticism, criticism is not a field of genuine learning. . . . One's "definite position" is one's weakness, the source of one's liability to error and prejudice, and to gain adherents to a definite position is only to multiply one's weakness like an infection. (Frye, p. 19)

> The modern student of critical theory is faced with a body of rhetoricians who speak of texture and frontal assaults, with students of history who deal with traditions and sources, with critics using material from psychology and anthropology, with Aristotelians, Coleridgeans, Thomists, Freudians, Jungians, Marxists, with students of myths, rituals, archetypes, metaphors, ambiguities, and significant forms. The student must either admit the principle of polysemous meaning, or choose one of these groups and then try to prove that all the others are less legitimate. The former is the way of scholarship, and leads to the advancement of learning; the latter is the way of pedantry. (Frye, p. 72)

These lines seemingly welcome, but actually discourage, the use of explanatory ideas in criticism. "Polysemous meaning" is recognized only in order to close off the possibility that any one line of investigation might be fruitfully pursued to its end. To have a definite position, no matter how correct, is to be "infected" with weakness, prejudice, and error, whereas to be tolerantly indifferent toward all definite positions, presumably including mistaken ones, is "the way of scholarship." Frye is quite emphatic about this. "All that the disinterested critic can do," when presented with the "color-filter" of an externally derived critical attitude, "is to murmur politely that it shows things in a new light and is indeed a most stimulating contribution to criticism" (Frye, p. 7). Frye himself illustrates his recommendation by glancingly alluding to a variety of frameworks, always with an understanding that they lie beyond the true business of criticism.

Professor Frye's widely accepted imperative, *Do not stray outside literature,* must be seen as territorial rather than intellectual. The avowed idea is to avoid indebtedness to other people's specialties, "for in that case the autonomy of criticism would . . . disappear, and the whole subject would be assimilated to something else" (Frye, p. 6). Once this apprehension is grasped, one can predict the degree of Frye's actual hospitality toward different lines of study. Works can, for example, be safely classified according to their patent resemblances and differences, but in order to say how those features came into being we would have to talk about motives, and there would be no assurance that the motives in question would prove properly "literary." Beneath, let us say, the urge to write an epic or a masque we might come across other urges at once more private and more universal than the literary taxonomist could account for. Thus it is not surprising that Frye repeatedly admonishes the disinterested critic to beware of all psychological explanations.

But this causal vacuum cannot be sustained; a critic who forswears deterministic thinking will inevitably fall back on a covert, wishful determinism bordering on tautology. In Frye's case this is particularly clear. "Poetry can only be made out of other poems," he says, "novels out of other novels. Literature shapes itself, and is not shaped externally . . ." (Frye, p. 97). "The true father or shaping spirit of the poem is the form of the poem itself, and this form is a manifestation of the universal spirit of poetry . . ." (Frye, p. 98); ". . . the central greatness of *Paradise Regained,* as a poem, is . . . the greatness of the theme itself, which Milton *passes on* to the reader from his source" (Frye, p. 96; italics in original); "the real difference between the original and the imitative poet is simply that the former is more profoundly imitative" (Frye, p. 97). Literature makes literature which makes literature; tradition itself is the fount of all inspiration and value. No questions need be asked about how the world's great stories gained their appeal, for the stories themselves are motivational forces. Indeed, Frye dares to hope that even the idea of the Oedipus complex will someday be exposed as nothing more than a misplaced compliment to the power of the Oedipus story: perhaps we shall decide "that the myth of Oedipus informed and gave structure to some psychological investigations at this point. *Freud would in that case be exceptional only in having been well read enough to spot the source of the myth*" (Frye, p. 353; italics added).

This vision of literature as its own progenitor is very far from being a unique indulgence. It is, in fact, a common fantasy among writers, a wish that art could be self-fathered, self-nurturing, self-referential, purified of its actual origins in discontent; and it is no less common among critics. Frye found a use for it in his brilliant study of Blake, virtually annihilating his identity as a critic while fusing himself with Blake's obscure private reality.[2] In that case a rapt surrender to the poet's wish for total imaginative control over the world provided an opportunity for valuable clarification. But such reverence for the all-sufficient text is obviously too narrow a foundation for a whole theory of criticism, and when Frye turns lawgiver he ends by providing an apology for more timid work, indeed for the most routine academic drudgery.

It is important to see that such a result is dictated by the very project of severing literature from its determinants. As Murray Krieger has shown, Frye follows the Arnoldian and Eliotic line of argument which makes artistic unity a substitute for the lost religious matrix, and which decides that in an age of dissociated sensibility this unity must be propped by a body of consciously appropriated belief.[3] Frye's novelty is to fortify the supposedly "anagogic" universe of a poem, not with overt dogmas, but with the rest of literature itself, considered as a great phalanx of works aligned by genre and period. The receding sea of faith has at least left *this* much behind. But as Freud said of Dostoevsky's final piety, lesser minds have reached the same position with less effort. Frye's emphasis on the autonomy of tradition and his simple equation of merit (as in *Paradise Regained*) with borrowed thematic content are all too congenial to critics who could never have written a page of *Fearful Symmetry*. While few professors would say outright that "literature shapes itself," fewer still have ventured beyond the confines of tradition and convention. Indeed, the fear of "going too far" with any hypothesis about literature has proved considerably stronger than the fear of arriving nowhere. Frye's suggestion that Freud himself may have made his name through motif-spotting, a talent we already encourage in our literary trainees, must be reassuring to scholars who would prefer not to raise any awkward questions.

Most literary curricula seem to rest on the assumption, implicit

2. *Fearful Symmetry: A Study of William Blake* (Princeton, 1947).
3. Murray Krieger, "The Critical Legacy of Matthew Arnold; Or, The Strange Brotherhood of T. S. Eliot, I. A. Richards, and Northrop Frye," *Southern Review*, n.s. V (April 1969), 457–474.

throughout *Anatomy of Criticism*, that the scholar-critic need only become conversant with a certain list of primary and secondary texts in order to begin contributing to knowledge. He should of course be trained in rhetoric and bibliography, but no mention is made of interpretive procedures for bringing some order into the wildly variant subjective responses evoked by any given work. Though first-rate critics like Wilson, Empson, Trilling, and Burke have not hesitated to make "extraliterary" sense of literature, the idea that we positively *ought* to do so is conceived as a threat to scholarly balance. The critic already knows what he is doing and will be all right if he can just keep himself from being drawn too much toward either what Frye has called "the myth of concern" or "the myth of detachment." (It was left for Northrop Frye to identify and endorse the ultimate English-department stance, detachment from the myth of detachment.)

Professor Frye claims that the mental process involved in literary criticism "is as coherent and progressive as the study of science," and he expects that his colleagues' efforts will be revealed as a unified scientific system, "the main principles of which are as yet unknown to us" (Frye, pp. 10–11). This discovery would, as he says, "certainly be convenient" (Frye, p. 11), and many academics will forgive him for going on to treat it as already established. Unfortunately, there seems to be no objective basis for this optimism. The history of literary study is transparently a history of intellectual and political fashion, never more so than in recent formalism and neo-religious moralism. Critics have arrived at no agreement whatever about the meaning of beauty, the criteria of value, or even the grossest facts about books and authors, such as whether Shakespeare was or wasn't stoical, whether Milton was or wasn't of the Devil's party, whether Blake was crazy or visionary or both, whether *The Golden Bowl* is an example of self-transcendence or of colossal arrogance and evasion. Unless one had decided in advance to find criticism "coherent and progressive," he would be hard pressed to justify calling it an intellectual discipline at all.

Such a justification would have to show that literary study, like other disciplines, is concerned with the differential evaluation of various styles of inquiry according to their relative success in making sense of the objects studied. But not only is this winnowing process singularly missing from criticism, it is condemned outright as needlessly zealous, intolerant, and unliterary. Each critic is free to adopt the "approach" that suits his fancy, and most of the approaches prove to be little more than analogical vocabularies lending an air of exactitude to whatever the critic feels like asserting. This is precisely why Professor Frye can urge us not to "choose one . . . and then try to prove that all the others are less legitimate." What does it matter whether we call ourselves Thomists or Aristotelians or phenomenologists, provided we don't take our method too solemnly or show impatience with our neighbor's? *Anatomy of Criticism* is in part a book of professional etiquette, expressing and inculcating the civility that makes literary eclecticism possible. That this civility is in practice anti-intellectual has gone unnoticed—a fact that begins to suggest the extent to which "English" has deafened itself to criteria of knowledge.

The tolerance of literary scholars for "polysemous meaning" is understandably strained by methods that claim to deal in causes and effects. It disappears altogether as soon as such a method is applied in earnest. A critic can allude to Marx now and then, but he had better not get too interested in exposing the class apologetics in cherished texts, much less in other critics' theories of meaning. Similarly, it is a badge of broad-mindedness to season a conventional argument with references to Freud, but the references will be calmly received only if they remain honorific. One may, to be sure, safely credit an author (even a pre-Freudian one) with having made use of "Freudian insights." This is not psychoanalytic discourse but a subtle prophylaxis against such discourse, for the fantasy materials that a Freudian would have ascribed to the unconscious source of the work itself have been promoted to the realm of conscious art, where all of us feel at home. To say that an author has endowed his hero with Freudian traits is no more psychoanalytic a statement than to say that he has evoked a pleasant landscape; in both cases the question of unconscious influence over the whole text is being avoided. And this avoidance is the minimal condition a critic must fulfill if he doesn't want to be regarded as unbalanced.

Thus there is less Freudian criticism extant than one might think, and most of it continues to be received either with hostile alarm or with those polite murmurs that Professor Frye advises us to utter in the presence of the single-minded. The reasons for this reception overlap with those explaining the virtual ban on Marxian analysis. Both Freud and Marx ask us to think about matters that not only partake óf alien disciplines, but are profoundly unsettling in their own right. While Freud may seem politically less iconoclastic than Marx, his method is in one sense more radical; it leaves the critic with less ground on which to strike a righteous attitude. Psychoanalytic principles bring into question the very possibility that a critic's relation to his texts could be fundamentally rational and disinterested.

Resistance to such self-appraisal assumes many forms, but it almost never assumes the form of meeting Freudian propositions on evidential grounds. From Wellek and Warren's icy and confused chapter on "Literature and Psychology" in 1949 to the present day, it is next to impossible to find a clear and informed discussion of psychoanalysis by a critic who does not employ it.[4] One hears instead that the Freudian revolution was won long ago and that we needn't make a fuss over it now, or that psychoanalysis has been replaced by any number of better systems, or that it neglects creativity or communication or religion or society or existential anguish or aesthetic textures. Such half-truths are usually followed by a retreat to homespun moralized psychology or to nebulous, dignified, quasi-metaphysical concepts such as Jung's, which, far from seeking to "explain" religion and art, seek to declare their sublime immunity from explanation.

Indeed, Jung has proved a godsend for many critics troubled by the menace of psychoanalysis, for he spent the better part of a lifetime coping with that menace in seductive and readily adaptable ways. Even someone who applies Jung's system with unfashionable explicitness and persistence will find himself free to retain an elevated notion of literature. To invoke that system is of course a revealing mark of indifference toward evidence, for as Edward Glover demonstrated, Jung's hypotheses are logically unnecessary and mutually contradictory; his methodological stance shifted con-

---

4. René Wellek and Austin Warren, *Theory of Literature* (New York, 1949), pp. 75–88. For more up-to-date thinking, purportedly sympathetic, see Lee T. Lemon, *The Partial Critics* (New York, 1965), p. 94: "Neither proper psychological definition of *archetype* nor the relative soundness of Freud's and Jung's views of the content of the unconscious need concern the literary critic directly. The only significant fact is that elements do get into poetry which can best be explained by psychoanalytic theory." The likelihood that *some* theory is potentially useful exhausts the critic's curiosity; since he has no way of choosing between Freud and Jung, he calls them both "psychoanalytic" and drops the subject.

tinually between claims of adherence to the strictest clinical principles and claims of rapport with ineffable mysteries; and for these reasons and others his version of neo-Platonism has made scant impact on any field of serious inquiry.[5] These, however, are points of small concern to the lapsed-religious humanist, whose own hopeful guesses about the uplifting value of literature are as fanciful as Jung's. Modern men in search of a soul can make wide allowance for one another's poetic leaps of faith.

This is not to say that critics who openly espouse Jungianism will escape the disapproval of their more cautious colleagues. The latter, failing to appreciate the circularity of Jung's mental journey, its intent of rescuing spiritual and cultural matters from destructive scrutiny, will find in the use of Jungian terms yet another instance of going too far. But because the offense is not so much empirical as social, it can be forestalled merely by using Jung's ideas without attribution or with suitable disclaimers. Token gestures of skepticism can become a means of escape from considerations of plausibility— as, for example, in Professor Frye's statement that the collective unconscious is "an unnecessary hypothesis in literary criticism" (Frye, p. 112), even while he has been developing an immanent and impersonal notion of creativity that seems to demand that very hypothesis.

Since good criticism appears to be largely a matter of sympathy, sensitivity, and pertinent learning, one might reasonably ask whether such vagueness over theory has much importance. Yet it does not seem too venturesome to propose that all scholars, even literary ones, could profit from being clear about what they believe and what they are doing. There is also a possibility that what many of them are doing is wrong both in its premises and in its educational impact. Behind the public façade of eclecticism there may lie a dogmatic avoidance of unacknowledged aspects of literary experience; behind the tactful withdrawal from theories, a disregard for knowledge; behind the celebration of traditional themes, an intolerance toward students who want to come to grips with their deepest responses.

These possibilities are in fact widely realized. The cardinal features of professional critical training as most of us know it are a suppression of affect and a displacement of attention from artistic

5. See Glover, *Freud or Jung* (London, 1950).

process onto motifs, genres, literary history (conceived not as the study of how books are influenced by objective conditions, but as chronology, borrowings, gossip, and a disembodied "history of ideas"), and the busywork of acquiring the skills and attitudes needed for circumspect research.[6] Actual criticism, in the familiar sense of making a case for the superiority of some works to others, is frowned upon as amateurishly subjective. Since sheer acquaintance with the body of Anglo-American literature is supremely valued, emphasis is laid on "working up" the designated genres and periods without concern over how literature moves us. As Professor Frye says with some enthusiasm, after showing how we can trace the devices of pastoral elegy from the Bible and the early Church and Theocritus and Vergil through Sidney, Spenser, Shakespeare, Milton, Shelley, Arnold, Whitman, and Dylan Thomas, "we can get a whole liberal education simply by picking up one conventional poem and following its archetypes as they stretch out into the rest of literature" (Frye, p. 100).[7]

One could hardly wish for a more vivid statement of the prevailing academic faith; all that need be added is that nobody believes it except those who propagate it. By now the humanizing pretensions of traditional literary study seem to have been questioned by everyone but its official custodians. But so long as the field prizes gentility over principled inquiry, no critique of those pretensions is likely to make much headway; one always runs against the tacit agreement that curators of culture needn't bother with ideas except as indulgences of taste or fashion.

At present it is generally true that students who reject this consensus must either feign acceptance of it or drop out of school. The survivors and inheritors of literary training tend to be those best adapted to dull, safe, provincial work, while the more creative and inquisitive students, having squandered valuable years on the graduate regimen expecting that it *must* have something to do with

6. On these matters see Louis Kampf's essay-review of three books of literary history in *History and Theory*, VI (1967), 72–88. See also R. J. Kaufmann, "On Knowing One's Place: A Humanistic Meditation," *Daedalus*, Summer 1969, pp. 699–713, and Allen Grossman, "Teaching Literature in a Discredited Civilization," *Massachusetts Review*, X (Summer 1969), 419–432.

7. Frye's "archetype" is not quite the same as Jung's; it is merely any "typical or recurring image" in literary tradition, and archetypal analysis is consequently "the study of conventions and genres" (Frye, p. 99).

the life of the imagination, are mastered at last by despair.[8] Nor is the despair confined to students. The occupational disease of "English," rarely acknowledged until recently, is a debilitating fear that literary scholarship as we have been practicing it is a useless and elitist pastime. If the fear is somewhat exaggerated, the exaggeration nevertheless springs from an entirely understandable bad conscience.

II.

The answer, then, to the question whether it is antihumanistic to look outside literature for principles of literary understanding must be a further question: What is meant by humanism? The humanism that purports to defend classical and Judeo-Christian values by cherishing the texts in which those values supposedly reside is indeed jeopardized by extraliterary knowledge, but such a humanism amounts to little more than the confusion of a book list with an education, and its practical results are hardly worth preserving. Suppose, however, that humanism were taken to mean a concern for knowing (and protecting) man as an evolved species, embarked on a unique and possibly self-abbreviated experiment in the substitution of learning for instinct. In that case there would be no need to build walls between one discipline and all others out of fear that the alleged autonomy of one's specialty might be challenged. On the contrary: the search for universals underlying all cultures and traditions would be everyone's business, and proof that one category of human production, such as literature, is functionally consistent with others would be welcomed as significant.

The starting point of this humanism might be a comparison of man to the nearest primates. Such a comparison seems at present to indicate that man's emergence was accompanied by the suppression of much of his forerunner's patterned behavior, the prolongation of his infantile dependency, the postponement of his sexual maturity but also a rich complication and intensification of his sex life, and the diversion of part of this heightened sexuality into sub-

8. It is supremely ironic that some frustrated students, deducing that any intellectual effort must be inimical to their neglected feelings, are now turning against "the mind" and discovering an ally in C. G. Jung—the Jung of numinosity, astrology, numerology, augury, alchemy, and the vulgarized Mysterious East.

stitutive aims and bonds. The delay and detour of instinctual discharge, while not in themselves an explanation of man's capacity to form concepts and modify his behavior experientially, are almost certainly preconditions for it; yet this same interference with animal function dooms man to self-disgust and neurosis, even making normal mating a precarious achievement for him. Each individual must recapitulate for himself, as if it had never been done before, the species' accommodation to social discipline, and this accommodation is always grudging, never finally settled before the moment of death. A true appreciation of man's works would take note of the renunciations and risks they inevitably entail.

Many lines of study could contribute to such an appreciation, but the postulates of Freudian psychoanalysis would be bound to command interest, for they alone have weighed the motivational effects of man's emergence as a species.[9] This was not Freud's original intent, but it was what he stumbled upon, with a disoriented retreat to fabulous reasoning, when he grasped the astonishing sameness of the repressed unconscious across all recorded eras and civilizations. Whatever its therapeutic or even its conceptual disadvantages, only psychoanalysis has registered the psychic costs involved in man's prolonged dependency and his improvising of culture out of thwarted desire.

Man, in a Freudian view, is the animal destined to be overimpressed by his parents, and neurosis is comprehensible as "abnormal attachment to the past."[10] Freud discovered that human beings can neither freely accept nor freely deny the parental demand that sexual and aggressive urges be tamed. All men, he saw, struggle not only against unregenerate impulses but also against their guilt for continuing to harbor those impulses. The fantasies and modes of infantile striving corresponding to the earliest experiences of nutrition, social training, and genital assertion are never wholly overcome

9. This point is elaborated by Weston La Barre, "Family and Symbol," in George F. Wilbur and Warner Muensterberger, eds., *Psychoanalysis and Culture: Essays in Honor of Géza Róheim* (New York, 1967), pp. 156–167. La Barre's *The Human Animal* (Chicago and London, 1960) and Alex Comfort's *The Nature of Human Nature* (New York, 1968) are helpful books for the layman.
10. Freud, "Five Lectures on Psycho-Analysis," *The Standard Edition of the Complete Psychological Works of Sigmund Freud*, ed. James Strachey, et al. (hereafter abbreviated S.E.), 24 vols. (London, 1953–   ), XI, 17.

and are reactivated when later crises strain the adaptive resources that have been pieced together through a trauma-marked development. It is not so much man's mortality as his inability to keep from being haunted by his repressed longings that makes him "a baby who is afraid of being left alone in the dark." [11] The prevalence of mass as well as individual delusion, the tendency of groups to unleash murderous hostility against other groups that have been projectively designated as embodying banished wishes, the orgies of ascetic penance and the rages for spiritual or material perfection that occupy much of recorded history exemplify the more general rule that men, tormented by the persistence of what they have forsworn, necessarily *regress together*.[12] They do so at their best as well as at their worst. A pooling of fantasies to impose bearable contours on the world seems to be a minimal requisite for all human achievement, even the achievement of those who work alone. By sanctioning certain regressions a culture enables its members to *reculer pour mieux sauter*.

This perspective indicates that the primary function of art may not be instructive or decorative or sedative. Originating in what Ernst Kris called a "regression in the service of the ego," [13] art uses symbolic manipulations to reconcile competing pressures. The artist is someone who provisionally relaxes the censorship regnant in waking life, forgoes some of his society's characteristic defenses, and allows the repressed a measure of representation, though (as in strictly unconscious symptom-formation) only in disguised and compromised form. His social role and his own equilibrium dictate a sign of victory for the ego, if not in "happy endings" then in the triumph of form over chaos, meaning over panic, mediated claims over naked conflict, purposeful action over sheer psychic spillage. In this sense the making and the apprehension of art works reenact

11. Géza Róheim, *The Origin and Function of Culture* (New York, 1943), p. 100.
12. See especially Erik H. Erikson, *Young Man Luther: A Study in Psychoanalysis and History* (New York, 1958) and *Childhood and Society* (2nd ed.; New York, 1963); and Norman Cohn, *The Pursuit of the Millennium* (Fairlawn, N.J., 1957) and *Warrant for Genocide: The Myth of the Jewish World Conspiracy and the Protocols of the Elders of Zion* (London, 1967). The last of these books may remind us that more than a methodological quarrel stands between those who analyze the projective content of myths and those who celebrate them as awesome powers.
13. See *Psychoanalytic Explorations in Art* (London, 1953).

the entire human project of making a tenuous cultural order where none existed before.

Assuming for the moment that this view is right, we can see that much "impersonal" literary criticism and theory tends to isolate and redouble the defensive activity in literature while ignoring its barely mastered elements of fantasy, desire, and anxiety. A criticism that explicitly or implicitly reduces art to some combination of moral content and abstract form and genre conventions is literally an anaesthetic criticism. It insulates the critic and his readers from a threat of affective disturbance—a threat that is perfectly real, for there is no reason to suppose that a reader's ego will prove more flexible and capacious than the artist's was. All literary criticism aims to make the reading experience more possible for us, but anaesthetic criticism assumes that this requires keeping caged the anxieties that the artist set free and then recaptured. The effect is often to transform the artist from a struggling fellow mortal into an authority figure, a dispenser of advice about virtue and harmony. "They all swear by the name of the great invalid," Thomas Mann said of any major writer's admirers, "thanks to whose madness they no longer need to be mad." [14]

Someone who wants to look more closely into literature's buried contest between impulse and inhibition will require a method for interpreting his own responses. As a richly overdetermined compromise formation, an art work can only be obliquely and dialectically truthful; so, too, our reaction to it will be a compromise demanded not only by the work's conflicting signals but also by the habitual bias of our ego. The nearest approximation to critical objectivity would seem to consist of gauging those factors both theoretically and intimately and of applying in reverse the principles by which artistic effects came about. This involves open preconceptions about psychic structure, disposition, and defenses and an expectation that certain thematic strands will prove important to follow because of their probable roots in early psychic development. Perhaps the key anticipation of psychoanalytic criticism is that art will borrow some of its real internal unity from repressed material, which "proliferates in the dark" in producing linked derivatives.[15]

Such preconceptions can of course be stigmatized as reduction-

14. Quoted by Roy P. Basler, *Sex, Symbolism, and Psychology in Literature* (New Brunswick, N.J., 1948), p. 4.
15. Freud, "Repression," *S.E.*, XIV, 149.

istic, but all systematic research is comparably governed; the only logical way of getting beyond common-sense impressions is to sharpen one's focus and then see whether new evidence has come into view and an intelligible order has been revealed. To apply deep-structural rules to literary analysis is no more intrinsically reductionistic than to apply them to the study of language.[16] The establishing of predictable patterns can become a basis for showing the intelligibility of expressions that seemed inert and arbitrary because the wrong questions were being asked about them. Thus the validation of a psychoanalytically oriented criticism rests on whether, at its best, it can make fuller sense of literary texts than could the most impressive instances of a rival criticism.

The likelihood of this result rests on the psychoanalytic anticipation that even the most anomalous details in a work of art will prove psychically functional. Being at bottom a theory of how conflicting demands are adjusted and merged, psychoanalysis is quite prepared for literature's mixed intentions, dissociations of affect from ideational content, hints of atonement for uncommitted acts, bursts of vindictiveness and sentimentality, and ironies that seem to occupy some middle ground between satire and self-criticism. In much literary commentary such phenomena are either overlooked or treated as nuisances to be forgiven or condemned, yet they are pervasive. ("A novel," said Randall Jarrell, "is a prose narrative of some length that has something wrong with it."[17]) The fact that

16. Indeed, the theoretical difference between Chomsky's linguistic rationalism and Skinner's linguistic behaviorism is entirely parallel to the difference between a psychoanalytic view of literature and an antimotivational view that treats any given work as a product of "influences" derived in an unknown manner from previous works. Like innate linguistic capacity, innate psychic disposition must be posited to account for ascertainable regularities. This is not, of course, to say that Chomsky's refutation of Skinner justifies Freud. The point is that a relatively "constrained" notion of psychic uniformity may prove flexible where a relatively "free" notion breaks down. Skinner's shunning of hypotheses about linguistic capacity leaves him with no choice but to ascribe an incredible causative weight to the mere hearing of words and sentences; so, too, literary theorists who sidestep the unconscious often end by deifying tradition and memory. See Noam Chomsky, "A Review of B. F. Skinner's *Verbal Behavior*," in Jerry A. Fodor and Jerrold J. Katz, eds., *The Structure of Language: Readings in the Philosophy of Language* (Englewood Cliffs, N.J., 1964), pp. 547–579.
17. Introduction to Christina Stead, *The Man Who Loved Children* (New York, Chicago, San Francisco, 1965), p. xl.

we can be moved by literary elements that are rationally incoherent or formally clumsy is puzzling to the nonpsychoanalytic commentator—so much so that T. S. Eliot, finding no adequate manifest referent for the clogged emotionality he perceived in *Hamlet*, reluctantly declared the play an artistic failure. Freudian discussion, by contrast, can locate the universality of the play's appeal and show how its very indirection, paralysis, and strangely overcharged language are enlisted in the task of coping with a powerful, relatively unelaborated Oedipal fantasy.[18]

Of course such a demonstration can never be more convincing than the reader wants it to be. Although psychoanalysis is not the wholly self-validating system described by some of its detractors,[19] the very nature of its attempt to interpose metaphorical psychic agencies between unconscious activity and overt behavior renders it unamenable to logical proof. Only those of its concepts that are closest to naked observation can be experimentally tested, and the few experiments thus far undertaken, while generally supportive of the theory, hardly close off alternative interpretations.[20] The skeptic is free to say, with the instrumentalists, that Freudian theory is unscientific because its assertions cannot be verified; or to join the positivists who relegate emotive matters to the harmless and meaningless realm of "poetic truth"; or to take refuge among the behaviorists who ensure that nothing so complex and uncontrolled as a human mind can become an object of their attention.

18. Academic critics have made characteristic rhetorical use of Ernest Jones's *Hamlet and Oedipus* (New York, 1949), taking its outdated scholarship and its literalism regarding fictional personages as reasons for dismissing the whole relevance of psychoanalysis to Shakespeare criticism. Meanwhile Jones's (and Freud's) central insight about the play has been confirmed and refined by other observers. See Simon O. Lesser, "Freud and *Hamlet* Again," *American Imago*, XII (Fall 1955), 207–220, and the studies summarized in Norman N. Holland, *Psychoanalysis and Shakespeare* (New York, Toronto, London, 1966).
19. On this point see David Rapaport, *The Structure of Psychoanalytic Theory* (New York, 1960), Abraham Kaplan, *The Conduct of Inquiry: Methodology for Behavioral Science* (San Francisco, 1964), and Michael Sherwood, *The Logic of Explanation in Psychoanalysis* (New York and London, 1969).
20. See especially E. Pumpian-Mindlin, ed., *Psychoanalysis as Science: The Dixon Lectures on the Scientific Status of Psychoanalysis* (Stanford, 1952); Helen D. Sargent, "Intrapsychic Change: Methodological Problems in Psychotherapy Research," *Psychiatry*, XXIV (1961), 93–108; and L. A. Gottschalk and A. H. Auerbach, eds., *Methods of Research in Psychotherapy* (New York, 1966).

All these versions of what C. Wright Mills called "abstracted empiricism" [21] shrug off the conclusions of psychoanalysis instead of attempting to replace them with better ones.

Unfortunately, Freud's achievement is entangled in an embarrassingly careless scientific tradition. The slowness of psychoanalysis to purge itself of unsubstantiated folklore and outmoded concepts cannot be denied. We no longer hear much about the primal crime, phylogenetic memory traces, Eros and Death, the Nirvana principle, or the infant's "primal hating" of the world, but we still find analysts deriving character traits solely from the vicissitudes of drives, dealing in hydraulically conceived sums of libido, and reifying Freud's oversimple tension-discharge model. [22] The virtual hibernation of psychoanalysis during the current period of revolutionary gains in natural science is cause for dismay. Yet there is no rival set of concepts covering the important ground that Freud appropriated seventy years ago. The literary student can hardly undertake a revision of clinical theory, but for the present he must try to ascertain which are its most essential and best verified points.

The main uncertainty facing a Freudian critic, however, is procedural rather than theoretical. The very abundance of "Freudian materials" in literature prompts him to ask what he should make of them, and here the theory cannot tell him which way to turn. Is the artist sicker, or is he better off, than those of us who observe his regressive forays at a distance? Nothing is easier than to "prove," using certain of Freud's premises, that art is a purely symptomatic activity, or to "prove" with equally Freudian premises that "the artist is not neurotic." The truth is that a literary critic is in a disadvantageous position for making such judgments. A text may open its fantasy life to him but it cannot, like an analyst's patient, react to his presence or delve for still hidden evidence that would support or refute his interpretive hunches. Indeed, because the regressiveness of art is necessarily more apparent to the analytic eye than its integrative and adaptive aspects are, psychoanalytic interpretation risks drawing excessively pathological conclusions. When this risk is put together with the uncertainties plaguing metapsychology

---

21. See *The Sociological Imagination* (New York, 1959).
22. See generally Norman S. Greenfield and William C. Lewis, eds., *Psychoanalysis and Current Biological Thought* (Madison and Milwaukee, 1965). The essays by Herbert Weiner, John D. Benjamin, and Robert R. Holt are especially important.

itself, one can see why Freudian criticism is always problematic and often inept.

This point has not been lost on psychoanalytic theorists of literature, who have looked for ways of putting Freudian discussion on a sounder logical and empirical basis. The results to date, however, have been somewhat quixotic. The only apparent means of ensuring against the literary equivalent of "wild analysis" is to suppress all interest in pathology, bypass ambiguities of theory, and concentrate on a circumscribed range of evidence. But as soon as this exchange of investigative freedom for a higher degree of certainty has been made, a trivialization seems to occur, and some of the spirit of psychoanalysis is lost. The very routine of one's method becomes a barrier to the deep involvement that should energize all criticism, Freudian criticism above all.

Not even the most coherent and ambitious attempt at a Freudian aesthetics, Norman N. Holland's *The Dynamics of Literary Response*,[23] avoids this pitfall. Holland assumes that literature, on the analogy of the dream and the joke, is essentially understandable as the disguising and discharging of an infantile fantasy—not, however, in the author's mind, which he deems too conjectural to bother with, but only in the reader's. "Literature transforms our primitive wishes and fears into significance, and this transformation gives us pleasure" (Holland, p. 30). If this is so, then something approaching scientific accuracy appears within the reach of criticism, for psychoanalysis tells us much of what we need to know about the two most relevant categories of understanding, namely fantasies and mechanisms of defense. Holland develops a theoretical model that does succeed in differentiating among our responses to various kinds of literature, from entertainments to works of calculated absurdity; this is a substantial contribution. Yet the effect is to promote a predictable form of discussion geared to the model's limited scope. Glossaries of readers' fantasies and defenses, illustrations of their possible combinations, and proof that any work can be assigned a spot in the scheme do not capture the literary enterprise much better than manuals of sex postures capture love. In both cases the inadvertently fostered attitude is resignation: Here we go again, what will it be this time?

This objection does not arise from the common but unreasonable

23. New York, 1968.

demand that a theory "feel like" what it describes; all theories are of necessity abstract. The quest for total certainty, however, seems to inhibit the first requisite of good criticism and good psychoanalysis, the capacity to be moved. A literary work may impress us with a complexity and economy, an energy and restraint, a precision and reverberation whose ultimate reference is not simply to the "nuclear fantasy" correctly isolated by Holland, but to the whole state of mind evoked by the text. Instead of presenting a disguised infantile wish that acquires "significance," great literature typically invites us to undergo a symbolic process of self-confrontation in which infantile solutions are resisted even as they are indulged. We identify with the pain as well as with the release involved in this process. "Beauty," as Rilke said, "is nothing but the beginning of terror that we are still just able to bear." [24] A criticism that cheerfully catalogs the unconscious tricks we play on ourselves and equates literary power with a judicious recipe of wishes and tactics, introjection and intellection, cannot avoid becoming a new version of anaesthesia—a version using Freud's terminology but lacking Freud's sympathy for the way great artists court unconscious engulfment in order to recreate the conditions of a human order.

This is to say that literature registers and arouses conflict, and that no theoretical preparation can spare a critic the necessity of submitting himself to that conflict. Norman Holland would, I am sure, agree with this statement, yet in practice he empties psychic defenses of their shame and anxiety and treats them much like the formal devices of rhetoric. When this is combined with ground rules discouraging biographical inquiry and value judgments, psychoanalytic discussion becomes what Holland has called "The Next New Criticism," a mere consolidation and deepening of the formalistic close reading of recent decades.[25] Such a tactful presentation seemingly makes room for us Freudians in the kingdom of polysemous meaning, but in actuality no one is placated. Conventional scholars remain quite aware that psychoanalysis constitutes a threat to their style of reading, and they are scandalized by the very claims

24. Quoted by Hanna Segal, "A Psycho-Analytical Approach to Aesthetics," *International Journal of Psycho-Analysis*, XXIII (1952), 206.

25. See *The Nation*, CXCII (1961), 339–341. Holland's chief authority for eschewing value judgments is Northrop Frye, whom he admires for having "cleared the air of a great deal of obscurantist smog" (*Dynamics*, p. xvi; see also pp. 196–197).

(for instance, that literature is after all much like joke-telling) by which Holland hopes to make Freudian criticism seem more agreeable.

Freudian criticism can become generally agreeable only by disavowing the idea of unconscious causation. Holland would never do this; he simply avoids authors' minds [26] and keeps his Freudianism well-mannered by showing magnanimity toward the shortcomings of "English." Yet those shortcomings must be directly challenged if "the connection between knowledge and the zest of life" [27] is to be preserved. Psychoanalysis would be yet another scholastic distraction from art if it were assimilated to the current ethos of academic departments. To move from collecting pastoral elegy motifs to collecting instances of phallic mothers would be a smaller step than most professors could imagine, a mere exchange of one indifferent taxonomy for another. The real value of literary psychoanalysis is that it can embolden us to be alone with books, to recognize our own image in them, and from that recognition to begin comprehending their hold over us.

The represented mind to which we respond in literary experience is not precisely the one we could infer from biographical data, but is improvised from what Keats called negative capability. This capability, however, is temperamentally limited by the persisting conflicts that must be managed in any creative process. The ego-state suffusing the work must borrow heavily from the "countercathected system"—that is, the cluster of defenses preventing inadmissible actions and expressions—that makes up the author's habitual character, and his career will escape redundancy only to the degree that he can vary his defenses. So, too, our ability to participate will rest on whether we can afford to trade part of our character-armor for an imagined equivalent. Fear of psychic dissolution, of surrender to the repressed, is thus the paramount obstacle both to creative freedom and to a reader's capacity for involvement.

It is in this light that we can grasp the significance of fixed genres, with their coded assurance that psychic activity will be patterned and resolved along familiar lines; the genre itself is a ready-made

26. That this is a consequence of Holland's model and not a personal limitation is apparent from his excellent essay, "H.D. and the 'Blameless Physician,'" *Contemporary Literature*, X (Autumn 1969), 474–506.
27. Alfred North Whitehead, *The Aims of Education* (New York, 1929), p. 139.

countercathected system. For this very reason, however, art that strives for originality is always restless within its formal borders and frequently generates new forms, which imitators are bound to misunderstand as embodying permanently valid principles of beauty.[28] While the works favored by posterity are not invariably those that defy tradition, their traditional elements always prove to have been adapted to a new vision of reality. This point is familiar in nonpsychological criticism; what psychoanalysis can show is that the new vision amounts to a reconciling of competing claims so as to fuse perception with the expression of conflict.

Criticism starting from an infantile fantasy instead of from this task of reconciliation will not be able to do justice to the cognitive aspect of literature, which is just as "psychoanalytic" as fantasy itself. The crucial difference between literary creation and symptom-formation resides in the extra demand we make of literature, that it confirm and extend our sense of truth. Whereas symptoms are rigidly stereotyped, are usually accompanied by guilt, and subtract from an individual's rapport with his surroundings, in the highest literary enjoyment we feel that our pleasure is being sanctioned by reality itself, whose principles have been set before us. This is an illusion, but the illusion can be practiced only by artists whose perceptiveness has not been obliterated by ego-needs. A work that flouts our conscious intelligence, as symptoms do, may have an "escape" interest but will be soon rejected for its crudeness or empty conventionality.

To recognize the importance of cognition is not, of course, to say that doses of unadulterated social or historical truth are found in literature and account for its power. Neutral-seeming literary material always conveys unconscious apologetics, and the latter turn out to be more compelling than any amount of faithful description. Hence the shallowness of criticism that evaluates books by their correspondence to approved political facts, and hence the folly of assuming that literature naïvely mirrors the conditions of the age in which it was written. Whatever historical knowledge we can glean from literature is knowledge of the way objective circumstances were

28. For a comparable argument from the standpoint of perception psychology, see Morse Peckham, *Man's Rage for Chaos: Biology, Behavior, and the Arts* (Philadelphia, 1965). In excluding psychodynamic factors, however, Peckham overrates the aesthetic importance of sheer perceptual novelty —a flaw of some moment, given the present state of the arts.

apprehended by one sensibility at the sufferance of all other psychic demands. This awareness can be illuminating once its restricted province is understood, but here again the proper point of vantage is neither fantasy nor facts, but the negotiating ego.[29]

Regarded psychoanalytically, literary works are very far from being simple lessons or exhortations decked out in poetic language; yet they *are* messages of a cryptic and intricate sort. Since our common plight is to be forever seeking acquittal from the fantasy-charges we have internalized as the price of ceasing to be infants, we share an eagerness for interpsychic transactions that seem to promise such an acquittal, or at least an abatement of guilt by means of establishing a confessional bond. Rather than being merely an unconscious release within the author or a similar release within the reader, literary process establishes a transitory complicity between the two. The forms this tie can assume are various. Milton's sensuality is hedged with law while Keats's is proclaimed as an imperious right, but both authors are posing ways for us to assert a measure of libidinal freedom. Swift implicates us in his aggression while Hemingway asks us to believe that life is castrating; both allow us to feel that our misanthropic sentiments are neither so unique nor so unfounded as we might have feared. Stendhal admits to a certain hypocrisy but easily wins our agreement that this is the way of the world; Joyce's Stephen tells us that his, and our own, creative ego must brush every hindrance from its path. In each instance we are invited, not to experience a fantasy, but to

29. Certain Freudian romantics, of whom the best known is Norman O. Brown, regard history itself as a gigantic tussle between the psychic forces posited by psychoanalysis. No such "psychologism" is being asserted here. A position like Brown's lends support to the accusation that psychoanalysis wants to replace other styles of observation by collapsing them into a general pathology. This is psychic determinism with a vengeance, but it is not psychoanalysis. Since my own essay may be subject to misunderstanding on this score, let me emphasize that psychoanalytic discourse properly seeks to show how individuals and groups *respond to* a totality of inner and outer conditions, and that for this task an awareness of nonpsychological forces is indispensable. (The point was made most clearly by Otto Fenichel, "The Drive to Amass Wealth," in his *Collected Papers,* Second Series [New York, 1954], pp. 89–108.) As applied to literature, this position not only welcomes but insists upon knowledge of every operative factor, including genre, convention, rhetorical devices, philosophical intent, audience, class, and personal background. What psychoanalysis disputes is not the usefulness of such information, but the equation of it with literary experience.

share a posture toward questionable impulses, and in the act of sharing to diffuse responsibility and stake out some unconscious territory free from the taxation of conscience.

Among the countless possibilities for literary exchange, one relationship seems frequent enough to merit special emphasis. An author often places his reader in the role of parent and begs his absolution. By revealing what has been on his mind, mixing oblique confession with a reassertion of commitment to decency and reality and beauty, and by involving the reader in everything he discloses, the author claims the right to be accepted as he is. But since everyone remains filial on the deep level where literature is registered, the reader does not use the communication quite as it was meant; he welcomes the represented self-exculpation, not as applying to someone else, but as a subtle brief in his own defense.

The tendency of critics to exaggerate the moral, social, or realistic content of literature becomes more comprehensible in this light. Every critic is first a reader who turns the text to the purposes of his beleaguered ego. By transmuting the author into a paragon of conscience or documentary literalism he completes the covering of his tracks; the literary self with which he has identified has been placed beyond reproach. Not even psychoanalytic theory, with its open attention to such unconscious tactics, is a sufficient preventative against their use. By bottling and labeling the repressed contents that Freud thought were so noxious, a Freudian can preclude the self-risk that literature asks of us. Literary art is then revealed as benign parlor magic and nothing more.

"The charm of knowledge would be small," said Nietzsche, "were it not that so much shame has to be overcome on the way to it." [30] Any system of propositions tends eventually to dissipate that shame, either by evading anxiety-provoking matters or by assimilating them to the sense of the ordinary. The latter course is obviously preferable if a choice must be made, yet knowledge about literature has a curious way of ceasing to be wholly true when such a regularization has been accomplished; the loss of uncertainty is also a loss of humanity. This is the kernel of truth in the widespread but largely foolish worry that psychoanalysis will "ruin" our favorite books. While literature is not so easily destroyed by critical remarks, any

---

30. *Beyond Good and Evil*, in *The Complete Works of Friedrich Nietzsche*, ed. Oscar Levy, 18 vols. (New York, 1964), XII, 85.

critic can temporarily make an engaging text seem dreary—not, however, by revealing too much of it, but by revealing too little and claiming this to be the whole. The very success of psychoanalytic theory in anticipating predictable aspects of literature leaves the Freudian peculiarly vulnerable to this coasting on his assumptions. His unusual advantage of method must be matched by an unusual susceptibility to the restless life of art if psychoanalysis is not to become a narcotic in his hands.

TWO ✒ CRIME AND FANTASY IN *GREAT EXPECTATIONS*

ALBERT D. HUTTER

I.

"Hold your noise!" cried a terrible voice, as a man started up from among the graves at the side of the church porch. "Keep still, you little devil, or I'll cut your throat!" [1]

The terrible voice belongs to Abel Magwitch. He descends upon Pip and the reader alike with tremendous suddenness and ferocity. Here, at the very outset of the novel, Magwitch bursts into Pip's thoughts like some imagined ogre of childhood, rising from "the distant savage lair from which the wind was rushing," rising from the marshes, starting up from among the Pirrip graves. "You young dog," he tells Pip, licking his lips, "what fat cheeks you ha' got. . . . Darn Me if I couldn't eat 'em" (I, 3). He goes on to describe the

---

1. Charles Dickens, *Great Expectations,* ed. Louis Crompton (Indianapolis and New York, 1964), p. 2; copyright © 1964 by The Bobbs-Merrill Company, Inc.; reprinted by permission of the publisher. All references are to this edition; chapter and page numbers appear in parentheses following quotations.

young man with him ("in comparison with which young man I am a Angel"):

> That young man hears the words I speak. That young man has a secret way pecooliar to himself, of getting at a boy, and at his heart, and at his liver. It is in wain for a boy to attempt to hide himself from that young man. A boy may lock his door, may be warm in bed, may tuck himself up, may draw the clothes over his head, may think himself comfortable and safe, but that young man will softly creep and creep his way to him and tear him open. I am a keeping that young man from harming of you at the present moment, with great difficulty. I find it wery hard to hold that young man off of your inside. (I, 4–5)

This opening incident is the basis for what Dickens called "the grotesque tragicomic conception," the relationship between Pip and Magwitch which inspired the book and which achieves a pivotal surprise in Chapter 39 when Magwitch returns.[2] Magwitch's reappearance in *Great Expectations* gives literal substance to the guilt and fears that haunt Pip from the opening chapter. Throughout the novel Pip's chance association with the convict overshadows his other relationships, his aspirations and pretensions.

At first Pip's terror and guilt over robbing a file and "wittles" appear to be the exaggerations of childhood. His terror is conveyed to the reader through surprise—as when Magwitch first appears, or when Pip opens his door to find "a party of soldiers with their muskets: one of whom held out a pair of handcuffs to me, saying, 'Here you are, look sharp, come on!'" (IV, 31). Yet there is enough humor in Dickens' description to distance our identification with Pip. We perceive Magwitch's exaggeration in describing his horrific young man; Pip cannot. As the novel progresses, however, the first encounter with Magwitch takes on overtones that mystify and disturb us as much as they do the protagonist.

Pip betrays Joe for the first time in the act of stealing Joe's file, and as a result he is tormented by guilt.[3] Later the file mysteriously

2. John Forster, *The Life of Charles Dickens*, ed. A. J. Hoppé, 2 vols. (London, 1966), II, 284–285.
3. Pip admits that "My state of mind regarding the pilfering . . . did not impel me to frank disclosure; . . . It was much upon my mind (particularly when I first saw him looking about for his file) that I ought to tell Joe the whole truth. Yet I did not, and for the reason that I mistrusted that if I did, he would think me worse than I was" (VI, 42–43).

turns up in the hands of a stranger who uses it as a swizzle stick to stir his rum and water. Although Pip is now older, and apprenticed to Joe, he still responds to this stranger and to the file itself as he had first responded to the convict. He thinks of "the strange man taking aim at me with his invisible gun" and of "the guilty coarse and common thing" his own convict associations have been. He dreads that the file will reappear when he least expects it (as in fact Magwitch does reappear in Chapter 39), and he dreams of it "coming at me out of a door, without seeing who held it," until he screams himself awake (X, 83).

Instead of the file, Magwitch's broken leg-iron turns up six chapters later as the weapon used to assault Mrs. Joe. Pip's immediate reaction to this crime is: "I was at first disposed to believe that *I* must have had some hand in the attack upon my sister" (XVI, 128), and he continues to feel responsible for the assault.[4] By now the file has become an obsession and a barrier between him and Joe. Pip's attempts to rationalize the theft and the necessity for keeping it secret are self-contradictory and unnecessarily defensive:

> the secret was such an old one now, had so grown into me and become a part of myself, that I could not tear it away. In addition to the dread that, having led up to so much mischief, it would be now more likely than ever to alienate Joe from me if he believed it, I had a further restraining dread that he would not believe it . . . (XVI, 130)

Through his guardian in London, a criminal lawyer, Pip continues to be thrown in contact with a world that he associates with Magwitch and that taints even his pursuit of Estella. Thus at one point when he is waiting for Estella, immediately after a tour through Newgate, he frantically tries to beat the prison dust from his clothes. Instead, the aura of prison clings to him:

> I consumed the whole time in thinking how strange it was that I should be encompassed by all this taint of prison and

---

4. Because he is Mrs. Joe's closest relation, and because of his obligations to her, Pip assumes that he was "a more legitimate object of suspicion than any one else" (XVI, 128). This is certainly a peculiar piece of reasoning. Later Pip is horrified at having inadvertently provided the weapon (XVI, 130).

crime; that, in my childhood out on our lonely marshes on a
winter evening I should have first encountered it; that, it
should have reappeared on two occasions, starting out like
a stain that has faded but not gone; that, it should in this new
way pervade my fortune and advancement. (XXXII, 285)

Magwitch proves to be not only Pip's benefactor but also the
father of Estella. We don't know this until Chapter 50; we simply
feel an inexplicable weight of criminality on Pip. But even when
Pip's connections with Magwitch are finally accounted for, his sense
of criminality and guilt remains unappeased and unexplained. His
hatred and disgust toward Magwitch linger on in peculiarly unresolved ways. Pip's immediate response to the returned convict, like
his later rejection of Magwitch's money,[5] is absolute: "The abhor-
rence in which I held the man, the dread I had of him, the repugnance with which I shrank from him, could not have been exceeded
if he had been some terrible beast" (XXXIX, 346).

The hero's initial fears of Magwitch are tied to an equally powerful hatred of him. The process of repressing this hatred and learning
to love his benefactor is only partially successful. In childhood Pip
tries to soothe his fears by imagining Magwitch transported or dead
(XIX).[6] When he reappears, Pip quarters him elsewhere and soon
hopes to ship him out of the country again. As Pip realizes that he
is the cause of Magwitch's illegal return, he fancies himself "in
some sort, as his murderer" (XLI, 370). Pip seems capable of loving
Magwitch only to the degree that Magwitch is helpless and endangered. Pip's solicitude is suspect when he comments, "it was
dreadful to think that I could not be sorry at heart for his being
badly hurt, since it was unquestionably best that he should die"
(LIV, 483–484). And in a peculiar, if suggestive, incident Pip be-

5. A powerful social stigma, of course, was attached to accepting money
from a convict. The conscious moral force of the novel, however, rejects
such prejudice and moves us toward an acceptance and love of Magwitch.
Dickens reveals that Magwitch's wealth was earned quite legally in New
South Wales (XXXIX, 347–348). But to the very last Pip refuses to think
of taking money from him. When Magwitch hints that Pip will have the
money after his death, Pip still rejects the thought and realizes with relief
that Magwitch's possessions would be forfeited to the Crown (LIV,
passim).
6. "My comfort was, that it happened a long time ago, and that he had
doubtless been transported a long way off, and that he was dead to me,
and might be veritably dead into the bargain" (XIX, 158).

lieves himself to be suspected of carrying poison to Magwitch.[7] It is very unlike Dickens to introduce this suspicion and then to drop it completely. As minor as the incident is, it reinforces our sense of Pip's lingering hostility toward Magwitch. This seems, in fact, the only way of accounting for it.

The relationship between Pip and Magwitch is obviously central to our understanding of the novel. A literal summary of its progress, however, does not adequately account for its power. Although we know that Dickens first conceived the novel in terms of these two figures and their effect on each other, we don't know why they so fascinated him. Pip's own reaction to Magwitch far exceeds anything Magwitch does to him; the haunting fear and hatred in their first encounter affect Pip throughout the novel, lingering in ways that Dickens himself may have been unaware of (as in the "poisoning incident"). Dickens' evident incapacity to provide an explanation for Pip's continuing guilt suggests that for both Pip and Dickens himself, the Pip-Magwitch relationship has deep unconscious roots. Magwitch, I believe, must be understood as Pip's father—or, more specifically, as that aspect of the father that both threatens and terrifies a child.

A number of passages strongly imply this relationship. "As I never saw my father or my mother," Pip tells us in Chapter 1, "and never saw any likeness of either of them . . . my first fancies regarding what they were like, were unreasonably derived from their tombstones" (I, 1). One paragraph later, Magwitch leaps at Pip from among the tombstones marking his parents' graves. And the chapter closes with Magwitch moving back toward the dead: "As I saw him go . . . he looked in my young eyes as if he were eluding the hands of the dead people, stretching up cautiously out of their graves, to get a twist upon his ankle and pull him in" (I, 5). When Magwitch returns from the colonies and Pip recoils from him, Magwitch makes it quite clear how he sees their relationship: "Look'ee here, Pip. I'm your second father. You're my son—more to me nor any son" (XXXIX, 346).

What is crucial here is not simply the suggestion or actual state-

7. "The daily visits I could make him were shortened now, and he was more strictly kept. Seeing, or fancying, that I was suspected of an intention of carrying poison to him, I asked to be searched before I sat down at his bedside" (LVI, 496–497).

ment of a father-son relationship, but the context of that relationship—the fear and guilt that so intensely accompany these two
scenes. Magwitch threatens to overwhelm Pip, either by brute force
or by love. Socially, Magwitch first drags Pip into the mud of his
own attempted escape, makes him a criminal accomplice, and then
goes to an opposite extreme of elevating Pip as high as his money
will carry the boy. Imagery relating to phallic strength and fear
of castration pervades these scenes with Magwitch and suggests
the source of their intensity. For example, Magwitch's return is
heralded by a detailed account of the weather:

> It was wretched weather; stormy and wet, stormy and wet;
> mud, mud, mud, deep in all the streets. . . . So furious had
> been the gusts, that high buildings in town had had the lead
> stripped off their roofs; and in the country, trees had been torn
> up, and sails of windmills carried away; and gloomy accounts
> had come in from the coast, of shipwreck and death. . . . We
> lived at the top of the last house, and the wind rushing up the
> river shook the house that night, like discharges of cannon or
> breakings of a sea. When the rain came with it and dashed
> against the windows, I thought . . . that I might have fancied
> myself in a storm-beaten light-house. . . . the staircase lamps
> were blown out; . . . [and] through the black windows (open-
> ing them ever so little was out of the question in the teeth
> of such wind and rain) I saw that the lamps in the court were
> blown out, and that the lamps on the bridges and the shore
> were shuddering, and that the coal fires in barges on the river
> were being carried away before the wind like red-hot splashes
> in the rain. (XXXIX, 339–340)

The repeated references to objects torn, pulled out at their roots,
stripped, and blown out, attacking the doors, windows, and passages of Pip's house, suggest a personal assault. Later Pip admits,
"In every rage of wind and rush of rain, I heard pursuers. . . . I
began either to imagine or recall that I had had mysterious warnings of this man's approach" (XXXIX, 350). The language of these
warnings implies that Magwitch's strength is phallic and that he
threatens Pip with both castration and a sexual attack on the passages of Pip's body. Thus Pip pulls back from Magwitch as if "he
had been some terrible beast," or, even more specifically: "I recoiled

from his touch as if he had been a snake." And again: "At a change in his manner as if he were even going to embrace me, I laid a hand upon his breast and put him away" (XXXIX, 347, 342). The first words Magwitch utters offer to slice Pip open, and Magwitch goes on to specify a few internal organs (heart and liver) on which he has particular designs. Magwitch's "young man" has similar aims, and is likely to appear even when Pip has locked his door and is safely tucked in bed; and Magwitch's emissary in Chapter 10 possesses the alarming phallic powers of "an invisible gun" forever pointed at Pip, as well as the stolen file. It was this file that reappeared in Pip's nightmare, held by some invisible hand (X, 83). That hand is surely Magwitch's, and in Chapter 39 we find that Magwitch "laid his hand on my shoulder. I shuddered at the thought that for anything I knew, his hand might be stained with blood" (348).

At the height of his anxiety over the storm Pip hears the sound of a church clock striking eleven, and Magwitch makes his appearance: "I was listening, and thinking how the wind assailed and tore it, when I heard a footstep on the stair." And Pip adds: "What nervous folly made me start, and awfully connect it with the footstep of my dead sister, matters not" (XXXIX, 340). It actually matters a great deal. Like the reference to Pip's carrying poison to Magwitch, this peculiar suggestion is made and then dropped. There is no apparent reason for Dickens to introduce it, and there is no apparent use made of it once it has been introduced. But I suggest that it intimates an unconscious connection between Magwitch, Joe, and Mrs. Joe: they enact various parental attitudes of an Oedipal triangle centering on Pip. Moreover, the pervasive sense of crime in the novel may be traced back, through the association with Magwitch, to the original crimes Pip commits: the theft of Joe's file, and the robbing of Mrs. Joe.

Mrs. Joe is represented in the most forbidding terms: "She was tall and bony, and almost always wore a coarse apron, fastened over her figure behind with two loops, and having a square impregnable bib in front, that was stuck full of pins and needles" (II, 7). That bib is the very essence of her as a woman: it makes her literally "impregnable," and minimizes the effect of anything stuck into her. It is against this formidable foster mother that Pip commits his first crime. He robs her, stealing at dawn into her kitchen pantry, probing into jars, uncovering dishes, and finally escaping with her "beautiful round compact pork pie" (II, 15). This intimation of an incestuous entering and robbing of the mother is developed in Pip's own guilt over the impending act when he comments: "I was in mortal terror of the young man who wanted my heart and liver; I was in mortal terror of my interlocutor with the iron leg; I was in mortal terror of myself, from whom an awful promise had been extracted" (II, 14). Most importantly, the first "crime" against Mrs. Joe is magnified into a genuine assault on her by Orlick, later in the novel. Julian Moynahan has suggested that Orlick (and later, Bentley Drummle) "enact an aggressive potential that the novel defines, through patterns of analogy and linked resemblances, as belonging in the end to Pip and to his unconscionably ambitious hopes." [8] He shows that Orlick commits the crime for which Pip has all the justification. Although he also shows that Orlick enacts an aggressively sexual side of Pip in his pursuit of Biddy, he does not see the attack on Mrs. Joe in this light.[9] The emphasis on the weapon, Mrs. Joe's falling and bleeding, and the subsequent, inexplicable propitiation of Orlick all suggest, however, that this attack carries strong sexual overtones. Particular attention is directed to the weapon used—"something blunt and heavy"—which turns out to be Magwitch's old leg-iron. And Pip laments: "It was horrible to think that I had provided the weapon, however undesignedly, but I could hardly think otherwise" (XVI, 129, 130).

Once the assault has been carried out, Mrs. Joe is a changed woman. She no longer torments Pip or Joe, and she positively plays up to Orlick:

> I confess that I expected to see my sister denounce him, and that I was disappointed by the different result. She manifested the greatest anxiety to be on good terms with him, was evidently much pleased by his being at length produced, and motioned that she would have him given something to drink. . . . and there was an air of humble propitiation in all she

8. Julian Moynahan, "The Hero's Guilt: The Case of *Great Expectations*," reprinted in *Assessing Great Expectations*, ed. Richard Lettis and William E. Morris (San Francisco, 1960), p. 163.
9. In his attack on Mrs. Joe and the robbery-assault of Pumblechook, "Orlick acts merely as Pip's instrument or weapon" (Moynahan, p. 161). Here, Moynahan's own language inadvertently suggests a sexually aggressive meaning to Orlick's role.

did, such as I have seen pervade the bearing of a child towards a hard master. (XVI, 133)[10]

Her hardness and lack of femininity have been assaulted and broken down with a vengeance. It is as if the formidable bib and forbidding air were themselves symbolic of the taboos of incest, and had been pierced by Orlick—but at a price. Mrs. Joe soon dies, while Pip's guilt continues to grow. Hearing Magwitch and thinking of Mrs. Joe, with the fearful storm raging outside, Pip brings an unconscious thread of the novel to a climax. Those footsteps arouse Pip's guilty conscience. Someone has come to avenge the crime against his dead sister.

To understand why that avenger is Magwitch—and not, for example, Joe, who is husband to Mrs. Joe and a more obvious father to Pip—we must recognize that ambivalent attitudes toward a single father have been split apart in this novel and divided between at least two father figures, Joe and Magwitch. Freud wrote:

> The relation of the boy to the father is, as we say, an "ambivalent" one (that is, composed of conflicting feelings of tenderness and hostility). In addition to the hate which wants to remove the father as a rival, a measure of tenderness for him also exists as a rule. Both attitudes of mind combine to produce identification with the father: the boy wants to be in his father's place because he admires him and wants to be like him, and also because he wishes to put him out of his way. At a certain moment the child comes to understand that the attempt to remove the father as a rival would be punished by the father with castration.[11]

In the imaginative world of Pip's childhood Magwitch is the castrating father—the "pirate," the "snake," the "terrible beast" come to cut the organs out of little Pip. The "measure of tenderness" and

10. The "bearing of a child" and "a hard master" are suggestive of pregnancy and erection.
11. Sigmund Freud, "Dostoevsky and Parricide," *The Standard Edition of the Complete Psychological Works of Sigmund Freud,* ed. James Strachey, *et al.* (hereafter abbreviated *S.E.*), 24 vols. (London, 1953–1966), XIV, 309–332.

"admiration" for the father are concentrated on Joe. As a result Joe is virtually feminized in his relations with Pip. The theft of his phallic file and its surrender to Magwitch dramatize Joe's weakness; they also locate the father's power—and potential for revenge—in Magwitch's hands.

Pip tells us that he always treated Joe as "a larger species of child, and as no more than my equal" (II, 7). Before he is exposed to Miss Havisham, before he develops his love for Estella and his social aspirations, Pip knows a kind of pastoral bliss beside Joe, emulating his work in the forge. Whenever he sees Joe after he has left for London, he is reminded of the "larks" they were to have had together and of the old quiet life by the forge that he has lost. He first describes Joe as "a mild, good-natured, sweet-tempered, easy-going, foolish, dear fellow—a sort of Hercules in strength, and also in weakness" (II, 6). Later he writes, "Joe laid his hand upon my shoulder with the touch of a woman. I have often thought him since like the steam-hammer, that can crush a man or pat an egg-shell, in his combination of strength with gentleness" (XVIII, 151–152). In dealing with Orlick Joe displays his most effective steam-hammer qualities, and Pip is lost in admiration: "if any man in that neighbourhood could stand up long against Joe, I never saw the man" (XV, 122). Only Joe's egg-shell tenderness, however, is directed toward Pip. At times this aspect of the blacksmith is carried to a ludicrous extreme. For example, at Mrs. Joe's funeral we find "Poor dear Joe, entangled in a little black cloak tied in a large bow under his chin . . . seated apart at the upper end of the room" (XXXV, 302).

A small boy's relationship to his father is defined between the polarities of killing and replacing him or submitting fully to his power. In the latter case he may solve the problem of incest and consequent fear of the father by deciding to take the mother's role himself, even imagining that he will bear the father's child.[12] This

12. See, for example, Freud's discussion of the "complete" Oedipus complex in "The Ego and the Id," *S.E.*, XIX, 12–59. The tendencies toward replacement of the mother via identification derive from what Freud termed the "inverted negative" response (p. 34). Two of Freud's longer case histories deal with versions of this response: the analysis of Schreber, "Psycho-Analytic Notes on an Autobiographical Account of a Case of Paranoia (Dementia Paranoides)," *S.E.*, XII, 9–82; and the "Wolf-man" case, "From the History of an Infantile Neurosis," *S.E.*, XVII, 7–122.

solution, clearly not part of Dickens' conscious intention, is nevertheless suggested at two points in the text. The comic and sad encounter between Joe and Pip in London is occasioned by a message from Miss Havisham. Joe comes down to London to pass it on, receives an uncomfortable welcome from Pip, and is made awkward and formal in his turn. But he is determined to relate his conversation with Miss Havisham. She had asked if he were in correspondence with Mr. Pip. "Having had a letter from you, I were able to say 'I am.' (When I married your sister, Sir, I said 'I will'; and when I answered your friend, Pip, I said, 'I am.')" (XXVII, 241). The comic allusion to a marriage comments ironically on Pip's coolness toward Joe: they have scarcely any contact now, and their once close union has been dissolved. Unconsciously, it suggests that their former tie was a kind of marriage.

Much earlier in the novel, when Pip and Joe are on the closest of terms, Pip scrawls out another letter for Joe. They are alone together, and Pip is learning how to write:

> "mI deEr JO i opE U r krWitE wEll i opE i shAl soN B haBelL 4 2 teeDge U JO aN theN wE shOrl B sO glOdd aN wEn i M preNgtD 2 u JO woT larX an blEvE ME inF xn PiP." (VII, 47)

Unlike such extra letters as the "r" in "krWitE" (which helps to reproduce a dialect sound in pronouncing the word), the "g" in "preNgtD" seems wholly gratuitous. But it makes the phrase look more like "pregnant to you" than "prenticed to you."

One further piece of textual evidence may help to demonstrate the unconscious splitting of attitudes toward the father in *Great Expectations*. Some twenty years ago there was an exchange of articles between John Butt and Humphry House. Butt had published Dickens' outline or plan for the conclusion of *Great Expectations*. He and House debated the exact dating of the plan and the use Dickens made of it. At one point, convinced by House's argument, Butt changed his earlier position and argued that the plan applied only to the final episodes of the novel:

> Other details help to confirm this view. Miss Havisham's lover was originally named "Compey," and so the name stands in Chapter 42 of the Wisbech MS. Later Dickens changed the

name to "Compeyson," and we can watch him in the act of adding the last three letters to the name in the manuscript of Chapter 45.[13]

"Compeyson" is also the form that appears in the manuscript plan: "Compeyson. How brought in?" Butt writes:

> But Compeyson had been "in" from the beginning of the novel, and he had been actively shadowing Pip and Magwitch from the first chapter of the final stage. Moreover Dickens had "brought in" his relationship to Miss Havisham while he was still calling him "Compey." "How brought in" must therefore refer to something else, and to what else can it refer but to Compeyson's part in the scene of Magwitch's capture? [14]

Butt's scholarship raises still another question: why should Dickens bother to change the name of this character at all, and what, if any, relationship does this have to the climactic scene on the river? The answer, I believe, lies in the unconscious meaning of the added suffix, and more generally in Compeyson's role as another of Pip's alter egos, like Orlick.

Compeyson is a confidence man, selfishly abusing the trust and love he inspires by posing as a gentleman, while Pip looks back on his own expectations and aspirations to be a gentleman as criminally selfish. Compeyson betrays Miss Havisham; Miss Havisham tries to dupe Pip, abusing both Estella and Pip in her desire for revenge. But most importantly, Compeyson's relationship to Magwitch is a projection of Pip's unconscious response to his benefactor. We have seen that Pip reveals a desire for Magwitch's death along with his terror of him. Compeyson tries to destroy Magwitch and is destroyed in turn.

When Pip aids Magwitch's attempted escape, late in the novel, he nervously comments on the convict's calm: "One would have supposed that it was I who was in danger, not he . . ." (LIV, 479). With the steamer bearing down upon them, Magwitch is apprehended from a customs galley, and he responds by reaching across and seizing a muffled figure shrinking back in a corner of the galley. The figure is Compeyson, who has pursued Magwitch and betrayed

13. John Butt, "Dickens's Plan for the Conclusion of *Great Expectations*," *The Dickensian*, XLV (Spring 1949), 78.
14. Butt, "Dickens's Plan," p. 79.

him. At that instant the steamer hits the two boats. These events occur so swiftly that Pip is struck by a blow and stunned unconscious during Compeyson's fight with Magwitch:

> Still in the same moment, I saw the face [i.e., Compeyson's] tilt backward with a white terror on it that I shall never forget, and heard a great cry on board the steamer and a loud splash in the water, and felt the boat sink from under me.
>
> It was but for an instant that I seemed to struggle with a thousand mill-weirs and a thousand flashes of light; that instant past, I was taken on board the galley. (LIV, 481)

Pip's struggle coincides exactly with the struggle between Magwitch and Compeyson. Magwitch later tells Pip that he and Compeyson "had gone down, fiercely locked in each other's arms, and that there had been a struggle under water, and that he had disengaged himself, struck out, and swam away" (LIV, 482–483). The simultaneity of the two events suggests a confusion between Pip and Compeyson which the plot as a whole reinforces.

Compeyson is thus a kind of scapegoat-Pip. Once he has been disposed of, Pip feels much closer to Magwitch: "for now my repugnance to him had all melted away" (LIV, 483).[15] It seems reasonable to suppose that Dickens played with the name "Compey" until he found a variation that sounded right, satisfying his unconscious sense of Compey's role in the novel. "Compey" is a patricidal "son," on whom the father takes appropriate vengeance.

Following this scene on the river the novel moves swiftly toward its conclusion. Magwitch dies in prison, and in the following chapter Pip contracts a fever.[16] He falls into a coma and appears to hallucinate:

15. As I have mentioned, however, his love for Magwitch is still ambivalent and takes peculiar turns. In the paragraph following this quotation Pip reasons that it was best that Magwitch die.

16. In Dickens' next novel, *Our Mutual Friend,* Eugene Wrayburn is beaten and nearly killed at the point where he seems to contemplate seducing the heroine. He, too, suffers a coma and prolonged illness and is then nursed by the heroine, whom he marries. Clearly Wrayburn is being punished for his would-be sins, and his illness and recovery signify expiation and a process of spiritual rebirth. This characteristically Dickensian pattern seems to be behind Pip's illness. The scene acted out between Compeyson and Magwitch is repeated here: Pip, the cause of Magwitch's return and therefore of his death, suffers punishment and a kind of death in his turn. He will then be reborn into Joe's arms.

. . . that I often lost my reason, that the time seemed interminable, that I confounded impossible existences with my own
identity; that I was a brick in the house wall, and yet entreat-
ing to be released from the giddy place where the builders
had set me; that I was a steel beam of a vast engine, clashing
and whirling over a gulf, and yet that I implored in my own
person to have the engine stopped, and my part in it hammered
off; that I passed through these phases of disease, I know of
my own remembrance, and did in some sort know at the time.
That I sometimes struggled with real people, in the belief that
they were murderers, and that I would all at once comprehend
that they meant to do me good, and would then sink exhausted
in their arms, and suffer them to lay me down, I also knew
at the time. But, above all, I knew that there was a constant
tendency in all these people—who, when I was very ill, would
present all kinds of extraordinary transformations of the human
face, and would be much dilated in size—above all, I say, I
knew that there was an extraordinary tendency in all these
people, sooner or later, to settle down into the likeness of Joe.
(LVII, 500–501)

Pip then wakes up to find Joe at his bedside, nursing him back to
health.

Julian Moynahan believes that Pip's hallucinations "articulate the
division in his character between helpless passivity and demonic
aggressiveness." [17] It is possible to be still more specific. All the
images in this passage refer to the dualities we have associated with
Magwitch and Joe, and to the response they elicit from Pip. The
important quality of the first image would appear to be the giddy
height that frightens Pip, possibly suggesting erection. Each of the
final two images unmistakably shows Pip repudiating his "rise," his
power within the vast engine, and begging instead for a symbolic
castration: "to have the engine stopped, and my part in it hammered
off." The next hallucination locates these fears more specifically: he
dreams of struggling with murderers who turn out to be friends.
In the preceding three chapters Magwitch has murdered Compeyson
and Pip has responded with a greater trust and love for the convict
than he had previously shown. In the hallucination the murderers-

17. Moynahan, "The Hero's Guilt," p. 166.

turned-friends look more and more like Joe. The fantasy anticipates the transition to a waking state, as Pip gradually focuses on his nurse, and it also reduplicates in miniature the larger transition of the novel: having left Joe, fought against Magwitch, and been reconciled to him, he is now about to return to Joe's care.

The final reflection is astonishingly specific. It shows that these pendulum swings of the novel reflect Pip's struggle with a powerful phallic father (Magwitch) and his desire to submit to a passive love of the much gentler Joe. "The human face" behaves like a human phallus: it transforms itself by dilating in size, by expanding and then contracting until it finally settles "down into the likeness of Joe."

The solution Pip seeks at the close of the novel is a figurative self-castration and a return to a childhood state of absolute dependence on Joe:

> I was slow to gain strength, but I did slowly and surely become less weak, and Joe stayed with me, and I fancied I was little Pip again.
>
> For, the tenderness of Joe was so beautifully proportioned to my need, that I was like a child in his hands. He would sit and talk to me . . . in the old unassertive protecting way . . . He did everything for me except the household work, for which he had engaged a very decent woman . . . (LVII, 505)

When Pip is able to leave London,

> an open carriage was got into the Lane, Joe wrapped me up, took me in his arms, carried me down to it, and put me in, as if I were still the small helpless creature to whom he had so abundantly given of the wealth of his great nature. . . . and I laid my head on Joe's shoulder, as I had laid it long ago when he had taken me to the Fair or where not, and it was too much for my young senses. (LVII, 505–506)

When he feels Joe once again growing distant with him, he accuses his own callous independence:

> Ah! Had I given Joe no reason to doubt my constancy, and to think that in prosperity I should grow cold to him and cast

> him off? Had I given Joe's innocent heart no cause to feel
> instinctively that as I got stronger, his hold upon me would be
> weaker . . . ? (LVII, 509)

Pip actually repeats a state of infancy when, with the father watch-
ing, he demonstrates his ability to walk: "See, Joe! I can walk
quite strongly. Now, you shall see me walk back by myself" (LVII,
509). When Joe answers him as "sir," Pip devises a regressive means
of recapturing their lost intimacy:

> The last word ["sir"] grated on me; but how could I remon-
> strate! I walked no further than the gate of the gardens, and
> then pretended to be weaker than I was, and asked Joe for
> his arm. (LVII, 509)

Although the final chapter of *Great Expectations* has Pip
leaving for Egypt and not returning for eleven years, we feel that
the real close of the novel occurs with his return to Joe and Biddy.
Pip had hoped to propose marriage to Biddy, but this would have
been a strange marriage, smacking of a child-parent relationship. He
intends to ask her if she "can receive me like a forgiven child (and
indeed I am as sorry, Biddy, and have as much need of a hushing
voice and a soothing hand) . . ." (LVII, 511). Biddy ends by
marrying Joe and becoming in a sense Pip's mother. Thus in the
final chapter, when Pip returns after eleven years to surprise Joe
and Biddy, he finds an infant "Pip" in his place:

> There, smoking his pipe in the old place by the kitchen fire-
> light, as hale and as strong as ever, though a little grey, sat
> Joe; and there, fenced into the corner with Joe's leg, and sitting
> on my own little stool looking at the fire, was——I again!
> "We giv' him the name of Pip for your sake, dear old chap,"
> said Joe, delighted when I took another stool by the child's
> side . . . (LIX, 521)

II.

Magwitch's function in the novel cannot be defined purely in terms
of a threatening, paternal relationship with Pip. He is also a victim

of society, the product of an expanding materialist economy that was itself criminally negligent of the lower classes it exploited. Magwitch's life history is a parable of Victorian economic life: he had been deserted from earliest memory, left to fend for himself, and forced into stealing merely in order to survive. He is seen as dirty, dangerous, and a hardened criminal by those who have shaped him and who wish to keep him at a distance—in prison or transported (XLII, passim).

It seems fitting, then, that he should be particularly associated with dirt. When Pip first sees him he is "smothered in mud" (I, 2); he calls himself a "dung-hill dog"; he fights Compeyson in a muddy ditch, twice escapes, and is twice captured in the mud flats of a Thames swamp; and he makes his reappearance in London when there is "mud, mud, mud, deep in all the streets" (XXXIX, 346, 339). One critic comments: "Mud is a peculiarly appropriate symbol for the class of society that Magwitch represents—the downtrodden and oppressed of life, all those victims of injustice whom society has tried to submerge. It is a natural image of the social dunghill in which violence and rebellion are fomented. . . ." [18] "Dunghill" is a well-chosen term, as Magwitch's effect on Pip is often described as one of soiling or staining.

In fact, the ideas and images associated with Magwitch—dirt, lack of self-control (revealed in his excesses of temper and revenge, of love for Pip), money and gifts—all partake of the psychoanalytic complex of anality.[19] It is not that Magwitch is himself an "anal personality" but rather that he evokes the particular range of associations originating in a child's attitude toward his feces. These images tell us that money is dirty, that a blatant need for it is demeaning, and that making it is itself a process that stains or pollutes. This attitude toward money certainly pervades Pip's snobbery, if not snobbery in general. The snob's poses of not soiling his hands, of holding his head high, and of turning up his nose are all characteristically "anal."

Pip turns down Magwitch's first gift, the two pound notes sent

18. John H. Hagan, Jr., "The Poor Labyrinth: The Theme of Social Justice in Dickens's 'Great Expectations,'" reprinted in Lettis and Morris, *Assessing Great Expectations,* p. 84.

19. See particularly Freud's "Character and Anal Erotism," *S.E.,* IX, 169–175, and "On the Transformations of Instinct as Exemplified in Anal Erotism," *S.E.,* XVII, 127–133; and Otto Fenichel, *The Psychoanalytic Theory of Neurosis* (New York, 1945), pp. 278–284, 487–488.

via another convict, with an obvious disgust for the dirt and foul associations he automatically attributes to them: "two fat sweltering one-pound notes that seemed to have been on terms of the warmest intimacy with all the cattle markets in the county" (X, 83). Such language indicates a further basis for Pip's revulsion toward Magwitch's second gift, the money of his great expectations. We have seen the unconscious association suggested earlier, linking Magwitch with a threatening image of the father. There is also the Victorian social stigma normally attached to dealings with or dependency on a criminal, and that stigma itself stresses an association between money and feces (the "dust piles" in *Our Mutual Friend*), which was strongly felt in the period and still more strongly defended against.

Jaggers' response to Magwitch, and to the poor and criminal classes in general, is characteristic of Victorian society's "successful" repression of the basis of its own wealth and expectations. Not accidentally, Jaggers is also a model of the anal personality—highly ordered, obstinate, and compulsively clean. His ritualistic cleanliness leaves the constant smell of "scented soap" on his hands, and leads to a scene like this:

> . . . he washed his clients off, as if he were a surgeon or a
> dentist. He had a closet in his room, fitted up for the purpose,
> which smelt of the scented soap like a perfumer's shop. It had
> an unusually large jack-towel on a roller inside the door, and
> he would wash his hands, and wipe them and dry them all over
> this towel, whenever he came in from a police-court or dis-
> missed a client from his room. When I and my friends repaired
> to him at six o'clock next day, he seemed to have been engaged
> on a case of a darker complexion than usual, for, we found him
> with his head butted into this closet, not only washing his
> hands, but laving his face and gargling his throat. And even
> when he had done all that, and had gone all round the jack-
> towel, he took out his penknife and scraped the case out of his
> nails before he put his coat on. (XXVI, 226–227)

This ritual defines the nature and basis of his self-control and moral fastidiousness. The normal requirements of his working day, his contact with clients, the law, prisons, people in general constantly threaten to soil him—much as Pip feels his existence strangely stained after leaving Jaggers' office or visiting Newgate, and feels this stain about to pollute his meeting with Estella. Jaggers' office is in Little Britain. The pollution of his daily life and his response to it are a microcosm of the business world of nineteenth-century Britain.

Like any successful figure in that world, Jaggers is also highly aggressive, but he is careful to keep his aggression under strict control. Jaggers' obvious exaggerations are built on the most sacred economic and ethical clichés of the period. The ambitious man of the era hoped to "rise" in the world, to thrust himself to the top of his economic and social group, yet he tried not to appear competitive, crude, ungentlemanly. The adjective "manly," as it was used by the Victorians, contained both aspects of this idea: male strength and power, plus a self-imposed restraint:

> There are many tests by which a gentleman may be known; but there is one that never fails—How does he *exercise power* over those subordinate to him? How does he conduct himself towards women and children? . . . Strength, and the consciousness of strength, in a righthearted man imparts a nobleness to his character; but he will be most careful how he uses it. . . . Gentleness is indeed the best test of gentlemanliness.[20]

The sense of conflict and repression built into such terminology mirrors the conflict at work in Jaggers and the world he symbolizes. The very physical appearance of the lawyer simultaneously asserts his masculinity and denies it:

> He was a burly man of an exceedingly dark complexion, with an exceedingly large head and a corresponding large hand. . . . He was prematurely bald on the top of his head, and had bushy black eyebrows that wouldn't lie down, but stood up bristling. His eyes were set very deep in his head, and were disagreeably sharp and suspicious. He had . . . strong black dots where his beard and whiskers would have been if he had let them. (XI, 87)

We are very aware of hair on his face which bristles with assertion, and we are even more aware of hair which isn't there—the early

---

20. Samuel Smiles, *Self Help; With Illustrations of Character, Conduct, and Perseverance* (Chicago, 1881), pp. 440–441.

baldness on a large head, the heavy beard which is kept back. His moral posture strikes the same note. As Wemmick repeatedly tells us, Jaggers is "always so high"—a phrase which implies his moral superiority and associates it with male power. Dickens' portrayal of Jaggers reveals the enormous discomfort occasioned by the lawyer's moral positions and clarifications. When he cross-examines Wopsle or disposes of a client he asserts himself to a point of total domination, but always with a strict self-control that seems to deny the assertiveness. When Pip comes to remonstrate with him, Jaggers immediately puts Pip on the defensive by absolving himself of any involvement, any interest at all. "Don't commit yourself . . . and don't commit any one. You understand—any one. Don't tell me anything. I don't want to know anything" (XL, 360). This phallic assertion and its immediate repression, characteristic of Jaggers and of the language of economic power in the period generally, are epitomized in Jaggers' most distinctive gesture. He throws out his great forefinger, and then bites it "accusingly."

Jaggers affects Pip in many ways that suggest a legitimized, and consequently a less overtly frightening, version of Magwitch. He is Magwitch's agent and spokesman for a good part of the novel. He distributes Magwitch's money to Pip and in the process he cleans it up until the time when Pip discovers its (dirty) source. As Pip's guardian, he behaves like a chiding, disapproving father. Between them Magwitch and Jaggers suggest opposite but related sides to Victorian economic life—the dirty and the clean, the criminal and the legitimate.

Their shared qualities offer additional insight into Pip's hallucinations in Chapter 57. There Pip feels himself giddily exposed, first as a brick and then as a steel beam of a vast engine, and begs to be removed from his height, to have the engine stopped and his "part in it hammered off" (LVII, 500). We can now see that his fear of phallic assertiveness and desire for symbolic castration have two related meanings. They signal, in his personal life, a shift in attitude toward the father, a movement from Magwitch to Joe. But the sense of a vast whirling engine or great house-wall in which he has been placed is also his and our sense of society as a whole. Julian Moynahan writes that

> the hero-victim cries for release from his unsought position of height and power, but cannot help himself from functioning

as a moving part of a monstrous apparatus. . . . In the narrative's full context this vast engine can be taken to represent at one and the same time the demonic side of the hero's career and a society that maintains its power intact by the continuous destruction of the hopes and lives of its weaker members.[21]

The imagery of Pip's hallucinations and even Moynahan's own language suggest an identical unconscious basis for individual and social attitudes in the novel. "The monstrous apparatus" is powerful and male, and its fierceness destroys what Moynahan aptly terms "its weaker members." Just as Pip fears to assert himself against Magwitch (and suffer the fate of Compeyson), so he fears to assert himself in society, to find work, to succeed, and to abuse the lower classes as society itself has abused Magwitch. The underlying pattern of phallic aggression and fear of castration is present in a social as well as a personal reading of this passage.

Jaggers' goal would seem to be total self-reliance: sufficient control over those people and objects around him to ensure his safety, his own freedom of action, and ultimately his dissociation from any human emotion. His actions exaggerate and parody the popular notions of self-reliance and self-help of the period. The "self-made man" is a man who owes his success to no one, who has perfect control over his own movements, over what he takes in and what he releases. In psychoanalytic terms the concept suggests an individual's desire for mastery of his body and of his very existence: he has made (created) himself. The adult solution to problems of independence and economic self-reliance will be excessively important to a man whose childhood contains conflict over related issues. Similarly, in a society where children grow up in competition with strong fathers (where the family structures tend to be markedly patriarchal), and where great stress is placed on cleanliness, toilet-training, and self-control, the family and business structures will be mutually reinforcing.

Financial independence thus becomes of paramount importance, whereas "any class of men that lives from hand to mouth will ever be an inferior class. They will necessarily remain impotent and helpless." [22] To avoid this impotence Smiles urges "the virtue of self-denial, than which nothing is so much calculated to give strength

21. Moynahan, "The Hero's Guilt," p. 167.
22. Smiles, *Self Help*, p. 324.

to the character." [23] The ideal of an economically independent man is attained by an adult version of toilet training, as Smiles's language makes clear:

> Economy, at bottom, is but the spirit of order applied in the administration of domestic affairs: it means management, regularity, prudence, and the avoidance of waste. . . .
> Economy also means the power of resisting present gratification for the purpose of securing a future good, and in this light it represents the ascendency of reason over the animal instincts.[24]

Smiles's thought reveals a combination of anal and genital attitudes that seems particularly Victorian. Helplessness and impotence result from a lack of wealth; self-denial gives strength and power to the individual. As he reminds his readers at one point, there are two classes of men: "those who have saved, and those who have spent." [25] The latter waste their power, the former are the industrial monarchs of society. Steven Marcus has shown how this "economic" mode of thought was part of the official Victorian doctrine of sexuality. Marcus describes Dr. William Acton's warnings against masturbation, concluding that Acton's apparently scientific advice is essentially fantasy, built on fear of sexuality:

> The fantasies that are at work here have to do with economics; the body is regarded as a productive system with only a limited amount of material at its disposal. And the model on which the notion of semen is formed is clearly that of money. Science, in the shape of Acton, is thus still expressing what had for long been a popular fantasy: up until the end of the nineteenth century the chief English colloquial expression for the orgasm was "to spend." . . . Furthermore, the economy envisaged in this idea is based on scarcity and has as its aim the accumulation of its own product.[26]

23. Smiles, p. 322.
24. Smiles, p. 327.
25. Smiles, p. 324.
26. Steven Marcus, *The Other Victorians* (New York, 1966), p. 22. Marcus approaches nineteenth-century medical bias through Freudian insight. But it is worth noting that Freud himself was practicing psychoanalysis before 1900, and he occasionally reflects prevalent Victorian prejudices.

Marcus goes on to suggest two ideas behind this Victorian fantasy: the fear of poverty and the tendency to regard the human body as a machine.

Dickens' novels demonstrate the pervasiveness of both ideas. Wills, gifts, hidden paternity, and recurrent great expectations are the concretely financial rewards lavished on his heroes, while economic disaster leads characters from every social class—Little Nell, Betty Higden, or the financial giant, Merdle—to death. Dorothy Van Ghent has shown that the mechanical view of people as things or parts of things and the animation of the inanimate inform the vision of *Great Expectations,* and are prominent as early as *Martin Chuzzlewit*.[27] Both Jaggers and Magwitch share in this mechanization: Jaggers forces Wemmick into a fixed pose of reticence known as his "post-office mouth"; and he is himself mechanically ritualistic in his cleanliness and in the accusatory gesture of his forefinger—a gesture that finally comes to stand for him. Magwitch virtually incorporates Pip as an extension of himself in his financial desire to "make a gentleman" out of the mire of his own life,[28] to clean and gild the degradation felt while accumulating money: "I mustn't see my gentleman a footing it in the mire of the streets; there mustn't be no mud on *his* boots" (XL, 357).

Psychoanalysis tells us that a child's first notion of his feces are that they are a part or extension of himself. With a boy they become associated in his mind with that part of himself he most fears to lose—the penis—and are thus closely linked to fears of castration. Holding on to feces, in a later stage of development, may result from an overwhelming fear of castration; if the Oedipal conflict strongly reinforces such fears, the solution may be to regress to an earlier mode of thought and an earlier conflict, to substitute feces for penis and hold on to the former as a means of protecting the

---

For example, his theory of the "actual neuroses" (see "On the Grounds for Detaching a Particular Syndrome from Neurasthenia Under the Description 'Anxiety Neurosis,'" S.E., III, 90–115) seems to reflect an unfounded prejudice against masturbation and coitus interruptus.

27. Dorothy Van Ghent, "The Dickens World: A View from Todgers's," in *The Dickens Critics,* ed. George Ford and Lauriat Lane (Ithaca, 1961), pp. 213–232, and *"Great Expectations": Form and Function in the English Novel* (New York, 1961), pp. 125–138.

28. Magwitch says to Pip, "I tell it, fur you to know as that there hunted dung-hill dog wot you kep life in, got his head so high that he could make a gentleman—and, Pip, you're him!" (XXXIX, 346).

latter. But psychoanalysis has shown that reversal is often used defensively in neurotic thought, and an opposite solution may also be used for the same problem: threatened with a fear of castration, the neurotic decides to give in, to relinquish the penis or to go back to the anal substitute and relinquish wealth.[29]

In *Great Expectations* the powerful and threatening fathers also control the source of Pip's wealth. We have already seen that Pip desires to be rid of both Magwitch and Jaggers but avoids open conflict with them. Fearing castration, he seeks a regressive solution —appeasement of the father along with denial of his own aggressive, incestuous wishes. So, too, he seeks to adopt an aloof and genteel attitude toward material possession, the attitude of the inept Matthew and Herbert Pocket, and finally he renounces altogether the money proffered by Magwitch. The business of a gentleman, it would seem, is no business at all, a denial of money-making which ought to lead to a denial of money itself—to poverty. The unconscious wish behind this aspect of the novel is a desire to reverse society's imposed pattern of phallic competition and economic control—to be generous, disinterested, and wholly above such competition.

And this is precisely how Dickens resolves Pip's business career. He credits Pip with one disinterested act: setting up Herbert Pocket in business. Pip rejects Magwitch's money with all its unpleasant

29. In Freud's "Wolf-man" case (see above, note 12) his patient had been seduced by an elder sister and he had responded with a mental reversal of the trauma, even feeling considerable guilt at his own (imagined) aggression toward that sister. He had witnessed intercourse between his parents, had felt it as an act of violence, and yet in his subsequent fantasies of the act had adopted his mother's role. He developed an anal fixation as part of his inverted solution to the Oedipus complex. Feces were imagined as substitutes for children and for the penis, and one memory sounds as if it had been lifted from *Great Expectations:* the subject's father gave his sister "two large bank notes" which were unconsciously interpreted as a sexual gift, an act of intercourse (p. 83).

Pip's relationship with Joe implies a desire—like that of Freud's subject—to replace the mother. Magwitch's violent and dirty reappearance, accompanied by imagery of the storm raging against the apertures and passages of Pip's rooms, is suggestive of "anal rape." Magwitch's wealth, epitomized by the "fat sweltering one-pound notes," provides the weapon for assaulting and appropriating Pip, who feels himself "pursued by the creature who had made me" (XL, 365). The unconscious implications here remain pertinent to Pip's whole social initiation and to his eventual repudiation of his fortune and implicit withdrawal from any form of economic competition. In this novel of social consciousness and growth, father-son relationships are critical because they determine social identity in a world dominated by men.

associations, but he manages to spend a portion of it on Herbert before he is made aware of those associations. The investment is sound. Pip can roll up his sleeves and go to work for Clarriker's, he can give up his independence and work for someone else, knowing all the time that he himself has created his employer. He is a self-made man. This act guarantees his own power while asserting his disinterestedness and lack of manipulation. The hero's realized expectations with Clarriker's gratify a wish for independence and success which is everywhere in the novel, beginning with its title, but the wish is gratified by what seems a deus ex machina. Pip achieves his expectations too easily, without actually suffering the price they appear to demand.

Pip's problems are caricatured and overcome in the portrayal of Wemmick. At work Wemmick is dominated by his employer, who places him in the outer office and makes him screen anyone who enters. His eating habits here epitomize the role he must adopt: "Wemmick was at his desk, lunching—and crunching—on a dry hard biscuit; pieces of which he threw from time to time into his slit of a mouth, as if he were posting them" (XXIV, 213). Everyone who enters and leaves the office is carefully checked and dealt with in the same manner. Wemmick turns himself into a machine in order to eat, to receive or give directions, to dispose of people and property. His ideal is to turn all possessions into portable property. At Walworth he has similarly built a fortress home, complete with drawbridge, whose entrances are narrow and protected, and are now under his exclusive control. Wemmick's identification with his snug retreat is the reverse of Pip's sense of exposure in his rooms on the evening of Magwitch's return. By controlling the entries and passages of his house Wemmick implicitly takes full control over himself.

The main difference between Wemmick's home and his office is his reversal of roles toward Jaggers and his own father. As Wemmick tells Pip, "Walworth is one place, and this office is another. Much as the Aged is one person, and Mr. Jaggers is another" (XXXVI, 315). The extreme contrast between Wemmick's father ("the Aged" or "Aged Parent") and Jaggers is strikingly similar to the split for Pip between his guardian-benefactor and Joe. Whereas Joe is good-hearted and tender (and intellectually and socially Pip's inferior), Wemmick's father is simply senile. This gives the son full control over him. What is euphemistically described as "the great nightly ceremony" is a ritual prepared by Wemmick presumably for his father's benefit:

> Proceeding into the Castle again, we found the Aged heating the poker, with expectant eyes, as a preliminary to the performance of this great nightly ceremony. Wemmick stood with his watch in his hand until the moment was come for him to take the red-hot poker from the Aged, and repair to the battery. He took it, and went out, and presently the Stinger went off with a bang that shook the crazy little box of a cottage as if it must fall to pieces . . . Upon this the Aged—who I believe would have been blown out of his arm-chair but for holding on by the elbows—cried out exultingly, "He's fired! I heered him!" (XXV, 224–225)

The hot poker, the gun, the explosion all emphasize the potency of Wemmick, who organizes the ceremony and fires the weapon— while his father grabs his chair for dear life. This scene may be a comic inversion of a primal scene. Instead of a boy's witnessing his parents copulating, and being terrified by what he takes to be their violence, the son himself now performs the "great nightly ceremony," and with parental approval. What is perfectly clear from the passage is an inversion of power from father to son. Wemmick is ideally tender and considerate of the Aged, and the Aged is ideally weakened and dependent on his son. There is no conflict because the Aged's senility is a most effective form of castration.

With Jaggers, Wemmick is another man, or son; he dramatically alters and splits his personality. While he and Pip are dining at Jaggers' home, Pip tries

> catching his eye now and then in a friendly way. But it was not to be done. He turned his eyes on Mr. Jaggers whenever he raised them from the table, and was as dry and distant to me as if there were twin Wemmicks and this was the wrong one. (XLVIII, 420)

As they are about to leave a transformation takes place:

> Even when we were groping among Mr. Jaggers's stock of boots for our hats, I felt that the right twin was on his way

back; and we had not gone half a dozen yards down Gerrard Street in the Walworth direction before I found that I was walking arm-in-arm with the right twin, and that the wrong twin had evaporated into the evening air.

"Well!" said Wemmick, "that's over! He's a wonderful man, without his living likeness; but I feel that I have to screw myself up when I dine with him—and I dine more comfortably unscrewed." (XLVIII, 423)

Wemmick can afford to be gentle and tender with his parent for the same reasons that Pip can afford to be "disinterested" in his position at Clarriker's; both are aware of their ultimate influence and control. Wemmick's exaggerated splitting of personalities between home and office is not only a profound comment on the gulf between moral and economic demands in the period, but also a filial strategy far more successful than Pip's. The aspects of Pip's psychic plight that must remain painfully repressed are made comically accessible to us through Wemmick. This is true, for example, of the very language used to describe Wemmick's father: "The Aged . . . might have passed for some clean old chief of a savage tribe, just oiled" (XXXVII, 321). The basis of humor here is the treatment of what would normally be a symbol of potency and domination (the chief of a savage tribe) as if he were a harmless ("clean," "old") sexual tool ("just oiled"). The surprising and clever description is a "bribe," an inducement to allow a release of aggression against a father figure.[30] And the humor also lets us enjoy the mechanization of a human being (oiled like a tool) which is so frightening at other points in the novel.

Pip's fortunate solution to his financial problems, however, is neither comic nor successful. It is rather symptomatic of Dickens' own difficulty in trying to offer a viable alternative to the social ills he has described. The overt solution to Pip's great expectations is ill prepared and unconvincing, while the implied solution is regressive: the appearance of a little Pip back at the forge, tended by Joe and by a new, loving Mrs. Joe, and with all the problems of economic competition and social identity comfortably reserved for a distant point in the future.

This ultimate failure to suggest radical reform prompted Humphry

30. See generally Freud's "Jokes and Their Relation to the Unconscious," *S.E.,* VIII, and particularly p. 132.

House to call the book "the clearest artistic triumph of the Victorian bourgeoisie on its own special ground." House accused Dickens of shirking "the implications of the reconciliation with Joe and Biddy," and of trying to assure us that "Pip is the same decent little fellow after all: but what if he had had no Herbert to fall back on . . . ? Dickens . . . takes Pip's new class position as established, and whisks him off to the East, where gentlemen grow like mushrooms." Yet House defends the ending aesthetically because the book "is the sincere, uncritical expression of a time when the whole class-drift was upwards and there was no reason to suppose that it would ever stop being so. The social ideals of Pip and Magwitch differ only in taste." [31]

I disagree. On the level of characterization, Dickens is quite critical of the upward class-drift of his society. The pressure of expectations tends to divide characters, to induce a separation between an external pose of correct aloofness and a covert aggression aiming at wealth and social supremacy. The few characters who fail to evidence this split—Matthew Pocket, for example—are dominated and lifeless. In *Great Expectations* the "correct" attitudes of the period have nothing like the emotional force of its criminality. Jaggers may manage, with great effort, to keep his hands clean of this criminal stain, but his success is hardly held up for emulation. Yet Dickens, for reasons that have never been satisfactorily explained, could not pursue the logic of his own implicit critique, either here or elsewhere in his works and life. His reactionary support of Carlyle in the Governor Eyre case, his contradictory positions on prison reform,[32] and his surprising repudiation of labor unions in *Hard Times* (1854) are characteristic turnabouts, attempts to deny the reform whose necessity he had demonstrated. The ending of *Great Expectations* is typical precisely because it is inconsistent. But why this ambivalence?

The case of *Hard Times* suggests a possible answer. *Hard Times* is as oriented toward social criticism and social reform as any novel Dickens wrote. It castigates industrial society as a whole and raises the common industrial worker to the status of hero. But when the workers' grievances seem to lead them to a justified and total revolt, Dickens introduces an inept caricature of a union organizer to

31. Humphry House, *The Dickens World* (London, 1965), pp. 156–157.
32. Philip Collins thoroughly discusses this question in *Dickens and Crime* (London, 1965).

discredit the obvious solution. In a chapter entitled "Men and Brothers," he contrasts the short and twisted figure of Slackbridge "with the great body of his hearers in their plain working clothes." Slackbridge "was above the mass in very little but the stage on which he stood. In many great respects he was essentially below them. He was not so honest, he was not so manly. . . ."[33] The imagery emphasizes Slackbridge's lack of masculinity, his shortness, his twistedness, and his "mongrel dress," [34] in comparison with the upright, "manly" workers in the hall. At the same time it emphasizes and deplores Slackbridge's attempt to raise and assert himself, either literally on the podium or by urging the men to crush their "masters" in a strike. The passage repudiates a rebellion against the industrial masters by denigrating the phallic power ("slack bridge") of the would-be leader of the rebellion, by implying castration or impotence as the necessary result of such a desire. Dickens here upholds the implicit contradiction in Victorian manliness. For the workers whom he idealizes, it means both strength *and* repression of that strength.

The clean, enduring, and self-controlled nature of his hero, Stephen Blackpool, reinforces this ideal. Stephen refuses to strike and is ostracized by his "brothers." In the following chapter, entitled "Men and Masters," Stephen also tries to maintain his independence from his overbearing employer, Mr. Bounderby. Implicitly he is seeking an equilibrium of ambivalent forces toward a father figure. Dickens is unwilling to have him either revolt entirely or become Bounderby's tool. Thus Stephen emerges as the epitome of "manliness," whose practical consequence is paralysis—he cannot revolt and he cannot work for Bounderby. In the end he leaves Coketown, is falsely accused of theft, and dies from his fall into the Old Hell Shaft.

The dissatisfying outcome of *Great Expectations* reflects not only Dickens' personal ambivalence but the unconscious contradictions of Victorian society with regard to money, the lower classes, and the upward class-drift described by Humphry House. In this shared

33. Charles Dickens, *Hard Times*, ed. George Ford and Sylvère Monod (New York: Norton, 1966), pp. 105–106. Citations by book, chapter, and page are in parentheses following quotations.
34. He was also described by Dickens as "shabby-genteel," although this was removed from the proofs (see p. 256, note 106.3 in the Norton Critical Edition cited in note 33). The phrase implies that Slackbridge is a false gentleman, much like Compeyson.

ambivalence lies the power as well as the limitation of Dickens' novel. It is felt throughout Pip's personal history and in the social allegory of his great expectations. Dickens offers us a profound insight into the psychology underlying Victorian social attitudes—a psychology he seems to have fully shared.

III.

The attempt to resolve social conflict in *Great Expectations* is only one of the problems of its final chapter. Dickens had submitted the last installment to Bulwer-Lytton, and allowed himself to be persuaded into a radical revision of the ending.[35] In its original (draft) version Pip's chance meeting with Estella simply leaves him with a sense that "suffering . . . had given her a heart to understand what my heart used to be" (LIX, 523). Bentley Drummle has died, but Estella has remarried. In the published ending Estella has not remarried, and there is a clear suggestion of a future marriage to Pip. Pip finds her in Miss Havisham's old ruined garden, they part hand in hand, and Pip sees "no shadow of another parting from her" (LIX, 526).

Our preference for one version or the other depends upon more than the plausibility of Pip's marriage to Estella. In order to accept the second ending we must take a wish, an impossible dream, as fact. Until the final chapter Dickens has made us feel Pip's hopeless idealization of a woman raised for revenge, raised—as Estella herself realizes—incapable of normal affections.

Dickens' heroines are always incomplete women. As his hero discovers the pretty young thing of his dreams to be a vacuous, spoiled child he attains a measure of self-understanding but is never reconciled to feminine imperfection. Rather, the woman herself is implausibly perfected, or simply replaced—as Dora Spenlow is replaced by Agnes Wickfield in *David Copperfield*. The very names of Dickens' heroines, culminating with the ironic Rosa Bud of *Edwin Drood,* suggest a self-parody of his tendency to create female china dolls. In *Great Expectations* Dickens seems particularly aware of his own limitations: instead of attempting to transform or eliminate

---

35. The original ending was first reprinted and discussed by Forster, II (1966), 289 and 441n.

Estella—at least until the final chapter—he uses her to dramatize Pip's self-delusion.

Dickens never really tries to portray Estella's emotions. She has been the object of other people's hopes and ideals, perhaps understanding them but incapable of a full response. "It seems," she tells Pip, "that there are sentiments, fancies—I don't know how to call them—which I am not able to comprehend. When you say you love me, I know what you mean, as a form of words; but nothing more. You address nothing in my breast, you touch nothing there" (XLIV, 390). Estella is Dickens' finest study of a beautiful and desired woman because she is seen so exclusively from without. She is created by those around her—by Miss Havisham, for whom she is an instrument of revenge, a more beautiful and invulnerable version of herself; and by Pip, for whom she is the ultimate great expectation, the princess awarded him by his fairy godmother. The second ending is dissonant because we suddenly see Estella from within, as really having a personality, and we are asked to believe that Pip's attitude toward her is completely altered.

From their first meeting, however, Pip's attraction for Estella is bound to a sense of her inaccessibility. "She seemed much older than I," he says on first meeting her, ". . . and beautiful and self-possessed; and she was as scornful of me as if she had been one-and-twenty, and a queen" (VIII, 59). Pip thus becomes obsessed with what he cannot have, and finds himself incapable of pursuing a more satisfactory love. When he later contrasts Biddy and Estella, he realizes that "Biddy was never insulting, or capricious . . . ; she would have derived only pain, and no pleasure, from giving me pain; she would far rather have wounded her own breast than mine. How could it be, then, that I did not like her much the better of the two?" (XVII, 140).

The answer is that his strongest attachments can only be maintained where there is little or no prospect of fulfillment. Only when Estella announces that she will marry Bentley Drummle does Pip make his own declaration. During this meeting, Pip admits that he has always loved her, has seen her everywhere ("on the river, on the sails of the ships, on the marshes, in the clouds . . .") and insists on the fact that "you must have done me far more good than harm, let me feel now what sharp distress I may" (XLIV, 393). But it is distress he has sought all along with Estella, and he fully indulges himself in it in this scene. He concludes:

> In what ecstasy of unhappiness I got these broken words
> out of myself, I don't know. The rhapsody welled up within
> me, like blood from an inward wound, and gushed out. I held
> her hand to my lips some lingering moments, and so I left her.
> But ever afterwards, I remembered—and soon afterwards with
> stronger reason—that while Estella looked at me merely with
> incredulous wonder, the spectral figure of Miss Havisham, her
> hand still covering her heart, seemed all resolved into a ghastly
> stare of pity and remorse. (XLIV, 393)

The passage is particularly revealing in two ways. First, its use of
contradictory language exposes the logic behind Pip's passion.
Unhappiness, his own rejection, is really a part of what he seeks in
Estella and the basis for his "ecstasy." Second, the transition from
Estella to Miss Havisham suggests a substitution of one for the other.

Estella and Miss Havisham become interchangeable. Throughout
this scene Pip finds Estella uncomprehending or unresponsive to
his words, while marking their profound effect on Miss Havisham.
Later, Miss Havisham sends for Pip to beg his forgiveness.[36] In the
process she undergoes a transformation, and sees herself as she
once was in the period before her disaster. She is changed from
an old hag to a woman, as Pip himself notes: "There was an earnest
womanly compassion for me in her new affection" (XLIX, 432).
Pip leaves her, walks into the old brewery, and sees a vision of her
hanging from a beam (434). This is a repetition of an earlier vision
(VIII, 68), and in both cases Pip had previously been bitterly
wounded by Estella's treatment of him. Yet he never maligns Estella
or wishes her ill; rather, his vengeance is projected onto Miss
Havisham.[37] And not only his vengeance, but his passion. His vision
so disturbs him that he returns to check on Miss Havisham, and
as he is about to leave he sees her burst into flame:

> I saw a great flaming light spring up. In the same moment I
> saw her running at me, shrieking, with a whirl of fire blazing

36. See XLIX, 430. In the final chapter Estella makes the same request and
    receives virtually the same answer (LIX, 525).
37. Moynahan, "The Hero's Guilt," pp. 163–165, shows that this vengeance
    is also due Miss Havisham in her own right. Moynahan sees Bentley
    Drummle as Pip's vengeful surrogate in Drummle's cruel treatment of
    Estella (pp. 161–162).

all about her, and soaring at least as many feet above her head as she was high. (XLIX, 434)

Pip covers her with his coats and the tablecloth, closes with her, and finds that

> we were on the ground struggling like desperate enemies, and that the closer I covered her, the more wildly she shrieked and tried to free herself; . . . I still held her forcibly down with all my strength, like a prisoner who might escape; and I doubt if I even knew who she was, or why we had struggled . . . Assistance was sent for, and I held her until it came, as if I unreasonably fancied (I think I did) that if I let her go, the fire would break out again and consume her. (XLIX, 434–435)

Although her dress is burned, she is covered in a white sheet and cotton and still has "something of her old ghastly bridal appearance" (435). She repeats three phrases over and over, asking Pip in the last to forgive her: "I leaned over her and touched her lips with mine, just as they said, not stopping for being touched, 'Take the pencil and write under my name, "I forgive her" ' " (XLIX, 436).

This change of heart and desire to be forgiven are similar to Mrs. Joe's behavior following her beating. As she sought to propitiate Orlick, so Miss Havisham continues to beg Pip's pardon. And as with the attack on Mrs. Joe, there is a sense here of sexual assault: Miss Havisham is shrieking and "inflamed." Pip holds her, covers her with his own body on the ground, and keeps her there even after the flames have gone out, for the fire within her may "break out again."

Miss Havisham and Estella are opposite versions of a single woman: the latter a virgin (unobtainable) ideal, the former a debased sexual object. Their exaggerated contrast is typically Victorian, yet it is rooted in a universal repression of childhood. All boys are forced, with varying success, to divorce sexual longing from a tender respect for their mothers. A common unconscious strategy is to imagine two figures, a "whore" sexually possessed by the father and an ideally spiritual "virgin."[38] Fairy tales display this

---

38. See Freud's "Contributions to the Psychology of Love," especially Parts I and II: "A Special Type of Choice of Object Made by Men," and "On the Universal Tendency to Debasement in the Sphere of Love" (*S.E.*, XI, 165–190).

split by depicting a disgusting old hag and a beautiful princess. And the world of Satis House is seen, especially by the boy Pip, as a fairyland where Miss Havisham is the presiding deity and Estella is the princess and the reward.[39]

On his first visit to Satis House Pip is met by Estella, who leads him to Miss Havisham's door and leaves him by himself in the dark hall. "This was very uncomfortable, and I was half afraid. However, the only thing to be done being to knock at the door, I knocked, and was told from within to enter." He goes into a room lighted entirely by candles, and discovers

> in an arm-chair, with an elbow resting on the table and her head leaning on that hand, . . . the strangest lady I have ever seen, or shall ever see.
>
> She was dressed in rich materials . . . all of white. . . . But, I saw that everything within my view which ought to be white, had been white long ago, and had lost its lustre, and was faded and yellow. I saw that the bride within the bridal dress had withered like the dress, and like the flowers, and had no brightness left but the brightness of her sunken eyes. I saw that the dress had been put upon the rounded figure of a young woman, and that the figure upon which it now hung loose, had shrunk to skin and bone. Once, I had been taken to see some ghastly waxwork at the Fair, representing I know not what impossible personage lying in state. Once, I had been taken to one of our old marsh churches to see a skeleton

39. Both Estella and Miss Havisham are seen as "queens" by Pip (VIII, 59; XXIX, 253), and Miss Havisham is twice referred to as his "fairy godmother" (169, 170).

The name "Satis House" is itself an ironic comment on the lack of satisfactions to be obtained there (see especially VIII, 59). It "had a great many iron bars to it. Some of the windows had been walled up; of those that remained, all the lower were rustily barred. There was a court-yard in front, and that was barred" (VIII, 57). The physical qualities of the house emphasize that it was once used; its entries and openings were once clear and have since been covered, barred, rusted. The same sense is conveyed by its "rank garden" and old brewery: once active and fermenting, the brewery's liquids have dried, its "uses and scents . . . have evaporated" (VIII, 67). These symbols imply a former sexual access or "entry," subsequent decay, and a continued taboo against Pip's entry. Estella warns Pip, "Better not try to brew beer there now, or it would turn out sour, boy" (59). The entire place is barricaded against robbers (VII, 54).

in the ashes of a rich dress, that had been dug out of a vault under the church pavement. Now, waxwork and skeleton seemed to have dark eyes that moved and looked at me. I should have cried out, if I could. (VIII, 60–61)

Symbols of purity and beauty (whiteness, the bridal dress, the rounded body of a young woman) are seen in terms of decay—yellowing, withering, shrinking, sinking—and finally death itself. With its repeated emphasis on the wedding and the physical changes in Miss Havisham, this rotting of dress and body ultimately makes itself felt as sexual decay. It carries a disgust which contradicts all the symbols of the wedding. The clocks are stopped *before* the marriage which never occurred, and everything Miss Havisham does, and is, emphasizes that the marriage was never consummated. This insistence on the fact that no marriage took place, together with the repeated imagery of sexual decay, suggests that the frozen clocks, the wedding cake and dress are products of reversal and denial.[40] Miss Havisham's literal story and symbolic trappings tell us that her existence has been defined by Compeyson's betrayal. The unconscious implication is that she has been sexually rotted by Compeyson. As fairy godmother to Pip, her physical and symbolic qualities derive from the same source as the old hag's ugliness in fairy tales: she is an extreme caricature of the sexually desired mother whom the child must vilify in order to reject.

Compeyson's role as "son" is as crucial here as it was in the climactic scene of Magwitch's capture. His betrayal of Miss Havisham is felt, at its deepest level, as the son's sexual betrayal of the mother. It is related to Pip's robbery of Mrs. Joe and Pip's later "grappling" with the burning Miss Havisham. In this sense Compeyson is a surrogate for Pip with Miss Havisham, much as Orlick was a surrogate for Pip in the attack on Mrs. Joe. The language describing Compeyson's betrayal once again bears this out. Pip tells us that Miss Havisham "had the appearance of having dropped, body and soul, within and without, under the weight of a crushing blow" (VIII, 64). Miss Havisham herself refers to her "wretched breast when it was first bleeding from [the] stabs" inflicted by Compeyson (XXXVIII, 329). And her brother Arthur has a similar

---

40. Some aspects of Miss Havisham's implied sexuality are less affected by a defensive reversal—like her feeding unseen in the night and a "ravenous intensity" in her affection for Estella (XXIX, 261, 258).

vision of her when he tells Compeyson, " 'she's standing in the corner at the foot of the bed, awful mad. And over where her heart's broke—*you* broke it!—there's drops of blood' " (XLII, 376).

The speaker in this last quotation is Magwitch, who is retelling to Pip what he overheard Arthur tell Compeyson. The complicated history of this piecemeal and thrice-removed narration of Miss Havisham's love affair with Compeyson is in sharp contrast to the climactic scene of Compeyson's final betrayal of Magwitch and his death. The contrast suggests that maternal relations in the underlying Oedipal conflict of the novel are far more repressed than the father conflicts described above. This is felt more generally in the absence of character or its complete distortion in all the major female figures. Mrs. Joe is seemingly unmotivated in her ill-treatment of Pip or her sudden reversal after being attacked, while Joe's sensibilities are delicately portrayed throughout (and particularly in scenes such as his visit to Pip in London). For all his coarseness Magwitch's character is strongly felt, whereas Estella is emotionally vacant. Miss Havisham is the richest creation among the women in the novel, and this richness is a direct result of her powerful unconscious appeal and of the conscious repression used to mask this appeal. Caricature here derives from a particularly strong degree of repression.

This view of Dickensian caricature may be clarified if it is contrasted with a more naked and less successful portrayal of a similar underlying fantasy. We have examined the passages in Chapter 8 of *Great Expectations* in which Pip first enters Satis House, meets the beautiful and queenlike Estella, is guided down dark passages of the house, and is left alone to enter a room without a trace of sunlight. The vision of whiteness and glitter that first greets him gives way to a sense of decay, and to the wizened, frightful figure of Miss Havisham seated in a chair. Compare this to the portion of *Hard Times* in which the hero, Stephen Blackpool, is seen entering his own home. Stephen is first accompanied by Rachael, an idealized woman who refuses to become his wife and who is an earlier and more saccharine version of Estella. After leaving her, Stephen proceeds home, lights his way by candle upstairs through the passages of a dark shop, and enters his own darkened room. He stumbles against something:

> As he recoiled, looking down at it, it raised itself up into the form of a woman in a sitting attitude. . . .

Such a woman! A disabled, drunken creature, barely able to preserve her sitting posture by steadying herself with one begrimed hand on the floor, while the other was so purposeless in trying to push away her tangled hair from her face, that it only blinded her the more with the dirt upon it. A creature so foul to look at, in her tatters, stains and splashes, but so much fouler than that in her moral infamy, that it was a shameful thing even to see her. (I.x.52)

The woman is Stephen's wife. A former friend of Rachael's when Stephen courted and married her, she has gradually become degraded and debauched (I.xiii.64). There is an unconscious logic to this sequence of events: the woman with whom the hero has sexual relations is seen as corrupted and corrupting. She becomes both a "dead woman" and a "demon" (I.xii.62). The woman who remains a loyal, platonic comrade through the years is gradually elevated to the status of angel (I.xiii.68). Stephen broods over the fact that his relations with Rachael are restricted and subjugated to "the infamous image" of his wife:

Filled with these thoughts—so filled that he had an unwholesome sense of growing larger, of being placed in some new and diseased relation towards the objects among which he passed, of seeing the iris round every misty light turn red—he went home for shelter. (I.xii.63)

The "sense of growing larger" implies erection: his aggressiveness and anger against his wife grow out of his sexual desire. This desire is seen as "unwholesome" and "diseased," tainting the objects around him, turning the very area in which he walks into one of red lanterns, of lust. His subsequent temptation to poison his whore of a wife (I.xiii) carries the same sexual force. If she should swallow the poison (as he hopes and fears), he will be responsible for poisoning (i.e., polluting) her, and he himself will be polluted by the act. But when he returns home, he finds Rachael by his wife, a heavenly force to minister to her and to protect him from temptation. The entire scene reads like a soap opera; Stephen cries out to Rachael, "Thou art an Angel. Bless thee, bless thee! . . . Thou changest me from bad to good. . . . it may be, thou hast saved my soul alive!" (I.xiii.68), and he kneels before her. The chapter concludes: "As the shining stars were to the heavy candle in the window, so was

Rachael, in the rugged fancy of this man, to the common experiences of his life" (I.xiii.69).

This imagery is repeated in the scene of Stephen's death, in the chapter entitled "The Starlight" (III.vi.201). Stephen has been crushed and mangled by a blatant symbol of destructive female sexuality—he falls into a deep, treacherous hole known as the "Old Hell Shaft." His rescue suggests a fetus being pulled from the womb: as he is extricated from the pit, attention focuses on a long rope, straining as it is wound coil upon coil, finally pulling him up in a bucket:

> A low murmur of pity went round the throng, and the women wept aloud, as this form, almost without form, was moved very slowly from its iron deliverance, and laid upon the bed of straw. At first, none but the surgeon went close to it. He did what he could in its adjustment on the couch . . . (III.vi.206)

And this chapter, too, concludes with a contrast between the ugly pit from which he has been delivered and the heavenly quality of Rachael, the angelic virginal woman, whom Stephen sees in the stars.[41]

The constant juxtaposition of Rachael and Mrs. Blackpool, with the contrasting imagery of angelic virginity and debased whoredom, has the same unconscious roots as the creations of Estella and Miss Havisham. But the latter are far more disguised in their conscious characterization and their relations with the hero. Whereas there seems to be no distance between Stephen's feelings for Rachael and the author's perception of them, Dickens makes us aware of the inherent problems in Pip's obsessive idealization of Estella. Similarly, while the sense of disgust attached to Blackpool's wife is fully indulged, the entire presentation of Miss Havisham is oblique and stylized. What might have been crude melodrama has been rendered artistically successful by the heightened work of psychic disguise.

Until the close of *Great Expectations* Dickens works brilliantly within the limits posed by his underlying assumptions about women. But at this point the ability to operate on two contradictory levels breaks down: he is unable to sustain an unconscious Oedipal fantasy in a significantly disguised form. The sexually charged "burning"

41. Rachael's frequent association with the stars provides another connection with "Estella."

scene between Miss Havisham and Pip anticipates Estella's debasement in her marriage to the brutal Bentley Drummle. The fantasy of possessing the mother, which results in the death of Miss Havisham, is then followed by a fight and an implicit murder of the son by the father (Compeyson's death on the river) and by Pip's own illness. From this point until its close the emotional force of the novel is nostalgic, implying a regressive, infantile solution rather than the adult solutions of economic independence and marriage.

One element of nostalgia has already been discussed: Pip's quite conscious desire to remain weak and childish with Joe after his illness, and his discovering himself again as Little Pip in the final chapter. The language of these last pages plays sentimentally on direct references to his boyhood: "Now let me go up and look at my old little room, and rest there a few minutes by myself," Pip tells Joe and Biddy before parting (LVIII, 520). Eleven years later he returns to touch "the latch of the old kitchen door," to see Joe "in the old place by the kitchen firelight" and to see himself again "on my own little stool" (LIX, 521).

Nostalgia, particularly at the close of Dickens' novels, suggests a desire to return to a pre-Oedipal state, free of conflict and at one with the mother. This is perhaps most clearly seen at the end of *Barnaby Rudge*. The idiot-hero, Barnaby, is described by his mother as a "loving child to me—never growing old or cold at heart, but needing my care and duty in his manly strength as in his cradletime." After the death of his villainous father, Barnaby achieves that state which every Dickens hero desires with varying degrees of explicitness or completeness: "Never was there a lighter-hearted husbandman, a creature more popular with young and old, a blither or more happy soul than Barnaby; and though he was free to ramble where he would, he never quitted Her, but was for evermore her stay and comfort." [42] The exalted "Her" is Barnaby's mother.

This implicit solution is achieved, somewhat less obviously, through Pip's thwarted proposal to Biddy, who becomes a loving mother to Little Pip. Mrs. Joe is replaced by a woman who has implicitly loved Pip prior to her attachment to his foster father, Joe. A "family romance" is thus suggested in which Pip "allows" the marriage of his own parents. Early in the novel Pip described his harsh treatment by Mrs. Joe in terms of "the ridgy effect of a wedding-ring, passing unsympathetically over the human coun-

---

42. Charles Dickens, *Barnaby Rudge* (London, 1961), Chapter XVII, p. 137; and Chapter the Last, p. 634.

tenance" (VII, 55). He rejoices when at the end, Biddy puts her "good matronly hand with which she had touched [the hand of Little Pip], into mine. There was something in the action and in the light pressure of Biddy's wedding-ring, that had a very pretty eloquence in it" (LIX, 521). That eloquent gesture, with all three of their hands touching, symbolizes the ideal relationship toward which Pip seeks a return. He could have been Biddy's lover and husband; through Little Pip he is both Biddy's son and her first "lover."

Biddy is Dickens' cure for the close of the novel. He originally seemed about to use her as he used Agnes Wickfield in *David Copperfield:* as a sisterly friend to the hero, in love with him throughout, who is discovered in time to console him with a love as much maternal as it is marital. Instead, while struggling with the insoluble problem of disposing satisfactorily of Estella, Dickens reveals in the use of Biddy and Little Pip the novel's deepest wish for regression.

This pronounced regressiveness does not, of course, make *Great Expectations* an aesthetic failure, but it does suggest inherent limits in Dickens' art and possibly in the terms of Victorian art in general.[43] Dickens' limitations are the very basis of his ingenuity: repression demands a constant succession of bizarrely brilliant psychic im-

---

43. However, Dickens' persistent tendency to split women into absolute categories of good and bad, virgin and whore, makes him something of an aesthetic conservative. Thackeray's portrayal of Becky Sharp and Amelia Sedley, in *Vanity Fair,* was a radical attack on this established Victorian attitude toward women. Becky becomes little more than a high-class whore, but retains the author's interest and much of his sympathy, while Dobbin is forced to devalue Amelia before their marriage can take place. In *Henry Esmond,* Thackeray dwelt on the hero's love for his foster mother, and received a strong Victorian reaction: "The reviewer . . . in *Blackwood's Magazine* wrote: 'Our most sacred sympathies are outraged and our best prejudices shocked by the leading feature of this tale.' The *Athenaeum's* reviewer was more explicit: Esmond's marriage to Rachel, he wrote, 'affects us somewhat like a marriage with his own mother. All the previous emotions of the piece return to haunt us.' . . . The *Athenaeum's* man was right: we are in the presence of a kind of incest . . ." (From Walter Allen's "Afterword" to the Signet edition [New York, 1964] of *The History of Henry Esmond, Esq.*, p. 473).

Several of Hardy's major novels attempt to confront Victorian prejudice toward women, and in Tess and Sue Bridehead he deals explicitly with the problems attached to a woman who has been sexually "soiled." Eliot and Meredith partake of this same exploration, which seems to culminate in the work of D. H. Lawrence. In the period surrounding the growth of psychoanalysis there is thus a growing self-awareness and a movement toward breaking down set sexual attitudes. Dickens' incapacity to challenge feminine stereotypes may help to account for his peculiar lack of direct influence on major writers of this century.

provisations. If *Great Expectations* is his finest novel, this may be because its incredibly intricate devices of plot and symbolism enabled him to imply here, more clearly than elsewhere, that beneath the hero's manifest guilt there lies a deeper guilt, felt but never articulated.

The trend of recent Dickens criticism has been to emphasize guilt and pervasive darkness in his work, particularly in his later novels. Moreover, critics like J. Hillis Miller have seen in these novels Dickens' increasingly mature perception both of his own attitudes and weaknesses and of the inherent contradictions of his age. If Dickens' world seems to take on a darker hue, we are told, it is because he has grown up, because he has rejected the infantile solutions of his early works. Miller sees "a reorientation toward the future and toward the free human spirit itself as the only true sources of value." [44]

We have seen, however, that Dickens' mature achievement is very much enmeshed in the child-parent relationships that occupy his earlier plots. Those relationships have been more deeply embedded in the late novels, provided with a form that gives scope to the underlying fantasies without giving them away. Dickens' success as a popular writer was based on his continued ability to transmit fantasies of universal appeal and power; his achievement as an artist grew with his varied and more prolonged exploration of these themes.

In *Great Expectations* the pervasive guilt and criminality, the bizarre women and the frustrated love of the hero consistently resonate on several levels. Pip's fears and desires extend to all of the novel's relationships, its minor characters, its comedy and caricature, and even to the business context of Little Britain and the socially shared attitudes toward women. The social dimension of *Great Expectations* cannot be ignored, but does not in itself account for the novel's power. Dickens has created a richly suggestive story of individual growth that reveals the deepest wishes and conflicts of its hero, of its author, and of an age to which we still respond.

44. J. Hillis Miller, *Charles Dickens: The World of His Novels* (Cambridge, Mass., 1958), p. 333. Miller maintains that Dickens has moved from a dependence on "the child-parent relation as an escape from isolation" in the early novels to "the more adult solution of romantic love" in *David Copperfield*. From *Bleak House* through *Our Mutual Friend* he traces the further development of an "adult view" of love (as denial and sacrifice).

THREE ∽ MOBY-DICK

DAVID LEVERENZ

> *. . . we weight the body, close*
> *Its eyes and heave it seaward whence it came,*
> *Where the heel-headed dog fish barks its nose*
> *On Ahab's void and forehead . . .*
> —ROBERT LOWELL,
> *"The Quaker Graveyard in Nantucket"*

I.

We come to this book well-weighted. Maybe our edition has a sizable introduction, not only telling us the plot and the cast of characters but filling us in with background, intentions, symbolic structures, and favorite passages. Or maybe we have simply heard about this greatest of American books, and expect a sea adventure, with Ahab and the White Whale in mortal combat. We sit down with our expectations. Then, right from the start, the book heaves us seaward in ways we don't know how to cope with. Even on our third or tenth reading, we are overwhelmed simply by its strangeness. We expect to grasp, but the "ungraspable phantom" takes us into its own hands.

Such feelings are easy to domesticate. On a seaward spin, the myths of the land seem especially attractive. But if we are to be honest to our experience of this "wicked book," we have to begin not with the land-commentaries which resolve uncertainties and inexplicabilities (often by making inexplicability itself the theme),

38763

but with our own sense of crumbling expectations. The strangeness separates us from what we have been told, what we remember, into a curious aloneness. The more alone we become, the more we clutch at our land community. But the book still heaves us seaward, toward that "void and forehead."

Take, for instance, our first expectation. Here is a fat book under our right thumb, a "great novel." Most such books begin with a scene, or a character, or an event, or a piece of moral philosophy. In fact, we are already serenely confident about this book's beginning, since everyone knows the first line. "Call me Ishmael." We'll open the book to this man's monologue, as he sweeps us into his sea adventure. So we open the book—and we find:

> The pale Usher—threadbare in coat, heart, body, and brain; I see him now. He was ever dusting his old lexicons and grammars, with a queer handkerchief, mockingly embellished with all the gay flags of all the known nations of the world. He loved to dust his old grammars; it somehow mildly reminded him of his mortality.[1]

But perhaps we rush past this odd figure, lovingly purifying his books, yet "mocking" all the "known" nations and notions they contain. We aren't aware of the connection between that outer blazonry and his inner aloneness, between the known and the unknown and "mortality"—not yet. Even the "sub-sub-librarian" whom we meet next, so pitiable in his "promiscuous" efforts to fathom what can be "known" about the whale, awakes our distant humor more than our identification. We are already more fascinated by the inscrutable soul who acknowledges the help of these men than by either of them or by the data they have supplied. Our tenuous identifications with the Usher and the Sub-Sub seem, on reflection, located more in his perceptions than in their reality. We are curious, above all, about the tensions and abeyances in this man's mind. Why has he created such an introduction to the book?

In this mood, we turn the pages to the first chapter. "Loomings." Again the portentous lack of certainty:

---

1. Norton Critical Edition, ed. Harrison Hayford and Hershel Parker (New York, 1967), p. 1. All references are to this edition; page numbers appear in parentheses following quotations.

Call me Ishmael. Some years ago—never mind how long
precisely—having little or no money in my purse, and nothing
particular to interest me on shore, I thought I would sail about
a little and see the watery part of the world. It is a way I have
of driving off the spleen, and regulating the circulation. Whenever I find myself growing grim about the mouth; whenever
it is a damp, drizzly November in my soul; whenever I find
myself involuntarily pausing before coffin warehouses, and
bringing up the rear of every funeral I meet; and especially
whenever my hypos get such an upper hand of me, that it
requires a strong moral principle to prevent me from deliberately stepping into the street, and methodically knocking people's hats off—then, I account it high time to get to sea as
soon as I can. This is my substitute for pistol and ball. With a
philosophical flourish Cato throws himself upon his sword; I
quietly take to the ship. There is nothing surprising in this. If
they but knew it, almost all men in their degree, some time or
other, cherish very nearly the same feelings towards the ocean
with me. (12)

Let us look at the movement of this famous "first" paragraph.

"Call me Ishmael." This name immediately evokes a train of
mental associations and takes us straightway to the editors' footnote:
the original book of the original gospel, Genesis, where we find the
story of Ishmael's banishment to the wilderness with his slave
mother, Hagar, by Abraham, his father, on orders of his father's
jealous wife. Our psychological ears prick up expectantly, and we
might even wonder if Ishmael's psychology, too, will show that a
"bad" mother has dominated his father and has driven him out to
lead a life of lonely exile, leadership, mortality, and mute aggression.

But in making these connections, we miss the real impact of these
simple words: they activate mental contingencies rather than physical reality. We immediately define the speaker by someone else,
his analogue in the gospel text he wishes to reconstitute. Only later,
upon more reflection, do we become aware that these three words
don't necessarily give his real name. We have leaped for meaning
and explanation to this label as much because of our own uncertainty as because of his blunt request. We still have no sense of his
face, his body, his hands, his expression. As before, his use of
seemingly straightforward words, even to name the most vividly

present object (himself), slips us imperceptibly into alien and speculative identities, and separates us from the particular in the name of the universal. "Ishmael" exists as a storyteller, a role allowing all emotions to be provisional. We'll never learn his last name; as with his God, we'll never see his face.

The next five sentences, as we would expect of someone sent away from his father's wife into the wilderness, or of someone who so loves to drink with Sub-Sub failures, define and elaborate his need for water. The voice seems calm, reflective, highly rhythmic and evenly balanced in its quiet explanations. "Some years ago," a four-syllable echo of "Call me Ishmael," breaks into a pattering hyphenation, "never mind how long precisely," which establishes the storyteller's stance once and for all while again reaffirming his absolute control over narrative material and his preference for the vague generality over the "promiscuous" particular. With that established, Ishmael gives us four groups of eight words each, a perfectly balanced introduction to his motives and theme:

> having little or no money in my purse,
> and nothing particular to interest me on shore,
> I thought I would sail about a little
> and see the watery part of the world.

How controlled, how self-depreciating yet inclusive of the self's possibilities! The split participial clause explains his motives: no money, boredom—simply and universally human. Then the main clause connects motive and act in syntax, rhythm, and jaunty repetition ("little . . . little"), and domesticates the land-sea dualism into just another "part of the world." The emptiness in the participial negatives, the sense of having nothing and going toward the unknown, seems lost in the breezy tone of voice. Yet the pattering of *t*'s, the alliterations and smooth connectives, the balance and control and the cavalierly diminutive mood seem curiously glib for such a radical change in life. This man Ishmael seems to want to remove the threat, not only from "the watery part of the world," but more deeply from the quiet acts of self-assertion that have preceded these four phrases. The more diminutive the self, the more manageable its object.

Still, it's just a story. We go on to another skillfully balanced progressive rhythm, which surprises us a little by giving us another explanation for an act we thought he'd already accounted for:

> It is a way I have
> of driving off the spleen
> and regulating the circulation.

The vagueness of the "It" reminds us slightly of the sudden intrusion of "mortality" into the Usher's mild occupation. Again the lack of particularity seems characteristic. But the generalized nouns, "spleen" and "circulation" (not "my spleen" and "my circulation"), and the balanced participles which so harmoniously counterbalance the double participial phrase at the beginning of the previous sentence all make it very easy to miss the message: he desperately needs to control his body. We meet his body for the first time, depersonalized and abstract to be sure, but protruding beyond the limits of his previous sentence, asserting a condition his language can't quite master. We begin to sense that under the careful tapestry of abstractions lies a fear of what would happen if he lost control, if that "spleen" weren't driven off, if that "circulation" weren't regulated.

This fear wildly surfaces in the next sentence. Now the rhythms are longer, the balance more extended, almost to the breaking point:

> Whenever I find myself growing grim about the mouth;
> whenever it is a damp, drizzly November in my soul;
> whenever I find myself involuntarily
>   pausing before coffin warehouses,
>   and bringing up the rear of every funeral I meet;
> and especially whenever my hypos get such an upper hand
>   of me,
>   that it requires a strong moral principle to prevent me
>   from deliberately stepping into the street,
>   and methodically knocking people's hats off—
> then,
> I account it high time
> to get to sea as soon as I can.

The need to explain has become lugubrious, while the real explanation seems more hidden than ever. Rather different from just having no money and being bored! With every new "whenever," another

Why floods our speculating minds. Yet order is rigorously maintained syntactically. With every phrase he takes another breath and tries to fit new words to the old pattern, hoping some explanation will satisfy. But the characteristic pattern has lost its repetitive stasis and now seems the vehicle for an increasingly compulsive movement toward disintegration. The split between mind and body has become absolute, as the mind passively "finds" the body "grim about the mouth," with a "drizzly November in my soul," and "finds" again the "involuntary" nature of the body's progression from that oral ambiguity toward death and aggression.

We can see why Ishmael needed to identify with the Usher's ability to be "mildly reminded of his mortality." The threat of these acts has nothing mild about it. His balanced assertion that he "deliberately" and "methodically" would "knock people's hats off," with its overtones of castrating an unknown aggressor, seems curiously incongruous, since his "hypos" rather than his "moral principle" control that deliberate methodology. Control has almost yielded to the stress of those "whenevers." Accordingly, his previously relaxed sense of generalized time has become an imperative present tense: "I account it high time to get to sea as soon as I can." The hard consonants seem to spit those words at us—ever quietly aggressive. But those last five words imply that other uncontrollable forces may prevent that conscious wish.

Somehow the aggressiveness of "Call me Ishmael" has become polymorphously perverse, as the mind passively flees the body's spasmodic acts of unhinging violence. So Ishmael gathers all that sentence together into a "this," and declares, "This is my substitute for pistol and ball." We know now that going to sea is a "substitute," or sublimation, for certain undirected aggressive drives. He admits that much. But the pistol and ball can be used in various ways, as we discover in the next unexpected sentence:

> With a philosophical flourish
> Cato throws himself upon his sword;
> I quietly take to the ship. (12)

Now the balance has returned, with the habit of identifying himself through an older, historical figure. So, too, order and calm of mind return, as he inexplicably internalizes his aggression. But what is he saying? Maybe that suicide is the mind's final way (the "philosophical flourish") of controlling the body, and going to sea is like suicide. Or maybe that we must react against suicide as the final acquiescence to "pistol and ball" by going to sea. Or, psychologically, that this penis (the "sword") must murder the self, to avoid the possibility of less narcissistic intercourse, and that going to sea "quietly" abandons the potency of "pistol and ball" for safer possibilities. Yet Cato killed himself to avoid capture by Caesar, and if Ishmael's wish is to avoid father-figures, then how can he seek the authoritarian submission to a sea captain that he "explains" later in this chapter?

We are fuddled. That semicolon seems such a simple connection, yet in fact it is no connection at all. But we do know that he is going to sea, and that his philosophical mind feels some disjunction from his aggressive body, and that these emotions are probably too personal for someone so characteristically controlled and restrained to vent. At least we have a sense of his unexpectedness and his individuality.

Or do we? "There is nothing surprising in this." The vagueness of "this" recurs, and with it a sudden recapitulation of his originally blunt tone. His explanation expands what we had thought to be a personal statement into a "looming" sense of the human condition:

> If they but knew it,
> almost all men in their degree,
> some time or other,
> cherish very nearly the same feelings towards the ocean
> with me.

Now the unknown sits squarely with *us*. Furthermore, all the negatives and acts of aggression directed against land-creatures and land-emotions are suddenly ascribed to our "feelings towards the ocean." Are we, too, drawn *to* water because of our reaction *against* shore? Is shore that closely identified with the bodily self, death, violence, suicide? Will sea be the mind's haven? The ambiguity won't tell us whether the ocean is cause or escape. Instead, we are left simply with Ishmael's characteristic depersonalization of emotion in the name of universal identification. We differ from him only in our lack of "knowledge."

The ironies begin to overwhelm us. How can we "cherish" such feelings when our hypos have "involuntarily" taken over our will?

Maybe we can do so as the Usher "loved" to dust his grammars—to remind us of how little we can control our mortality. But how can we come out with such positive emotions when negatives rule the paragraph? How are we "with" Ishmael at all?

If knowledge is certainty, then Ishmael is certainly right to imply we have little knowledge—especially of *him,* his roots, his ground. The paragraph gives us only his motives for *dis*locating himself in space, and it offers us no way to locate him "precisely" in time, either. "Ishmael" and "Cato" come from very different times and cultures. Every reference to time generalizes rather than specifies: "Some years ago"; the chorus of "whenevers"; the subtle modulation of past into present tense; the "some time or other" in which we, too, feel these emotions. Ironically again, though, we can locate him in his one reference to *mental* time—the "damp, drizzly November in my soul." As we learn in the next chapter, this wintry feeling corresponds to his December reality. But the tenuousness of this correspondence indicates the chasm between mental state and physical being that shapes this paragraph. It also emblemizes the fluid maneuvering of our own identifications. From the philosophic voice "Ishmael," we reel through spleen, death-obsession, violence, and suicide and amazingly conclude with ourselves. Yet there is "nothing surprising in this." It all has to do with our feelings toward the ocean.

The rest of the chapter elaborates or "explains" the mystery of those feelings and offers two long and mutually contradictory sweeps of meaning. The first ends in a solipsistic universe; the second, in the otherness of the whale.

The movement from I-ness ("Call me Ishmael") to the universal You-ness that ends the first paragraph has brought Ishmael back to his calm, confident role as storyteller; and as he lists for us the land-people magnetically attracted to water, we almost forget the conflicts driving him from land. He loves to include all mankind in his mild fatalism. In fact, the next few paragraphs live largely in the second person. The water-gazers, the crowds of stationary and lemming-like landsmen, the necessity for water even in the most idyllic pastoral, the ancient divinity of water—all these lead away from the bodily anxieties toward the intellectual certitude that *we* see them. Our minds are one with his vision. True, this certitude rests on the inexplicable nature of what it perceives. But the appositional force of the seeing, the characteristic composite quality of Ishmael's presentation as he lists what seem to be all possible alternatives, gives us a passive and acquiescent feeling of confidence in his voice. We cease trying to answer the questions and accept them as answers themselves. After all, as we learned in the first paragraph, he differs from us only in that he knows what we all unknowingly cherish.

Yet this passive acquiescence in the shift from self to universality ends, as we'll learn again in "The Mast-Head," "with one half-throttled shriek" (140). Instead of leading us inexorably to water, the pulsing questions take us to Narcissus:

> Surely all this is not without meaning. And still deeper the meaning of that story of Narcissus, who because he could not grasp the tormenting, mild image he saw in the fountain, plunged into it and was drowned. But that same image, we ourselves see in all rivers and oceans. It is the image of the ungraspable phantom of life; and this is the key to it all. (14)

Now we have it! That image, "unknown" yet attractive to Narcissus, was his own reflection. So the unknown is simply ourselves, and our need for water is just a need to come into relationship with ourselves. Our body is out there, in the water, waiting to receive us when we at last dive and . . . drown. In ourselves? Is this another way of saying that the image of the body will overmaster the moral mind? Yet Ishmael took to sea to *escape* that self, to avoid throwing himself on his sword. So, he has assured us, do we. Paradoxes, paradoxes. The phantom becomes ungraspable once more. Is it the return of the repressed? How can Ishmael advance such universal solipsism when the rhetorical thrust of these paragraphs has depended on the gulf between I and You? The tensions between knowledge, water, and self can't be resolved so easily, despite his hunger for unity. The "pistol and ball" began not in self-intercourse but in aggression. Even on the most philosophic level of mind, where all these visions take place, we feel an otherness that can't be grasped by such abstractions.

So he takes another tack. Back to the I, and the body. "Now, when I say that I am in the habit of going to sea whenever I begin to grow hazy about the eyes, and begin to be over conscious of my lungs . . ." (14). The recapitulation subtly subverts the intellectual universality by reasserting his fear of being overaware of his individual body. One can be "over conscious" in many ways, and he seems to have touched on most of them. Characteristically, he then defines his role at sea by negatives: he'll never be a passenger, or Commodore, or Captain, or Cook. These roles of individual command or leadership require responsibility for others besides himself, and independence—not solipsism—is all he craves. He'll be "a simple sailor, right before the mast, plumb down into the forecastle, aloft there to the royal mast-head" (14). Each of these balanced phrases locates his body in a natural sailor's identity and context, while subtly stripping that identity of everything but sailorhood.

Once established as that simple sailor, Ishmael offers his characteristic array of explanations. Why, for instance, does he tolerate lack of independence in a sailor's life? If one holds to an individual identity, whether as the descendant of some "old established family" or as "a country schoolmaster," the transition "requires a strong decoction of Seneca and the Stoics to enable you to grin and bear it" (15). But that individual identity is what Ishmael is trying to escape. As a "slave," he can enjoy universal communion with slaves, much as he can fraternize with the poor Sub-Subs, knowing that his mental essence remains inviolate:

> Well, then, however the old sea-captains may order me about —however they may thump and punch me about, I have the satisfaction of knowing that it is all right; that everybody else is one way or other served in much the same way—either in a physical or metaphysical point of view, that is; and so the universal thump is passed round, and all hands should rub each other's shoulder-blades, and be content. (15)

The "satisfaction of knowing" soothes all physical pain. We meet this homosexual resolution of passive dependency often in Ishmael's narrative, especially in the notorious "A Squeeze of the Hand." Such dependency offers rewards while not requiring self-expenditure. Just as Ishmael supposedly goes to sea simply out of boredom and lack of money, so being a sailor offers the simple joys of money, "wholesome exercise and pure air of the forecastle deck" (15). What other motives could we need?

Even the tone of voice tells us. Ishmael is obviously playing games. He is flippant to the point of irreverence—"The act of paying is perhaps the most uncomfortable infliction that the two orchard thieves entailed upon us" (15)—and he disengages himself from his own explanations through incongruous appositions. We can be closer to the headwinds of nature on the forecastle deck than back with the captain; "that is, if you never violate the Pythagorean maxim" (15) not to eat beans. He denies the uniqueness of his situation by constantly adopting these universal perspectives, often through such humor. Just as Adam and Eve become simply those "orchard thieves," so this whole voyage appears on the scrolls of the Fates between many other events:

> "*Grand Contested Election for the Presidency*
> *of the United States.*
> "WHALING VOYAGE BY ONE ISHMAEL.
> "BLOODY BATTLE IN AFGHANISTAN." (16)

His greatest dependency rests with those Fates, not with himself. His motives are theirs, not his own. So far have we come from solipsism that all the explanations he offers are simply a way of biding time, funning with words, while "those stage managers" (16) order him about metaphysically like the "old hunks of a sea-captain" (15) who physically represents them.

Having finally established that he has no free will or motive whatsoever beyond those given to all men by the whims of Fate, and having indicated that all these explanations are simply "the wholesome exercise and pure air" of a sailor who has happened to be a wordsmith schoolmaster, Ishmael seems to have come full circle with his narcissism. The tussle between his need for independence and his need for dependence comes to rest in a mild fatalism. But "Loomings" concludes with still another abrupt twist, which at once reestablishes his individuality and connects it irretrievably to its identification with otherness. The paradox of Ishmael's being is that his self can find uniqueness only through the strangeness of the whale.

The Usher, we remember, loved to dust his books; it reminded him of his mortality. The Sub-Sub's commentator loves to sit with that failure and commiserate over wine. Both of these introductory situations evoke a kind of narcissistic pleasure by distancing inner conflicts into external objects. But the whale means something far different to Ishmael: a compulsive quest, not a calm mirror-comment. Furthermore, the whale at last breaks the charmed circle of

Ishmael's universal self and reveals the aloneness under his games and "curiosity":

> With other men, perhaps, such things would not have been inducements; but as for me, I am tormented with an everlasting itch for things remote. I love to sail forbidden seas, and land on barbarous coasts. Not ignoring what is good, I am quick to perceive a horror, and could still be social with it—would they let me—since it is but well to be on friendly terms with all the inmates of the place one lodges in. (16)

It could be Thoreau talking, except for that "would they let me." Yet even Thoreau would have domesticated his language more, just as he restricted to Concord his "itch for things remote." Ishmael's search for strangeness and independence has been carefully masked by the fun and games of his abstractions, his departicularized identifications, and his philosophy of solipsistic fatalism. Now, though, we can see that all his mental effort has come to a single-minded rest in one image:

> and in the wild conceits that swayed me to my purpose, two and two there floated into my inmost soul, endless processions of the whale, and, midmost of them all, one grand hooded phantom, like a snow hill in the air. (16)

There the chapter closes, with "the ungraspable phantom of life" breaching once more, this time offering no comforting clue to the meaning or "the key to it all." Narcissus has yielded again to the unknown.

We feel stranded, yes, but we are not stranded with paradox alone. By now we have a good sense of the dualisms that frame Ishmael's temper. We know that a yearning for knowledge or intercourse grounds his fatalistic narcissism, just as we have sensed the passive (and oral) dependency under his blunt and humorous oral aggressiveness. We have felt the controlled rhythms of balanced apposition and explanation disintegrate into opposition, or blind Fate, or the inexplicability of the "ungraspable phantom." His "knowledge" differentiates him from us; yet we sense that Ishmael's mind will be all of him we *can* "know." In flight from his body, he uses abstractions to universalize the particular and to dislocate himself from particular place and time and identity, in the name of a stoic perspective and self-deflation. Nevertheless, we have caught enough of the feared chaos behind his strict verbal control to sense what his body represents to him and how much he wants to be in touch with natural manhood. His mind cries for sailorhood, as the landsmen seek the sea. If he could only, like the Usher, accept his mortality! But his speculative temperament mocks and perplexes any accepting certainties. Instead, Ishmael embarks on the story of his quest for the "one grand hooded phantom" that focuses his inmost motives.

This quest will have three stages: Queequeg, Ahab, and the whale. Each stage brings Ishmael's search for strangeness and his obsession with the body into closer and closer conjunction. At the same time it fragments his own identity into those three figures and shifts our identification with his mental processes to those love-hate objects. First Queequeg engages us as the epitome of the natural male body. Then Ahab's "monomania" puts the male body into desperate intercourse with the whale. By the climax, Ishmael's voice has ceased all explanation, and he becomes a translucently passive observer of that primal scene.

But the whale itself ambiguously embodies Ishmael's tensions and desires as well, and brings to a faceless completion the two aspects of his quest that we have already seen in "Loomings." First, his wish to be Narcissus becomes the wish for potency. The search for the whale seems almost literally an attempt to find out where sperm really lies. This is the beginning of Ishmael's quest for knowledge." In that sense the whale becomes the ultimate, uncontrollable body, savagely venting its "spleen" on mind. But secondly, the whale embodies the strange otherness that Ishmael seeks. The psychology of this double symbolism will take us beyond the three stages of his two-sided quest to the ambivalences that have brought violence and aggression to his mind, leaving him an orphan on the natural body's coffin.

II.

As the first stage of Ishmael's search for potent identity and strange intercourse, Queequeg arouses anxiety only to dispel it in the joy of natural being. Since the "Spouter-Inn" is full, Ishmael agrees to share a bed with this "harpooneer," whom he hasn't yet seen. We can sense his vaguely circling anxieties just in the observations he makes while waiting for supper and the appearance of his bedmate. He sees "a ruminating tar" carving the table

> with his jack-knife, stooping over and diligently working away at the space between his legs. He was trying his hand at a ship under full sail, but he didn't make much headway, I thought. (22)

This masturbatory projection indicates something of Ishmael's own preoccupied "headway." More to the point, at dinner he learns from his "diabolically" grinning landlord that his "dark complexioned" harpooneer "eats nothing but steaks, and likes 'em rare" (22). The strangeness quotient of the man who can so potently wield a harpoon and orally gratify himself increases to the point of uneasiness, and Ishmael privately decides the man will have to undress before he does.

As bedtime approaches, this uneasiness reaches a fever pitch of sexual fear:

> It was fair to presume that being a harpooneer, his linen or woollen, as the case might be, would not be of the tidiest, certainly none of the finest. I began to twitch all over. Besides, it was getting late, and any decent harpooneer ought to be home and going bed-wards. Suppose now, he should tumble in upon me at midnight—how could I tell from what vile hole he had been coming? (24)

To be "coming" from a "vile hole" into untidy sheets shocks Ishmael so much that he thinks of sleeping on a bench, or of locking the man out. The body's ways unnerve this man of rarefied and speculative temperament. What could be worse, then, than to find that this harpooneer is out peddling the body of the mind itself, selling his "head" in the streets?

> "Can't sell his head?—What sort of a bamboozling story is this you are telling me?" getting into a towering rage. "Do you pretend to say, landlord, that this harpooneer is actually en-

gaged this blessed Saturday night, or rather Sunday morning, in peddling his head around this town?" (25)

Ishmael's fears for his safety at the hands of madness get him madder and madder himself, with great comic effect.

But our laughter depends on Ishmael's impotent lack of knowledge, his dependency on the landlord (as on the Usher and the Sub-Sub) for oral information, and his excessive anxiety over a strange body who could sell heads. We can laugh because the landlord, with his diabolical smile, controls our security in the midst of Ishmael's paranoia, and because Ishmael himself presents the situation with his characteristically self-depreciating irony, "as cool as Mt. Hecla [an active volcano] in a snow storm" (26). We identify with his need to be cool and his state of being hot, and laugh at the contradiction. But the problem of potency remains.

Meanwhile, Ishmael, steeled for the night, goes to the harpooneer's room to wait. There he finds still more sexual trauma, as he tries on what looks like "a large door mat, ornamented at the edges with little tinkling tags something like the stained porcupine quills round an Indian moccasin" (27). In the middle of this entrance to a "door" which is surrounded by strange prickly Indian foliage, he finds "a hole or slit . . . the same as in South American ponchos" (27–28). The strangeness of this doubly foreign object fascinates him:

> I put it on, to try it, and it weighed me down like a hamper, being uncommonly shaggy and thick, and I thought a little damp, as though this mysterious harpooneer had been wearing it of a rainy day. I went up in it to a bit of glass stuck against the wall, and I never saw such a sight in my life. I tore myself out of it in such a hurry that I gave myself a kink in the neck. (28)

In their first skirmish, the mirror of mental narcissism bests physical intercourse after only the briefest titillation. Ishmael returns to his characteristic posture of sitting and thinking—"about this head-peddling harpooneer, and his door mat" (28). Both these objects now seem equally strange, and we as landsmen fully empathize with Ishmael's confusions. Though his tone of voice in "Loomings" was worldly-wise, we have already sensed that in his body he is the merest innocent, exposed on this quest to traumas he can describe only with the most foreign metaphors.

Now that this mood of sexual anxiety has been established, the man comes—with head in hand. More and more he seems strange, as Ishmael projects new hypotheses onto his features:

> Such a face! It was of a dark, purplish, yellow color, here and there stuck over with large, blackish looking squares. Yes, it's just as I thought, he's a terrible bedfellow; he's been in a fight, got dreadfully cut, and here he is, just from the surgeon. (28)

But no—the squares are "stains of some sort or other" (28). Perhaps he was a white man captured by cannibals in the South Seas; "perhaps the sun there produced these extraordinary effects upon the skin" (29). Meanwhile, the man calmly takes off his "new beaver hat" and reveals no hair whatsoever except for a "small scalp-knot twisted up on his forehead. His bald purplish head now looked for all the world like a mildewed skull" (29). At the sight of this "bald purplish" object emerging from "new beaver" with an erection, Ishmael immediately thinks of death and decay. He would have "bolted out of it quicker than ever I bolted a dinner"—except that (of course!) "the stranger stood between me and the door" (29).

Again, as with the landlord, Ishmael impotently depends on the control of a stranger, and so do we. We wait while this "savage" goes through some odd religious rituals with an "idol," "a curious little deformed image with a hunch on its back, and exactly the color of a three days' old Congo baby" (30). We feel curiously quiet while the worship of this deformed "baby" goes on, almost voyeuristic in our passive perception of this fire ritual. But the "uncomfortableness" remains. Though religious in his way, the savage has been called Devil too many times for us not to taint him with our own religious frame. Our moral, sexual, and oral anxieties await his next move, while Ishmael carefully frames something to say. And while Ishmael so carefully thinks of the right words in the right order, "this wild cannibal, tomahawk between his teeth, sprang into bed with me" (31).

This stunning moment highlights the comedy of Ishmael's introduction to physical strangeness and potency. The fear of losing his head and of being controlled by the aggressive anger of his body, as we have seen in "Loomings," calls forth intricate verbal defenses.

Here, however, they all break down into action. "I sang out, I could not help it now; and giving a sudden grunt of astonishment he began feeling me" (31). We identify with Ishmael's mental confusions and also with the savage's equally strange discovery. Incongruity piled on incongruity, capped by castration anxiety and homosexuality in the intimacy of bed, resolves peacefully into the landlord's appearance. " 'Don't be afraid now,' said he, grinning again. 'Queequeg here wouldn't harm a hair of your head' " (31). Then Queequeg takes over, with his calm "knowledge." As Queequeg "politely motioned me to get into bed—rolling over to one side as much as to say—I won't touch a leg of ye . . ." (32), Ishmael's castration anxiety over losing his head-potency subsides into his first genuine friendship. His mind has at last stopped churning out assumptions, and narcissistic self-projections have given way to a kind of innocent intercourse, stripped of all sexual taint.

In other words, Queequeg's oddness has been satisfactorily explained. He's simply a savage, with a well-defined religion, social role, and sense of himself. Now that Ishmael knows this, he can watch Queequeg's strange dressing ritual with benign interest, as his bedmate first puts on his beaver hat, then jams himself under the bed for the very private act of putting on his boots. Ishmael explains these acts of foreign phallicism:

> . . . Queequeg, do you see, was a creature in the transition state—neither caterpillar nor butterfly. He was just enough civilized to show off his outlandishness in the strangest possible manner. His education was not yet completed. He was an undergraduate. (34)

The labels add up to comfortable stability, without any of the threatening unknown about them: domesticated nature in the frame of civilized Western education. In this mood Queequeg soon becomes, as a later chapter puts it, "A Bosom Friend." Ishmael admires the "calm self-collectedness of simplicity" in savages and finds Queequeg "entirely at his ease; preserving the utmost serenity; content with his own companionship; always equal to himself" (52). Naturally Ishmael explains this self-control in terms of the mind. "Surely this was a touch of fine philosophy; though no doubt he had never heard there was such a thing as that" (52). But more to the point, Queequeg's natural body has complemented Ishmael's mind. It has even redeemed it and made it whole. This new strangeness is wholly welcome:

> . . . I began to be sensible of strange feelings. I felt a melting in me. No more my splintered heart and maddened hand were turned against the wolfish world. This soothing savage had redeemed it. There he sat, his very indifference speaking a nature in which there lurked no civilized hypocrisies and bland deceits. Wild he was; a very sight of sights to see; yet I began to feel myself mysteriously drawn towards him. And those same things that would have repelled most others, they were the very magnets that thus drew me. (53)

We hear the echoes of "Loomings" and before, from the Sub-Sub's "splintered heart" to the "itch for things remote" separating Ishmael from his fellows. In the arms of Queequeg's strange potency, Ishmael can adopt the passive, feminine, wifely identity at last, and be sheltered in that innocent fellowship.

How can this transition occur so smoothly, with so much joy for Ishmael and so much comic spirit for us? From paranoia to spiritual intercourse requires only one step: the removal of phallic anxiety. The threat of physical intercourse with a woman (the "vile hole" or the "door mat") must yield to man-to-man submissiveness. As soon as we see Queequeg's manhood in a submissive frame, whether bowing to Yojo, the idol resembling a three-day-old deformed Congo baby, or accepting the landlord's decree, or getting under the bed to put on his boots, or deferring to Ishmael's head (by Yojo's whim) in the matter of choosing a boat, we can tolerate the assertion of his body in spontaneous manly skill, as he saves a young tormentor from drowning by his "long living arc of a leap" ("Wheelbarrow"), or as he hits the small oil slick "eye" dead center with his harpoon, or as he spears steaks whole at the table.

Furthermore, Queequeg's oral, cannibalistic gusto with those steaks or with his pipe can delight Ishmael only so long as the aggressiveness remains securely pinned to the apron of Mother Nature. And so it does, to the end. Much later, in "Cistern and Buckets," as Queequeg saves Tashtego by diving into the very head of the whale, we see him at last for what he has been from the beginning: a midwife whose "courage and great skill in obstetrics" (290) deliver Ishmael as well as Tashtego from the "teeth" of threats far greater than natural man. He never initiates but only helps and furthers natural process.

Queequeg's connection with nature needs to be stressed, because it marks such a contrast with Ahab. Even in his skin, so mottled by the sun, Queequeg is the submissive incarnation of the actions of natural forces. His legs, we learn in "The Spouter-Inn," "were marked, as if a parcel of dark green frogs were running up the trunks of young palms" (29). He has few of the mental skills conventionally associated with civilization. In fact, because he can't read, he alone notices Ishmael enter Father Mapple's chapel, while others are reading the epitaphs. Among these "frigid inscriptions" he notices life directly where others, more like Ishmael, are preoccupied with death and the past. Occasionally this lack of expertise seems very funny, as when he flips uncomprehendingly through a book and whistles prodigiously after every fifty pages. But this procedure itself makes us see books in a more primary light, as objects rather than functions, and his oral pleasure undercuts our sophisticated smile with its simplicity. Or rather, it fulfills our smile, as his body brings Ishmael's mind into this new world. As we have seen, the savage's "very indifference" speaks "a nature in which there lurked no civilized hypocrisies and bland deceits" (53). Books will never remind Queequeg, as they do the threadbare Usher, of his mortality.

In this frame of natural law, in fact, Queequeg can conquer mortality through his own will. Late in the narrative, when some casks have sprung a leak, Queequeg goes down to investigate, "like a green spotted lizard at the bottom of a well" (395). He lapses into a fever as a result of that intercourse with the "well, or an icehouse" (395), and asks for a coffin to be made. But when it has been shaped, and occupied by its tenant-to-be, Queequeg decides he wants to recover, and he does. Death to him has nothing to do with the simple body:

> In a word, it was Queequeg's conceit, that if a man made up his mind to live, mere sickness could not kill him: nothing but a whale, or a gale, or some violent, ungovernable, unintelligent destroyer of that sort. (398)

Much more than Thoreau, Queequeg is the fleshly embodiment of Emerson's transcendental philosophy, and this self-reliance makes him godlike to his head-servant, the philosopher. As Ishmael says in "A Bosom Friend," Queequeg's head

> reminded me of General Washington's head, as seen in the popular busts of him. It had the same long regularly graded retreating slope from above the brows, which were likewise very projecting, like two long promontories thickly wooded on top. Queequeg was George Washington cannibalistically developed. (52)

The image of the father-figure strikes us so forcefully that we miss the frame in which the image lives. George Washington has become a natural geological phenomenon, and the father's will simply expresses nature's laws.

So Queequeg's body embodies nature to Ishmael, and potency as well. The first stage of the quest seems to promise a journey of redemption, as Ishmael's teeming mind at least finds a body worthy of its companionship. The strangeness and "spleen" of nature seem to have been tamed. But this "joint stock company of two" (271) depends on a submissiveness to natural forces. What would happen if a hero could be found who could will himself into confrontation with those forces and tolerate the aggressiveness that Ishmael sublimates into mental conundrums?

III.

Queequeg's will can easily triumph over death by natural causes, but only because his nature lacks mind. Ahab desperately seeks the mind at the heart of things. When Queequeg blithely emerges from his coffin and walks the deck, Ishmael rejoices to see his dear friend alive again in his sun-scorched skin. He also sees the mystic tattooing on that skin. But only Ahab seeks to know what that tattooing means:

> And this tattooing, had been the work of a departed prophet and seer of his island, . . . so that Queequeg in his own proper person was a riddle to unfold; a wondrous work in one volume; but whose mysteries not even himself could read, though his own live heart beat against them; and these mysteries were

therefore destined in the end to moulder away with the living parchment whereon they were inscribed, and so be unsolved to the last. And this thought it must have been which suggested to Ahab that wild exclamation of his, when one morning turning away from surveying poor Queequeg—"Oh, devilish tantalization of the gods!" (399)

Ahab feels that the Other has a mind, malignant or beneficent, and he "bursts his hot heart's shell" upon its unknowable face.

In other words, the second stage of Ishmael's quest moves us from passive acceptance of a mind-body dualism to an aggressive attempt to bring mind and body into "knowledge." Otherness transforms Ahab, as selfness embodies Queequeg. We can see the difference simply in our first views of the two men. For Queequeg, our apprehension far outdistances the reality of his entrance. We expect a cannibal and we meet a natural animal, benignly submissive to his "three-day-old baby." The sun has mottled his skin, as nature has shaped his character. But when "Reality outran apprehension" and "Captain Ahab stood upon his quarter-deck" (109), we see the captain's body in imagery of unnatural and destructive processes, not natural harmonies. If Queequeg is a naturally landscaped George Washington, Ahab is that Washington after a forest fire:

> There seemed no sign of common bodily illness about him, nor of the recovery from any. He looked like a man cut away from the stake, when the fire has overrunningly wasted all the limbs without consuming them, or taking away one particle from their compacted aged robustness. (109–110)

The sun hasn't just tinged his skin. It has embraced every atom of him. This impact of destructive forces has brought him beyond Queequeg's acquiescent joint-stock religion of nature to the status of a work of art, permanent in mind and form:

> His whole high, broad form, seemed made of solid bronze, and shaped in an unalterable mould, like Cellini's cast Perseus. Threading its way out from among his grey hairs, and continuing right down one side of his tawny scorched face and neck, till it disappeared in his clothing, you saw a slender rod-like mark, lividly whitish. It resembled that perpendicular

seam sometimes made in the straight, lofty trunk of a great
tree, when the upper lightning tearingly darts down it, and
without wrenching a single twig, peels and grooves out the
bark from top to bottom, ere running off into the soil, leaving
the tree still greenly alive, but branded. (110)

Otherness has scarred what once was harmoniously organic. Was
this brand a birthmark, or did it come upon him "in an elemental
strife at sea"? (110). No one knows, though everyone suspects.
Narcissus and otherness are now so interlocked in Ahab that the
self's body, seemingly unchanged, has been permanently invested
with the fiery potencies of the gods.
     Queequeg's innocent submissiveness has become Ahab's sexual
erectness:

> His bone leg steadied in that hole; one arm elevated, and
> holding by a shroud; Captain Ahab stood erect, looking straight
> out beyond the ship's ever-pitching prow. There was an infinity
> of firmest fortitude, a determinate, unsurrenderable wilfulness,
> in the fixed and fearless, forward dedication of that glance.
> (110–111)

But the conflicts and fears that come with sexual potential, as we
have seen already with Ishmael's fears of Queequeg, surround that
erectness with castration (the "bone leg") and the "shroud." More
spiritually, the joy and spontaneity that characterize Queequeg have
given way to repressed and kingly suffering, expressed in religious
terms:

> Not a word he spoke; nor did his officers say aught to him;
> . . . Ahab stood before them with a crucifixion in his face;
> in all the nameless regal overbearing dignity of some mighty
> woe. (111)

To be so erect brings not only the loss of a leg, but also the need
to redeem that loss by will alone. "Ah, God!" we hear in "The Chart,"

> what trances of torments does that man endure who is con-
> sumed with one unachieved revengeful desire. He sleeps with

clenched hands; and wakes with his own bloody nails in his palms. (174)

Not only crucified, but self-crucified, Ahab reconstitutes himself as his own religion to confront the "hell" that "in himself yawned beneath him" (174) and the sea monster embodying that hell. Like Perseus, he hopes to slay the Medusa and hold up her severed, snaky head.

The erection of the will, then, subjects the body to emasculation in ways that only the sea knows how to do. Queequeg, so domesticated in his potency, takes our land vocabulary and land-identifications to the shore, but Ishmael's first visit to the *Pequod* launches us into a loneliness more stark, directed, and compelling. " 'Marchant service be damned,' " Peleg berates him. " 'Talk not that lingo to me. Dost see that leg?—I'll take that leg away from thy stern, if ever thou talkest of the marchant service to me again' " (68–69). This threat of losing a "leg" is Ishmael's introduction to the world of whaling, and Ahab, through his "crucifixion," takes upon himself those anxieties and identifications aroused by the sea.

Even the language of natural metaphor, so pervasive in Melville, changes with Ahab. Queequeg is a friendly animal, but Ahab demands to be master. In bed that first morning, Queequeg "shook himself all over like a Newfoundland dog just from the water" (34), and later we see him "swimming like a dog" (61) to save a drowning man. But Ahab's relation to the water begins in mental loneliness, not physical camaraderie. When Stubb comes up to the quarterdeck to complain that Ahab's ivory heel is keeping the men awake, Ahab's response forever separates him from domestic emotions of kindness and sympathy:

> "Below to thy nightly grave; where such as ye sleep between shrouds, to use ye to the filling one at last. —Down, dog, and kennel!" (113)

When we do see Ahab as an animal, the metaphors take us to the wild heart of the wilderness: a bear, a "mute, maned sea-lion," a "heart-stricken moose," a leader of prairie wolves. Or we see him in metaphors of stark natural process, aloof from civilization, like "the clouds that layer upon layer were piled upon his brow, as ever all clouds choose the loftiest peaks to pile themselves upon" (111).

Or we see him most unnaturally, as pure machine, "humming to himself" with "a sound so strangely muffled and inarticulate that it seemed the mechanical humming of the wheels of his vitality in him" (142).[2] Electric as the lightning that has grooved his soul, rigid and inflexible as that bronze statue, even in the fairest and most benign swirls of natural warmth, Ahab bends every natural emotion to one unnatural motive:

> Swerve me? The path to my fixed purpose is laid with iron rails, whereon my soul is grooved to run. Over unsounded gorges, through the rifled hearts of mountains, under torrents' beds, unerringly I rush! Naught's an obstacle, naught's an angle to the iron way! (147)

In the stress of this resolve, Ahab's potency seems one with his narcissism and his mind. His lonely, lunging soul projects a world. He has a loudly proclaimed love-hate relationship with God and the sun, the two most conspicuous projections of his potency needs, and in both cases he seeks to resolve these needs by solipsizing the objects. "For a long time, now," we are told in "The Grand Armada," "the circus-running sun has raced within his fiery ring, and needs no sustenance but what's in himself. So Ahab" (319). This masturbatory wish fulfillment has its oral component, as Ahab seeks to feed his flame:

> Though nominally included in the census of Christendom, he was still an alien to it. He lived in the world, as the last of the Grisly Bears lived in settled Missouri. And as when Spring and Summer had departed, that wild Logan of the woods, burying himself in the hollow of a tree, lived out the winter there, sucking his own paws; so, in his inclement, howling old age, Ahab's soul, shut up in the caved trunk of his body, there fed upon the sullen paws of its gloom! (134).

2. Thomas Woodson, in "Ahab's Greatness: Prometheus as Narcissus," *Journal of English Literary History*, XXXIII (September 1966), 358, notes that early metaphors compare Ahab "to a cannonball, a pyramid, a mortar, a railway train, a hurricane, and a tornado. Later we see him as a javelin, a harpoon, an anvil, a scythe, a mechanical vise, a seam of iron, a piece of steel."

But the impact of this image is spiritual, not corporeal. Ahab seeks mental intercourse, if only with his own mind. That is to him what steaks are to Queequeg. Where Thoreau calmly rhetoricizes about the mind's descent into the body to redeem it, Ahab actually attempts that redemption, and in a far more genital mode. The price is an aloneness more intense than anywhere else in American fiction, and a godlessness that desperately seeks the self for its divinity. " 'Talk not to me of blasphemy, man; I'd strike the sun if it insulted me' " (144), Ahab cries in "The Quarter-Deck." Even down to his nickname, "Old Thunder," he strives to overmaster God by incorporating God's universe into his own mind.

At first this love-hate relationship with potency projections seems to be riddled with father-conflict. Ahab as devil seeks both to emulate and to undermine the father whom the Puritans reconstituted. " 'He's a grand, ungodly, god-like man, Captain Ahab' " (76), Captain Peleg informs Ishmael in "The Ship," and Ahab's god differs strikingly from Queequeg's babyish Yojo in the depth of his inscrutable malignity. Yojo, we learn at the beginning of that chapter, is "a rather good sort of god, who perhaps meant well enough upon the whole, but in all cases did not succeed in his benevolent designs" (66). The god of Ahab, however, is the God of Father Mapple, "chiefly known to me by Thy rod" (51), without the trust of that land-father's submissiveness. As Ahab cries to the lightning much later, in "The Candles," "thou art but my fiery father; my sweet mother, I know not. Oh, cruel! what hast thou done with her? There lies my puzzle . . ." (417). No feminine softness soothes the "slender rod-like mark" by which Ahab has been "known" and branded.

And yet this narcissistic projection of himself into the father's potency leads directly to that "puzzle": his quest for otherness, intercourse. When Ahab's consummate need for "knowledge" meets the inscrutable wall of his lack, he projects himself onto that wall by his own fiery light. The shadow-figures cavort and couple in their "pasteboard masks" (144). But all the while he knows that something exists in those shadows not himself, not god, which keeps him stillborn inside his soul:

> "If man will strike, strike through the mask! How can the prisoner reach outside except by thrusting through the wall? To me, the white whale is that wall, shoved near to me. Some-

times I think there's naught beyond. But 'tis enough. He tasks me; he heaps me; I see in him outrageous strength, with an inscrutable malice sinewing it. That inscrutable thing is chiefly what I hate; and be the white whale agent, or be the white whale principal, I will wreak that hate upon him." (144)

The unknown "tasks" him beyond all the self-projections he can know or invent. His "intense bigotry of purpose" (141) allows none of the quietly ironic satisfaction Ishmael receives from those futile arrays of "explanations" and words. As soon as Ahab throws away his pipe, we sense that land satisfactions and land potencies have nothing to do with his needs.

Queequeg can be happy with his own pipe and in his own skin, but Ahab needs to penetrate that unknown wall and receive nourishment from sources other than "the sullen paws of his gloom." Locked into his body, he solipsistically feeds only for lack of that nourishment, and continually hungers for the origin, or source, or Egypt that will give him birth and knowledge at last.[3] He grasps at Pip, the young black boy abandoned in the middle of the sea, as at one who has seen something of God's truth. " 'I do suck most wondrous philosophies from thee!' " he cries in "Ahab and the Carpenter." " 'Some unknown conduits from the unknown worlds must empty into thee!' " (433). But the nourishment Ahab receives from the unknown appears only as self-projection. Striving desperately for potency, he wills his body to confront what has emasculated it, physically focusing all the aggressions that Ishmael represses into words. Jonah was devoured for a simple act of disobedience, and found salvation through submission to the god whose agent devoured him. This, to Father Mapple, is the essence of faith. But Ahab's disobedience takes the more sexual form of self-erection,

3. "Nineteenth-century man, so earnestly obsessed with extending his mental and physical control over all the vast deserts and oceans of the planet, confronts more starkly than his predecessors the *otherness* of nature, and part of him recoils in terror. At the same time he exuberantly revives his faith in irrational knowledge, in the mysterious correspondence of mind and matter; he absorbs nature into himself, coloring it with his own spirit: the result is solipsism. Ahab . . . is a Prometheus whose fire consumes him; . . . he is also a Narcissus" (Woodson, "Ahab's Greatness," pp. 361–362). See Dorothée M. Finkelstein, *Melville's Orienda* (New Haven, Conn., 1961) and H. Bruce Franklin, *The Wake of the Gods: Melville's Mythology* (Stanford, 1963) for Melville's use of non-European myths and themes to communicate that otherness.

and his consequent castration breeds an entirely new kind of potency: madness and monomaniacal revenge.

Where "reason" and "explanation" are the pasteboard masks of impotence, only madness can reconstitute the spirit in the face of the body's defeat:

> If such a furious trope may stand, his special lunacy stormed his general sanity, and carried it, and turned all its concentred cannon upon its own mad mark; so that far from having lost his strength, Ahab, to that one end, did now possess a thousand fold more potency than ever he had sanely brought to bear upon any one reasonable object. (161)

Geological and military tropes combine to transform the "narrow-flowing" natural potency of monomania into the self-encapsulated, unnatural, and "thousand fold" more potent goal of revengeful intercourse:

> There is a wisdom that is woe; but there is a woe that is madness. And there is a Catskill eagle in some souls that can alike dive down into the blackest gorges, and soar out of them again and become invisible in the sunny spaces. And even if he for ever flies within the gorge, that gorge is in the mountains; so that even in his lowest swoop the mountain eagle is still higher than other birds upon the plain, even though they soar. (355)

The joint-stock land-philosophy which structured the "rational" purpose for the *Pequod*'s voyage has been replaced by this madness and solitary flight, as the "joint-owners" of the *Pequod* have been usurped on the sea by Ahab.

To fix the eye and soul on one object and one object only, incessantly and obsessively, is Ahab's way of maintaining erectness in the face of a conspiring universe. Even in moments of sleep, this purposeful erectness never disappears. One night, when Starbuck happens upon his captain in the cabin, he sees Ahab

> with closed eyes sitting straight in his floor-screwed chair; . . .
> Though the body was erect, the head was thrown back so that

the closed eyes were pointed towards the needle of the tell-tale that swung from a beam in the ceiling.

Terrible old man! thought Starbuck with a shudder, sleeping in this gale, still thou steadfastly eyest thy purpose. (202)

Like Jonathan Edwards, whose eyes fixed on the bell rope at the back of the church for the duration of his sermons, Ahab points himself toward that telltale. But unlike the bell rope, the telltale offers no promise of heavenly direction. He looks to the fathers incessantly, as sun or god or lightning, for that sanctuary. But he finds potency only in his own madness. The fathers remain inscrutably ambiguous, invisible, while he projects his own needs onto their masks.

In fact, as we learn immediately after the "furious trope" of Ahab's monomaniacal madness, father has already been buried beneath the phallic stridency of our surface life:

> Winding far down from within the very heart of this spiked Hotel de Cluny where we here stand—however grand and wonderful, now quit it;—and take your way, ye nobler, sadder souls, to those vast Roman halls of Thermes; where far beneath the fantastic towers of man's upper earth, his root of grandeur, his whole awful essence sits in bearded state; an antique buried beneath antiquities, and throned on torsocs! (161).

Furthermore, the gods are actually "mocking" this father-figure, as the Usher's handkerchief whisks its mocking flags over dust:

> So with a broken throne, the great gods mock that captive king; so like a Caryatid, he patient sits, upholding on his frozen brow the piled entablatures of ages. (161)

Nevertheless, he is our father, and he holds the secret of our fate:

> Wind ye down there, ye prouder, sadder souls! question that proud, sad king! A family likeness! aye, he did beget ye, ye young exiled royalties; and from your grim sire only will the old State-secret come. (161)

Ahab has "some glimpse of this, namely: all my means are sane, my motive and my object mad" (161). But our sense of that madness depends on the father's fate, this plaything of the gods who sits on that "broken throne," his head upholding all civilization. Clearly these gods are forces that have overmastered the father, and toy with him even as we sympathize with our "family likeness."

Devouring himself for lack of adequate nourishment elsewhere, incapable of accepting the submissive land-nourishment of money (though he can transform a doubloon for his own purposes), Ahab feeds only on revenge. The spirit enters the lists as champion for the helpless body. "Oh, Ahab!" Ishmael cries in "The Specksynder," "what shall be grand in thee, it must needs be plucked at from the skies, and dived for in the deep, and featured in the unbodied air!" (130). And what his spirit fights defines, as it defies, this "poor old whale-hunter's" identity.

In the act of intercourse, he had been symbolically castrated, "blindly seeking with a six inch blade to reach the fathom-deep life of the whale" (159). Ever since, his identity has been shaped by that malicious act:

> The White Whale swam before him as the monomaniac incarnation of all those malicious agencies which some deep men feel eating in them, till they are left living on with half a heart and half a lung. . . . He piled upon the whale's white hump the sum of all the general rage and hate felt by his whole race from Adam down; and then, as if his chest had been a mortar, he burst his hot heart's shell upon it. (160)

On this "bursting" spirit the second stage of Ishmael's quest depends. Ahab focuses the rage that only a mind jarred loose from its body can feel. On land, Queequeg had seemed the epitome of harmonic bodily potency through devout mental acquiescence to the natural order of things. But the individual mind, such as Ishmael's, cries for deeper selfhood. Though Ishmael represses his tensions into a cadenced lockstep of aggressive ironies and rational explanations, his hero dares to reconstitute himself as "Old Thunder," the father, and confront directly what has been maliciously "devouring" him inside. The white whale isn't just the objective correlative for Ahab's masochism. It has been the source and ground of that self-punishment as well.

IV.

Yet Moby Dick comes to us invested with even more mystery and ambiguity, as the third stage takes Ishmael farther and farther out to sea. We have been given only land-frames with which to comprehend both Queequeg and Ahab. At the height of our sexual anxiety concerning the head-peddler, the landlord can give fatherly reassurance and security. Ahab, as a sea-borne father, outruns the explanations of Peleg and the shrouded prophecies of Elijah; yet, as Peleg says at the start, " 'stricken, blasted, if he be, Ahab has his humanities!' " (77). These "humanities" allow us landsmen our identification with his fight for potency and intercourse.

But with the whale we are entirely at sea. The frames of the fathers, most securely hammered into place by Father Mapple, can no longer hold the picture of this strangeness. Though we are told what the white whale "means" to the various human figures keening after it, that meaning seems as various and ambiguous as the doubloon Ahab has nailed to the mast. Mental efforts to comprehend physical fact slide at last into Pip's "I look, you look, he looks" 362, and the mind becomes capable only of self-projection. On land, the pasteboard masks hold their place, and shared narcissism can be called communication. Men can romance reality. But the sea calls all that language, and all efforts of the mind itself, into question.

Even our first two seeming glimpses of the white whale mislead us. As the first item in the Usher's etymology told us, when we speak Whale in this language we deliver that which is not true. In "The Spirit-Spout," Fedallah sees "a silvery jet" that "looked celestial; seemed some plumed and glittering god uprising from the sea" (199). Night after night this god lures the *Pequod* on, and some of the seamen swear that

> that unnearable spout was cast by one self-same whale; and that whale, Moby Dick. For a time, there reigned, too, a sense of peculiar dread at this flitting apparition, as if it were treacherously beckoning us on and on, in order that the monster might turn round upon us, and rend us at last in the remotest and most savage seas.
>
> These temporary apprehensions, so vague but so awful, de-

rived a wondrous potency from the contrasting serenity of the weather, in which, beneath all its blue blandness, some thought there lurked a devilish charm . . . (201)

But this spirit-spout eventually disappears, leaving only the vague resonances of godhead, spirit, and potent liquid to associate with that "monster" and with the man who pursues it. Our first phantom brush with "Moby Dick" brings potency and strangeness together, but without any taint of the body.

Our next encounter, however, confronts us with that body in all its impalpability:

> In the distance, a great white mass lazily rose, and rising higher and higher, and disentangling itself from the azure, at last gleamed before our prow like a snow-slide, new slid from the hills. Thus glistening for a moment, as slowly it subsided, and sank. Then once more arose, and silently gleamed. It seemed not a whale; and yet is this Moby Dick? thought Daggoo. Again the phantom went down, but on re-appearing once more, with a stiletto-like cry that startled every man from his nod, the negro yelled out—"There! there again! there she breaches! right ahead! The White Whale, the White Whale!" (236)

Soon the creature loses that label, and sits identityless on the sea:

> A vast pulpy mass, furlongs in length and breadth, of a glancing cream-color, lay floating on the water, innumerable long arms radiating from its centre, and curling and twisting like a nest of anacondas, as if blindly to clutch at any hapless object within reach. No perceptible face or front did it have; no conceivable token of either sensation or instinct; but undulated there on the billows, an unearthly, formless, chance-like apparition of life. (237)

"As with a low sucking sound it slowly disappeared again" (237), we learn from Starbuck that this creature is the "great live squid," the food of the sperm whale. Orality dominates our impression of this "pulpy mass . . . of a glancing cream-color." But this new aspect of the white whale proves as chimerical as the spirit-spout, and the landless, "unearthly" body also disappears into the sea.

So the dualism we have come to expect seems amply fulfilled. The white whale incarnates the mind-godhead-potency that Ahab craves and the bodily nourishment that Ishmael seeks. Yet neither side of the dualism can be pinned on the whale. Each slides into a wrong hypothesis about this "ungraspable phantom." The poles reflect human needs, not objective reality, even as they gather magnetic momentum in the quest for this hidden creature. Through one hundred and thirty-two chapters we move into identification with Ahab's possessed mind, seeking to comprehend the whale's invisible malice. In those same chapters, we also take instruction from Ishmael in all the particulars of the whale's body. The "cetology" chapters offer a counterpoint to Ahab's monomania, in the characteristic Ishmael mode of impartial control and knowledgeable disquisition. If the white whale remains ungraspable, we are given a "body of knowledge" enough to glut the most voracious mental appetite. Yet even in the midst of this mass of detail, we sense the pasteboard mask. It brings the body to the head, but Ahab's head has already been lodestoned by the body. As we flip impatiently through the cetological chapters, we begin to suspect that this "body of knowledge," like so many others, is little more than a holding action against the unknown.

The whale's strangeness gathers potency despite all "promiscuous" Sub-Sub efforts to fathom its identity. Only Ahab recognizes it as an adversary with a being forcefully and savagely separate from the land, and even he needs to project that identity as a mirror mind, a god. Both Ishmael and Ahab seek manhood, and specifically seek to reconstitute manhood in religious terms, through this whale. In "The Advocate," Ishmael muses on "the sperm whale's vast tail," and remarks how different our fear of that tail is from our willingness, on land, to engage in the most fearsome military maneuvers. The contrast, he implies, is simple: "For what are the comprehensible terrors of man compared with the interlinked terrors and wonders of God!" (99). But that same incomprehensibility of those "interlinked terrors and wonders" forever estranges us from certain knowledge, no matter how closely we approach the unknowable god-whale. As we are told at the end of "The Tail,"

> Dissect him how I may, then, I but go skin deep; I know him not, and never will. But if I know not even the tail of this whale, how understand his head? much more, how comprehend

his face, when face he has none? Thou shalt see my back parts, my tail, he seems to say, but my face shall not be seen. But I cannot completely make out his back parts; and hint what he will about his face, I say again he has no face. (318)

The Biblical overtones of this divine facelessness [4] give us perverse security, as if we "know what that means" even though we also know the tail, that potent symbol of male manhood, is only a pasteboard mask for a more unknowable essence. We need to pray, as Pip prays to the "big white God aloft there somewhere in yon darkness" (155). But the whale's otherness seems terrifyingly unresponsive to human needs.

When we meet the whale at last, in the three days of chase, we experience the final breakdown into incomprehensible strangeness. As Moby Dick first appears, with "his silent spout" and his "high sparkling hump," the "credulous mariners" think again of "the same silent spout they had so long ago beheld in the moonlit Atlantic and Indian Oceans" (446). We see him in terrestrial, pastoral terms of smoothness, orality, and civilized abundance:

> As they neared him, the ocean grew still more smooth; seemed drawing a carpet over its waves; seemed a noon-meadow, so serenely it spread. At length the breathless hunter came so nigh his seemingly unsuspecting prey, that his entire dazzling hump was distinctly visible, sliding along the sea as if an isolated thing, and continually set in a revolving ring of finest, fleecy, greenish foam. (447)

Birds feather the sea on the bubbles that "danced by his side," "and like to some flag-staff rising from the painted hull of an argosy, the tall but shattered pole of a recent lance projected from the white whale's back . . ." (447). No wonder that, in this context of mutually harmonious pleasure, the whale should recall the first climactic metaphor in Ishmael's description of "The Whiteness of the Whale":

> Not the white bull Jupiter swimming away with ravished Europa clinging to his graceful horns; his lovely, leering eyes

4. Jeremiah 18:17.

sideways intent upon the maid; with smooth bewitching fleet-
ness, rippling straight for the nuptial bower in Crete; not Jove,
not that great majesty Supreme! did surpass the glorified White
Whale as he so divinely swam. (447)

The spirit-spout, too, had "seemed some plumed and glittering god
uprising from the sea." But this first stage of divinity lives mainly in
man's perception, and depends on the fact that Moby Dick is "still
withholding from sight the full terrors of his submerged trunk,
entirely hiding the wrenched hideousness of his jaw" (448). He
is a "grand god," his body comparable to "Virginia's Natural Bridge"
(448) as he lofts himself out of the water before going down.

These land connectives take on more ominous associations, however, as Moby Dick rises again, like a "white weasel" from the
"undiscoverable bottom" (448), directly beneath Ahab's boat. Now
we see only the threat from his "open mouth and scrolled jaw.
. . . The glittering mouth yawned beneath the boat like an
open-doored marble tomb . . ." (448), as the whale takes the
bows and toys with "the slight cedar as a mildly cruel cat her
mouse" (449). We sense for the first time what Ahab has always
known: the source of the "feline madness" (161) that possesses him.
The "ever-contracting circles" (450) the whale makes around
Ahab's bubble-like head, stranded where he fell from the boat,
might even suggest Ishmael's first reason for going to sea: "It is a
way I have of driving off the spleen, and regulating the circulation."
The Whale, now an embodiment of circling spleen, brings the return
of the repressed body that Ishmael has been both questing for and
fleeing. At last potency and otherness have been conjoined. Ahab
and Queequeg, mind and body, have come to final intercourse.

With what? With the male body, in a sadistic recapitulation of the
marriage bed of Ishmael and Queequeg? The wish fulfillment of
those homosexual overtures remains a leitmotif, but that is not the
main theme. Projections of narcissistic potency have given way to
the threatening intimacy with the whale's jaw. The spirit-spout
has become pure body at last, without any male safety. Breaching the length of his body to begin the second day of the chase,
Moby Dick "booms his entire bulk into the pure element of air, . . .
his act of defiance" (455) against that air's purity. Against this
breach and the whale's subsequent attack on his boat, Ahab's last
defense, like Ishmael's last explanation of his motives in "Loomings,"

is a driven fatalism. With his leg " 'all splintered to pieces, Stubb,' " he accepts his identification with his lost bone:

> "But even with a broken bone, old Ahab is untouched; and I account no living bone of mine one jot more me, than this dead one that's lost. Nor white whale, nor man, nor fiend, can so much as graze old Ahab in his own proper and inaccessible being." (458)

While the splinter continues to "gore" him, he tells Starbuck that " 'This whole act's immutably decreed. . . . I am the Fates' lieutenant; I act under orders' " (459). But the fates are less kind to him than "those stage managers" were to Ishmael in "Loomings." Ahab's "own proper and inaccessible being," that last wish-fulfillment infirmity of a noble mind, comes into climactic intercourse with the body's otherness on the third day.

" 'Would now the wind but had a body,' " Ahab cries before the whale shows himself on that last day; " 'but all the things that most exasperate and outrage mortal man, all these things are bodiless, but only bodiless as objects, not as agents' " (461). It is the mind of the whale's body that creates the otherness, he knows; "maddened by yesterday's fresh irons that corroded in him, Moby Dick seemed combinedly possessed by all the angels that fell from heaven" (464). The only vocabulary Ishmael has for otherness is the religious one of the angels' defiant rebellion against the godhead. But we sense that the whale's demonology has roots beyond the holy fathers altogether. After the whale has rammed the *Pequod* with "his predestinating head," Ahab at last gives up his most "inaccessible being," his fatherhood, his potency aspirations, and his yearning for the light, as he recognizes to the full how completely his soul has been bound to the whale. " 'I turn my body from the sun' "(468).

His phallic body-surrogate, the ship, is sinking:

> "Oh! ye three unsurrendered spires of mine; thou uncracked keel; and only god-bullied hull; . . . death-glorious ship! must ye then perish, and without me? Am I cut off from the last fond pride of meanest shipwrecked captains? Oh, lonely death on lonely life. Oh, now I feel my topmost greatness lies in my topmost grief." (468)

"Cut off" from all but that lonely grief, he cries out his last few spasms of vengeance: " 'let me then tow to pieces, while still chasing thee, though tied to thee, thou damned whale! *Thus*, I give up the spear!' " (468). His manhood flies with the harpoon; the line fouls;

> the flying turn caught him round the neck, and voicelessly as Turkish mutes bowstring their victim, he was shot out of the boat, ere the crew knew he was gone. (468)

This passive voice, or voicelessness, dominates his end, after all aggression has been spent to impotence. Knowledge, too, falters into a simple awareness of loss, "ere the crew knew he was gone" (468).

Ishmael had begun his narrative in the aggressive mode, with the strong feeling that he wanted to be "methodically knocking people's hats off." In "The Hat," "one of those red-billed savage sea-hawks" had in fact snatched Ahab's hat, and dropped it from a "vast height into the sea" (440–441). Nature's potency scores where man's cannot. But now all phallicness collapses into the sea. In the throes of the sinking ship, as "concentric circles seized the lone boat iself" and "carried the smallest chip of the Pequod out of sight," Tashtego still stands at the last "few inches of the erect spar yet visible" and tries to nail a flag to the spar:

> A sky-hawk that tauntingly had followed the main-truck downwards from its natural home among the stars, pecking at the flag, and incommoding Tashtego there; this bird now chanced to intercept its broad fluttering wing between the hammer and the wood; and simultaneously feeling that etherial thrill, the submerged savage beneath, in his death-grasp, kept his hammer frozen there; and so the bird of heaven, with archangelic shrieks, and his imperial beak thrust upwards, and his whole captive form folded in the flag of Ahab, went down with his ship, which, like Satan, would not sink to hell till she had dragged a living part of heaven along with her, and helmeted herself with it. (469)

All this heavenly aspiration has been devoured at last by "the yet yawning gulf" of the sea, and the whale that embodies the sea. Now "all collapsed, and the great shroud of the sea rolled on as it rolled five thousand years ago" (469).

V.

It would be easy to say that father has been castrated by mother, as so many other American books have implied. After all, Father Mapple's sermon is delivered to an audience of widows. But Ahab isn't just Father Mapple at sea. He is the possibility of human potency itself. The phallic human body has already been emasculated into mind, and only Ahab tries to bend that mind to the service of reconstituting the body. That effort has led to the destruction of mind itself, with all its transcendental defenses against the possibility of physical death. The idea that "my body is but the lees of my better being" (41) depends on a flight from individuality into universality, the mental leap so characteristic of Ishmael's rhetoric. A man standing at such a mental "Mast-Head" "loses his identity; takes the mystic ocean at his feet for the visible image of that deep, blue, bottomless soul, pervading mankind and nature . . ." (140). But this universality of soul leads only to the "one half-throttled shriek" as "you drop through that transparent air into the summer sea, no more to rise for ever" (140).

The pasteboard masks may seem bathed in love, but, as we learned in "The Whiteness of the Whale," "the invisible spheres were formed in fright" (169). Death at sea, the "speechlessly quick chaotic bundling of a man into Eternity" (41), can barely shore up Eternity against such frightful speechlessness. An ultimately phallic man, such as Bulkington, that brawny six-footer in whose eyes "floated some reminiscences that did not seem to give him much joy," "slipped away unobserved" (23) from the land-climax of his shipmates' revelry to return to the lonely confrontation of that truth at sea. He, like an unconscious Ahab, realizes that the only alternative to castration now is to transform the castration itself into potency. "Take heart, take heart, O Bulkington!" Ishmael apostrophizes in "The Lee Shore." "Bear thee grimly, demigod! Up from the spray of thy ocean-perishing—straight up, leaps thy apotheosis!" (98). But this phallicness, whether of Bulkington's truth-seeking or of Ahab's monomania, ends at the same spot as the Usher's flag-covered handkerchief: mute mortality.

If the father-figures incarnate not only fatherhood but the possibility of human potency itself, the whale just as clearly embodies more than motherhood. He is a he, with the body that Ahab and Ishmael long for. Yet he is also nonhuman, feline and devouring, always surrounded with cream and milkiness that can never be touched. The quest for potency has ended with the helpless awareness that all real potency lives in the whale's ambiguous identity, not in the human mind. Insofar as he embodies the castrating maternal principle, the whale is in effect a product of filial vengeance: Melville has rendered the mother inhuman.

We can see this inhuman potency most obviously in the muteness of the whale. The manhood of words, incarnate in Father Mapple's sermon, structures all Ishmael's attempts to "know" the whale's strangeness. But speech is paternal, and real oral gratification cannot be controlled by the fathers any longer. Unlike Jonah or Tashtego, Ahab wasn't delivered from the whale. " 'Speak, thou vast and venerable head,' " mutters Ahab in "The Sphynx," as he looks at the whale Stubb has decapitated:

> "Of all divers, thou hast dived the deepest. . . . Thou hast been where bell or diver never went; hast slept by many a sailor's side, where sleepless mothers would give their lives to lay them down. Thou saw'st the locked lovers when leaping from their flaming ship; heart to heart they sank beneath the exulting wave; true to each other, when heaven seemed false to them. . . . O head! thou hast seen enough to split the planets and make an infidel of Abraham, and not one syllable is thine!" (264)

With vast relief he hears the cry, "Sail ho!" "suddenly erecting himself" to human illusions that a "lively cry" can "almost convert a better man" (264) to faith. The chapter ends with his apostrophe to universal connectedness in the sweep of that faith:

> "O Nature, and O soul of man! how far beyond all utterance are your linked analogies! not the smallest atom stirs or lives in matter, but has its cunning duplicate in mind." (264)

But here as everywhere else, whether in Ahab or Ishmael, the rage for connection wells from the fear of separateness and deprivation.

The whale offers no words and no communion. In fact, we learn in "The Prairie," "the Sperm Whale has no tongue, or at least it is so exceedingly small, as to be incapable of protrusion" (292). His genius "is declared in his doing nothing particular to prove it" (292). The whale is so securely strong that it need not prove anything, beyond negation. If we compare its skull phrenologically to a man's, as Ishmael does in the next chapter, we see the depth of that "potency":

> . . . in phrenological phrase you would say—This man had no self-esteem, and no veneration. And by those negations, considered along with the affirmative fact of his prodigious bulk and power, you can best form to yourself the truest, though not the most exhilarating conception of what the most exalted potency is. (293–294)

This potency or genius or fascination "is moreover declared in his pyramidical silence" (292). The silence of not needing to do anything to prove your genius, of not needing at all, takes us back to our origins in the sphinx and pyramid, those nonphallic, ambiguously maternal, unrelentingly and inhumanly inscrutable creations of the dead.

The often described "high, pyramidical white hump" of Moby Dick, his most striking feature, clearly associates these origins with the breast, but always in that context of untouchable strangeness. Though Ishmael seems obsessed with getting to the source of things from the moment he chooses to sail from Nantucket rather than New Bedford, his land-way of knowing through words leaves him utterly stranded. He realizes from the beginning that the sea, and especially whaling, has to do with the mother as well as potency. "One way and another," he tells us in "The Advocate," whaling

> has begotten events so remarkable in themselves, and so continuously momentous in their sequential issues, that whaling may well be regarded as that Egyptian mother, who bore offspring themselves pregnant from her womb. (99)

More specifically, he realizes that the ship embodies maternal security. As he goes on to say of Australia, "The whale-ship is the true mother of that now mighty colony" (100). Clearly the *Pequod*, selected over the "Devil-dam" and the "Tit-bit," attracts him because of that historic security: its robust age, its connections with the history of civilization. As the Pequod tribe of Indians was overmastered by the Puritan fathers, so, perhaps, Ahab can control his ship and man can overmaster the whale. Whether we see this ship "bearing down upon her boats with outstretched sails, like a wild hen after her screaming brood" (193), or fading at the last "as in the gaseous Fata Morgana" (469), we feel its links to the land. But what Ishmael doesn't want to realize is the gulf between land-love and sea-fright. His style, so like Cotton Mather's in its civilized associations, strives vainly to bridge the gap. The *Pequod*, as land-mother, is viciously attacked at last by its sea counterpart, "seemingly seeing in it the source of all his persecutions; bethinking it—it may be—a larger and nobler foe . . ." (466). The known mother dies by the head of the unknown.

Another way to describe that development is to see that all the land-mothers can easily be controlled. The sailors can easily encompass Mrs. Hussey and Aunt Charity, those laughably human bundles of ineffectuality. Even the *Pequod*, that "cannibal of a craft, tricking herself forth in the chased bones of her enemies," decked out "like one continuous jaw" (67) as she heads more directly for her sea-borne confrontation, is dominated by Ahab. The ship and her community, though the bonds seem shaped more and more by fright as she spins seaward, keep a communal connectedness alive, more fragmented but not very different in kind from the feelings that Ishmael ascribes to Father Mapple for his pulpit:

> Yes, for replenished with the meat and wine of the word, to the faithful man of God, this pulpit, I see, is a self-containing strong-hold—a lofty Ehrenbreitstein, with a perennial well of water within the walls. (43)

Wholly at sea, however, these walls turn inward into isolation, as the fathers lose control.

Similarly, if land-mothers can be controlled by fathers, the white whale's manhood veils as it expresses its domination by Mother Nature. His isolate potency is a pasteboard mask for her mute unknowableness:

> Almost universally, a lone whale—as a solitary Leviathan is called—proves an ancient one. Like venerable moss-bearded Daniel Boone, he will have no one near him but Nature herself; and her he takes to wife in the wilderness of waters, and the

> best of wives she is, though she keeps so many moody secrets.
> (330)

This "best of wives," in the land-metaphor, turns brutish at sea:

> Like a savage tigress that tossing in the jungle overlays her
> own cubs, so the sea dashes even the mightiest whales against
> the rocks, and leaves them there side by side with the split
> wrecks of ships. No mercy, no power but its own controls it.
> Panting and snorting like a mad battle steed that has lost its
> rider, the masterless ocean overruns the globe. (235)

Like a mother who randomly kills her children, the "masterless" sea
toys even with whales. Man's only defense against her emasculating
power is to create "a self-containing stronghold—a lofty Ehren-
breitstein" in himself:

> For as this appalling ocean surrounds the verdant land, so in
> the soul of man there lies one insular Tahiti, full of peace
> and joy, but encompassed by all the horrors of the half known
> life. God keep thee! Push not off from that isle, thou canst never
> return! (236)

Ishmael often thinks of himself in that dichotomy of inner potency
and outer enslavement, and even declares in "Nightgown," after
experiencing the bliss of lying with Queequeg "like the one warm
spark in the heart of an arctic crystal," that "no man can ever feel
his own identity aright except his eyes be closed . . ." (55). Elsewhere, in "The Blanket," he specifically associates the quality of
inner dissociation with an erection:

> Oh, man! admire and model thyself after the whale! Do thou,
> too, remain warm among ice. Do thou, too, live in this world
> without being of it. Be cool at the equator; keep thy blood
> fluid at the Pole. Like the great dome of St. Peter's, and like
> the great whale, retain, O man! in all seasons a temperature
> of thine own. (261)

"But how easy and how hopeless," he playfully concludes, "to teach these fine things! Of erections, how few are domed like St. Peter's! of creatures, how few vast as the whale!" (261).[5]

But the fate of this erect inwardness has nothing playful about it. Bulkington may find his apotheosis in landlessness, at the price of physical perishing, but how different is his situation from the fate of Pip, who was left abandoned on the sea "like a hurried traveller's trunk"? (346). "The intense concentration of self in the middle of such a heartless immensity, my God! who can tell it?" (347). Unlike Bulkington, he lives. "The sea had jeeringly kept his finite body up, but drowned the infinite of his soul" (347):

> Not drowned entirely, though. Rather carried down alive to wondrous depths, where strange shapes of the unwarped primal world glided to and fro before his passive eyes; and the miser-merman, Wisdom, revealed his hoarded heaps; and among the joyous, heartless, ever-juvenile eternities, Pip saw the multitudinous, God-omnipresent, coral insects, that out of the firmament of waters heaved the colossal orbs. He saw God's foot upon the treadle of the loom, and spoke it; and therefore his shipmates called him mad. (347)

"Make me, O Lord, thy Spinning Wheele compleat." Edward Taylor's request for God to make him a feminine instrument has been transformed into a vision of God himself as a kind of omnipresent phallic Whistler's mother, treadling the loom of his hoarded nourishment. Here at last is knowledge, dived for and found, but it destroys our insular Tahiti. "Warmest climes but nurse the cruellest fangs," we learn in "The Candles": "the tiger of Bengal crouches in spiced groves of ceaseless verdure" (413). No matter what inwardness we seek to project onto an indifferent world, the world emasculates the mind.

At last we have the basic tension of *Moby-Dick* before us. The double-bladed quest for strangeness and potency has become, like Cato's, a sword that turns on the bearer. We now know that strange-

5. Robert Shulman's article, "The Serious Functions of Melville's Phallic Jokes," *American Literature*, XXXIII (May 1961), 179–194, shows how these jokes assert the values of the creative individual against civilized society, while they also emphasize defiant aggression. Henry A. Murray claims, in "In Nomine Diaboli," *New England Quarterly*, XXIV (December 1951), 435–452, that this aggression was directed "at his mother's God and the society that shaped her."

ness and narcissism are one, both dependent on the otherness of the mother's body. Even the father's mind, so emphatically potent, expresses that otherness in the "feline" quality of its monomania. Ahab has been possessed, as he recognizes in his cry to the lightning:

> "Though but a point at best; whencesoe'er I came; wheresoe'er I go; yet while I earthly live, the queenly personality lives in me, and feels her royal rights" (417).

There's no insular Tahiti, we at last have to admit, that can shelter us from the fusion of incest-wish and incest-fear at bedrock in this book. The fear of being possessed by the self's body, as Ishmael conveys it in the first paragraph of "Loomings," slowly becomes displaced by the awareness that the self's body has already been possessed by the other body that gave it birth. Only the mind seems human, and it stays so just to go mad.

The mother's sexuality, in other words, stands as lodestone for man's aggression, his narcissistic defenses, and his sense of deprivation. True, much of the wish fulfillment in the story depends on a regression from sexuality to a homosexual insulation. "Come; let us squeeze hands all round," Ishmael cries in "A Squeeze of the Hand"; "nay, let us all squeeze ourselves into each other; let us squeeze ourselves universally into the very milk and sperm of kindness!" (349). Every ship they meet on the way is possessed by some fated otherness except for one: the Bachelor, whose "captain stood erect on the ship's elevated quarter-deck" (408) while the crew rejoiced at the overflowing sperm that filled everything on board "except the captain's pantaloons pockets, and those he reserved to thrust his hands into, in self-complacent testimony of his entire satisfaction" (407). But real intercourse brings no such potent fusion of the "milk and sperm of kindness," no such loss of selfhood into universal sameness. It brings malice and fright.[6] The last hopeful fantasy, in "The Symphony," depicts the sea as a pastoral, masculine god, heaving "as Samson's chest in his sleep" (442). But even

---

6. In *The Trying-Out of Moby-Dick* (Boston, 1949), Howard P. Vincent conjectures (p. 46) that the first plot "was that of a conflict between two men, an officer and a common sailor," like "The Town-Ho's Story" or so many of Melville's other books. Then, in his reworking, Melville allowed the aggression to turn toward the whale.

here, as Ahab warms to the air and "the step-mother world, so long cruel—forbidding—now threw affectionate arms round his stubborn neck" (443), we are vividly aware of what Delilah did to Samson, and of Ahab's fated end.[7] Neither milk nor sperm nor kindness can be possessed by man. Even at the height of homosexual gratification, the sperm they squeeze is never their own.

Under emasculation lurks oral deprivation, managed aggressively. The omnipresent fascination with cannibalism extends even (and especially) to the most transcendental habits of mind. As we learn in "The Chapel," "Faith, like a jackal, feeds among the tombs, and even from these dead doubts she gathers her most vital hope" (41). In fact, Ishmael not so subtly calls philosophy itself into question along the same female lines:

> So soon as I hear that such or such a man gives himself out for a philosopher, I conclude that, like the dyspeptic old woman, he must have "broken his digester." (52–53)

Moreover, all religion seems similarly suspect. As he digressively declares to Queequeg, "hell is an idea first born on an undigested apple-dumpling; and since then perpetuated through the hereditary dyspepsias nurtured by Ramadans" (82). The demonology so pervasive in this book grows from a more seriously broken "digester." This time the apple of knowledge has been dumplinged by Eve, and fed to Adam and his serpent over God's open grave.

All meaning, connection, depends on this nourishment from a maternal universe. Without it, the mind fragments. With it, as we are told of the fighting Quakers in "The Ship," man can seize "a bold and nervous lofty language" (71). How apt a description of Ishmael's own style! A man who, through lonely self-sufficiency, has

> been led to think untraditionally and independently; receiving all nature's sweet or savage impressions fresh from her own virgin, voluntary, and confiding breast . . . that man makes

7. A. Sandberg makes similar connections for Melville's short stories in "Erotic Patterns in 'The Paradise of Bachelors and the Tartarus of Maids,'" *Literature and Psychology*, XVIII, No. 1 (1968), 2–8. For the "orally-fixated narrator," the vagina is dirty, sex is violent, "heterosexual contact is brutal, homosexual is loving."

one in a whole nation's census—a mighty pageant creature, formed for noble tragedies. (71)

But even with that "virgin, voluntary, and confiding breast," this man has "what seems a half wilful over-ruling morbidness at the bottom of his nature":

> For all men tragically great are made so through a certain morbidness. Be sure of this, O young ambition, all mortal greatness is but disease. (71)

Those minds that try to find meaning are rooted in disease. Yet without that effort, not even a stump is left to call man's own. We hear in "The Doubloon" that

> some certain significance lurks in all things, else all things are little worth, and the round world itself but an empty cipher, except to sell by the cartload, as they do hills about Boston, to fill up some morass in the Milky Way. (358)

The final fate of land is to fill up that hole in the Milky Way. There, too, is the resting place of "the milk and sperm of kindness."

In the one childhood recollection Ishmael gives us, these conflicts become more clear. As Queequeg envelops him in bed, his sensations parallel an earlier time when his stepmother—whom he slips into calling "my mother"—"dragged me by the legs out of the chimney" that he was trying to climb. In penalty for this act, he was sent to bed at two P.M., on "the longest day in the year in our hemisphere" (32):

> At last I must have fallen into a troubled nightmare of a doze; and slowly waking from it—half steeped in dreams—I opened my eyes, and the before sun-lit room was now wrapped in outer darkness. Instantly I felt a shock running through all my frame; nothing was to be seen, and nothing was to be heard; but a supernatural hand seemed placed in mine. My arm hung over the counterpane, and the nameless, unimaginable, silent form or phantom, to which the hand belonged, seemed closely seated by my bed-side. For what seemed ages piled on ages, I lay there, frozen with the most awful fears,

not daring to drag away my hand; yet ever thinking that if I
could but stir it one single inch, the horrid spell would be
broken. (33)

His resentment against his mother had been transformed, as in fact
the book transforms aggression, into the act of intercourse itself.
His "hand" had connected with the otherness of the "silent form or
phantom" whom we meet in so many guises throughout, and he
could not "stir it one single inch." The phantom possessed him. What
began as an aggressive, phallic act (ascending the chimney) lost
its sunlight and in the darkness became pure impotent terror. To
be "wrapped in outer darkness" left him "frozen," with none of the
chimney's heat he was striving to emulate. Nothing rose in that final
confrontation. With relief, then, Ishmael returns to the "reality" of
Queequeg's arm and homosexual submission.

Stubb's dream confronts the conflicts even more directly. Stubb,
too, has been more or less sent to "kennel" by Ahab, as Ishmael was
quarantined by his stepmother, for venturing above his place. Here
again aggression leads to castration, and what begins as the male
identity of Ahab ends as a pyramidical female strangeness:

> "Such a queer dream, King-Post, I never had. You know the old
> man's ivory leg, well I dreamed he kicked me with it; and
> when I tried to kick back, upon my soul, my little man, I kicked
> my leg right off! And then, presto! Ahab seemed a pyramid,
> and I, like a blazing fool, kept kicking at it." (115)

But the dream doesn't end there. As Stubb debates with himself
over the merits of being kicked with a living member or a dead
member, " 'a sort of badger-haired old merman, with a hump on his
back, takes me by the shoulders, and slews me round' " (115). Pip's
merman, with his hoards of wisdom-gold, will lead to the vision of
God's foot on the treadle of the loom. This merman makes the
anality of the mother's sexual retentiveness more obvious.[8] When
Stubb asks if the merman wants a kick, too,

8. Even in "Loomings," we remember, Ishmael was playfully afraid of
Nature's "winds from astern" (15). These fears of the mother's sexual
transformation of oral retentiveness might also underlie the obsession
with the power of the whale's tail.

"he turned round his stern to me, bent over, and dragging up
a lot of seaweed he had for a clout—what do you think, I saw?
—why thunder alive, man, his stern was stuck full of marlin-
spikes, with the points out." (115)

Faced with this phallic yet vaginal ass, Stubb makes discretion the
better part of valor, just as Ishmael jerks his head out of Queequeg's
"doormat" as soon as he sees himself in the mirror. "'Wise Stubb,'"
the merman says, "and kept muttering it all the time, a sort of eating of his own gums like a chimney hag" (115). This "chimney
hag," not unlike the hag who pulled Ishmael out of the chimney,
then convinces Stubb that it's a great honor to be kicked by the
ivory leg of a great man who is also a pyramid:

"In old England the greatest lords think it great glory to be
slapped by a queen, and made garter-knights of; but, be *your*
boast, Stubb, that ye were kicked by old Ahab, and made a
wise man of." (116)

Again, wisdom comes—as with Pip—from submissive intercourse
with this aggressive "queen" or her surrogate merman. After all,
as the title for this chapter tells us, the source for the dream itself
is "Queen Mab."

All these conflicts and developments are recapitulated in "The
Gilder." Typically, Ishmael begins in a benignly reflective mood,
"under an abated sun," in his whaling boat,

so sociably mixing with the soft waves themselves, that like
hearth-stone cats they purr against the gunwale; these are the
times of dreamy quietude, when beholding the tranquil beauty
and brilliancy of the ocean's skin, one forgets the tiger heart
that pants beneath it; and would not willingly remember, that
this velvet paw but conceals a remorseless fang. (405)

"These are the times," he continues, "when in his whale-boat the
rover softly feels a certain filial, confident, land-like feeling towards
the sea; that he regards it as so much flowery earth . . ." (405).
The pastoral mood creates the expected land connectedness, all in
the mind, of course, as "fact and fancy, half-way meeting, interpene-
trate, and form one seamless whole" (406). Even "the cool dew of
the life immortal" (406) seems momentarily graspable.

But at the center of this insularity death gnaws its way into our certainties. That threat of unknown origin, unknown demise, turns the mental oneness into a spiritual fatherlessness:

> Where lies the final harbor, whence we unmoor no more? In what rapt ether sails the world, of which the weariest will never weary? Where is the foundling's father hidden? Our souls are like those orphans whose unwedded mothers die in bearing them: the secret of our paternity lies in their grave, and we must there to learn it. (406)

From the father's whole to the mother's hole is a step no greater than pronouncing "whale" on land and then at sea. Whether that hole is mentally interpreted as the mother's grave, the mother's vagina, the mother's mouth, or that morass in the Milky Way, the end result is to leave Ishmael an orphan, alone on Queequeg's coffin. To have that word "orphan" conclude *Moby-Dick* destroys forever the needed oneness, whether homosexual or narcissistic or philosophical or just human, that structures all our interpretations of the quest. The mother's otherness leaves no ground for reconciliation or "rebirth." Ishmael can connect only with the empty death-box made from the splintered wood of an absent land, as he floats like Pip in the middle of that heartless immensity.

VI.

I have slighted the scholarly and critical interpretations of *Moby-Dick* until now because in the main they offer land-views of a sea experience. It would be easy to put together a collage of quotations from Stanley Edgar Hyman, Henry Murray, F. O. Matthiessen, Richard Chase, and Newton Arvin, to name only the most prominent of those who have discussed Melville's psychology in terms of the search for the father or the castration by an ambiguous parent figure or the pervasive mother-son dependency.[9] Charles Kligerman, in his

9. See Hyman, "Melville the Scrivener," *New Mexico Quarterly*, XXIII (Winter 1953), 381–415; Murray, "In Nomine Diaboli," *New England Quarterly*, XXIV (December 1951), 435–452; Matthiessen, *American Renaissance* (New York, 1941); Chase, *Herman Melville: A Critical Study* (New York, 1949); Arvin, *Herman Melville* (New York, 1950).

essay on "The Psychology of Herman Melville" in *The Psycho-analytic Review* (April 1953), succinctly illuminates Melville's fear of the Bad Mother and his use of homosexual father-conflict as an escape from the mother-conflict that only *Moby-Dick* confronts. But almost without exception, literary critics have desexualized and de-individualized these conflicts. They turn the book into an exercise in mental forms, or "consciousness." [10] The mother becomes abstract and mythified, a static phenomenological category rather than the dynamic physical reality Ishmael so fears.

Writers as interesting and various as Charles Feidelson, Milton Stern, and Paul Brodtkorb all implicitly accept Ishmael's defensive flight into the mind as the only reality.[11] What we have seen as intercourse they treat as "perception." It is a rare Melville critic who will admit how "wicked" a book Melville wrote, and how Ishmael's orphaned end subverts everything Bulkington "stands" for. Our urge for unity is too strong. Even James Guetti, whose *The Limits of Metaphor* (Ithaca, 1967) nicely details the ways in which Melville's language circles back onto itself in a narcissistic artifice helpless before the inexpressible, accepts this standoff as the "meaning" of the book, as if the mental defense against intercourse (it's "unknowable") had become a tangible wall.[12] This search for meaning undeniably catches Melville's own search. As Alfred Kazin has said, "the most remarkable feat of language in the book is Melville's ability to make us see that man is not a blank slate passively open to events, but a mind that constantly seeks meaning in everything it encounters." [13] We have seen the desires that underlie that search. But as Kazin goes on to observe, there's the "little lower layer" that the mind can't reach, no matter how desperately it strives:

10. See especially James Baird, *Ishmael* (Baltimore, 1966), a Jungian study, and H. Bruce Franklin's *The Wake of the Gods: Melville's Mythology* (Stanford, 1963).
11. See Feidelson, *Symbolism and American Literature* (Chicago, 1953); Stern, *The Fine Hammered Steel of Herman Melville* (Urbana, Ill., 1957); Brodtkorb, *Ishmael's White World: A Phenomenological Reading of Moby Dick* (New Haven, 1965).
12. Edward H. Rosenberry's *Melville and the Comic Spirit* (Cambridge, Mass., 1955) discusses humor in terms of ambivalence but robs that word of much of its tension by making it little more than intellectual incongruity. Like Guetti, Rosenberry accepts the implied dualism as stasis and fact, not as wish-fulfillment retreat from dynamic interaction.
13. "Ishmael and Ahab," *The Atlantic*, CXCVIII (November 1956), 82.

. . . there is in Melville a cold, final, ferocious hopelessness, a kind of ecstatic masochism, that delights in punishing man . . . In all these scenes, there is an ecstasy in horror, the horror of nature in itself, nature "pure," without God or man: the void.

Against the horror of confronting this "void," most critics content themselves with intellectualized interpretations.

We can find ample excuse in *Moby-Dick* itself for this retreat. The book is deeply flawed by its tendency to transform intercourse into dualisms or narcissisms, though not nearly to the extent we find that transformation elsewhere in American literature. Too often the book *does* become, in I. A. Richards' phrase, merely a machine to think with. The head and the body touch too little in action, too much in philosophy. Because of Melville's puritanical bent toward making the word flesh, his characters slide too easily into their metaphoric equivalents or their fated categories, without the over-determined sense of interaction that makes real tragedy. Sometimes the scenes seem arbitrarily grouped, as if the stage director had left his script at home and was trying to recreate it in the manner of the great—say, *King Lear*. One chapter on Ahab's soul, then a couple on the flesh of whaling lore, then maybe some byplay between Stubb and a flunky. After a while we feel on the periphery of some cosmic thumb-twiddling, as these static entities wait for the source of real action to emerge.

Melville's own need to schematize his conflicts orients us toward those "meanings" and intellectual connections. But the "meaning-ful" scenes seem connected in parallel, not in organic development. Our narrator needs to control the body, and so he controls words as the body's metaphor, while the body's muteness stays hidden. In choosing the metaphoric plane, Melville comes close to losing the primal interactiveness of self and other, father and mother, man and nature. Metaphoric connectives become tangible, and he begins to lecture like the Puritan fathers, to "the divine inert."

Probably the clearest example of this tendency to impose abstract dualisms on more complex interactions is Melville's constant sermon-izing about Ahab's demonology. We can more or less ignore the pretentiousness of Elijah's and Fedallah's predictions, although that structure of foreknowledge reflects Melville's need to control the unknowable primal interaction through fatalism. But to see everything in terms of God and the devil, as Ahab and by implication Melville ask us to do, abstracts and homosexualizes the real tensions. The conflict between manhood and strangeness becomes merely the mental dualism of faithful and infidel. Then the tussle can be consigned, as Lawrance Thompson would have it, to a "quarrel with God," in a basically transcendental arena where Melville as a "spoiled child" can use God as a scapegoat for his frustrations.[14]

Melville's weakness for "meaning" also affects our relation to Moby Dick. Yes, the "one grand hooded phantom" is the penis. Yes, the hump like a snow hill is the breast. Yes, the broad wrinkled forehead is the mind. Yes, all human forms of potency have thus come to center on this one inhuman creature. But in the process, identity has become so fragmented and abstracted that the physical whale seems lost in the human cravings that spur it on. Maybe I am saying in more intellectual guise what several women have expressed to me about why they don't like *Moby-Dick*. They resent being dehumanized into projections of male potency or pedestaled otherness. Mother becomes the projection of a lack, not a vivid presence. The ambiguities and ambivalences seem merely intellectual, as if Ishmael were retreating to the ingrown potency he knows best: words, words, and more words. His Usher knew better.

Yet in this weakness is the book's deepest strength. Style holds our fundamental response, as always, and Melville's words hold all the tensions that sometimes seem slighted in action. When style and plot conjoin, the fusion takes our breath away. The structure of the quest leaves room for much defensiveness, but no one can put down the Epilogue without feeling drained, touched, exhausted by a contact that has overmastered us with involvement.

And yet, and yet. Style, potency, words, philosophy, aggression, humanity—what survives that sexual confrontation? Only the bleak recognition that all our lunges at universality just bare our aloneness:

> Buoyed up by that coffin, for almost one whole day and night, I floated on a soft and dirge-like main. The unharming sharks, they glided by as if with padlocks on their mouths; the savage sea-hawks sailed with sheathed beaks. On the second day, a sail drew near, nearer, and picked me up at last. It was the

14. *Melville's Quarrel with God* (Princeton, 1952).

devious-cruising Rachel, that in her retracing search after her missing children, only found another orphan. (470)

I, too, feel seduced and abandoned. It was "a damp, drizzly November in my soul" at the start, and now what do I have? Even the mouths are "sheathed" and padlocked. After all the words have soared like the sea hawks, I am left with a simple child's consciousness of loss.

Charles Gluck, a ten-year-old American boy, has caught that feeling:

November

The birds have all flown
And I am alone
In the big sky's mouth.[15]

To live with that aloneness, in that big sky, has been the American experience.

15. *Miracles,* ed. Richard Lewis (New York, 1966), p. 132; copyright © 1966 by Richard Lewis; reprinted by permission of Simon & Schuster, Inc.

FOUR 〜 JAMES JOYCE

From Stephen to Bloom

SHELDON R. BRIVIC

> . . . it is my hope that some thoroughly competent
> psychoanalyst may arise to give us a study of his
> books, which are life itself. . . .
>
> —ITALO SVEVO, James Joyce

I. INTRODUCTION

The meaning of Joyce's works, particularly *A Portrait of the Artist as a Young Man* and *Ulysses,* can be described in terms of one central problem of relationship. The relationships of Stephen Dedalus, Leopold Bloom, and Molly Bloom to their world and to each other are so framed in Joyce's fiction as to signify larger issues: the connections between the artist and his object, between spiritual and material things, between man and woman, parent and child, one human being and another. All these issues may be seen as aspects of the essential issue of Joyce's work: how to find a proper mode of relationship.

The idea of relationship as a unifying concept in Joyce's work is suggested by S. L. Goldberg's *The Classical Temper* (London, 1961), which, in my opinion and the opinions of others, is the finest book on

Ulysses.[1] Goldberg points out (pp. 69–70) that Stephen's aesthetic theory, in its description of the artist's relation to his subject, is based upon passages from St. Thomas Aquinas that describe the relation of the individual soul to the universe. Goldberg sees Stephen's attempts to define a proper mode of connection between the artist and his subject as efforts to solve the central Joycean problem of how to find a fruitful, constructive mode of relation to the world. And Goldberg uses a term from *Stephen Hero*, "the classical temper," to describe the solution to this problem that he finds in *Ulysses*.

This classical temper is an attitude of calm acceptance of the world. It is opposed by the early Stephen to the unrealistic romantic temper, which is always striving after what is unattainable.[2] The classical temper represents a solution for Goldberg because it is firmly connected, in touch with the people and objects of material reality. Thus, it solves the problem of alienation which *Ulysses* inherits from the *Portrait*.

The difficulty about finding a solution involving the classical temper in *Ulysses*, as well as in *Portrait*, is that the relationships in these works remain sundered: Stephen is not reconciled to Ireland or to any of his physical or spiritual parents; Bloom does not achieve any apparently meaningful contact with Stephen, with Molly, or with his world. The characters seem to be at least as badly out of touch at the close of *Ulysses* as they were at the start. In many ways they are worse off, for Stephen gives up his home, his job, and his friends in the course of the novel, and Bloom is cuckolded.[3] If Joyce wanted to show reconciliation or contact, why didn't he do so? And yet there are many hints—mythological parallels, astrological signs, dreams, coincidences, and other details—which suggest that some sort of communion takes place relating the characters to each other and to their world in a positive way. Thus, the novel suggests a positive ending even though the action that it shows ends negatively.

1. *The Classical Temper: A Study of James Joyce's Ulysses* (London, 1961) is referred to as the best book on *Ulysses* by both A. Walton Litz, *The Art of James Joyce: Method and Design in Ulysses and Finnegans Wake* (New York, 1964), p. viii, and Marvin Magalaner, "Introduction," *A James Joyce Miscellany, Third Series* (Carbondale, Ill., 1962), p. xi.
2. *Stephen Hero* (Norfolk, Conn., 1959), pp. 78–79.
3. Stanley Sultan argues persuasively that Bloom is cuckolded for the first time on June 16, 1904, in his *The Argument of Ulysses* (Columbus, 1964), pp. 431–433.

This contradiction is at the root of what might be called the most serious interpretive problem in Joyce criticism. For we have to know how Joyce's works end if we are to determine what they say, and the sort of ambiguity that is present at the end of *Ulysses* is also present at the conclusion of the *Portrait*—a conclusion that may be either triumph or catastrophe for Stephen—and at the ends of all of Joyce's major works.[4] Moreover, this ambiguity of ending is directly related to another question, much vexed among Joyceans— that of Joyce's irony. If the endings of the two novels are hopeful, then Joyce is sympathetic to Stephen and Bloom and their aspirations; if they are pessimistic endings, Joyce is deeply ironic.

Many critics regard *Portrait* and *Ulysses* as negative statements, describing them either as tragedy or as devastating satire.[5] Others, including Goldberg, have constructed theses according to which *Ulysses* indicates that Stephen, Bloom, and Molly will somehow be reconciled or reformed after the last page as a result of their experiences with each other in the course of the novel.[6] All these theses, however, are unsatisfactory contrivances based on hopes and hints. They can only be sustained by ignoring the great bulk of negative indication in *Ulysses*. It is noteworthy that Goldberg, the most consistent and systematic of these critics, actually goes so far as to deny the validity of substantial portions of *Ulysses*, claiming that Joyce was aesthetically mistaken when he wrote certain scenes and episodes because they do not fit Goldberg's conception of the novel.[7]

A way of resolving the positive and negative views of the ending of *Ulysses* is suggested in Arnold Goldman's recent *The Joyce Paradox* (Evanston, Ill., 1966). Goldman says (pp. 43–50, 107) that in *Ulysses*, as in *Dubliners* and the *Portrait*, two possibilities exist side

4. Is Gabriel Conroy dead or reborn at the end of "The Dead"? Is Richard Rowan victorious or defeated at the end of *Exiles*? In *Finnegans Wake* the ambiguity is so pervasive that no simple pair of terms could describe it, so ingrained that any attempt at resolution is pointless.

5. Hugh Kenner, *Dublin's Joyce* (London, 1956); Darcy O'Brien, *The Conscience of James Joyce* (Princeton, 1968); Richard M. Kain, *Fabulous Voyager: James Joyce's Ulysses* (Chicago, 1947); Carl Gustav Jung, "*Ulysses*, A Monologue," *Nimbus* II (June–August 1953), 7–20.

6. Goldberg, *Temper* and *James Joyce* (Edinburgh, 1962); William York Tindall, *James Joyce: His Way of Interpreting the Modern World* (New York, 1950) and *A Reader's Guide to James Joyce* (New York, 1959); Sultan, *Argument*.

7. *Temper*, pp. 139–143, 257–259, and passim.

by side. There is a possibility that the characters can change and resolve their problems, but there is also a possibility that they are fixed in their personalities and can never escape their eternal human conflicts and divisions. Goldman shows that evidence for both of these conclusions exists in the texts and says that the view any reader takes depends upon his intellectual and literary allegiances. I believe that Goldman is correct in finding two coexistent endings in Joyce's works, but he does not really consider what this dualism indicates about Joyce's own values and conflicts.

The paradox described by Goldman can be explained in terms of the conception of Joyce's works as studies of a central problem of relationship: the solution Joyce presents in *Portrait* and *Ulysses* is that the protagonist paradoxically achieves a mode of creative relation to his world and to others by means of separation. Thus, Stephen will be able to relate to Ireland productively, to create an artistic image of it, because he separates himself from it. As he puts it, "the shortest way to Tara was *via* Holyhead." [8] Similarly, the relationship of Stephen and Bloom will have a positive effect upon them because the two men, son and father, part from each other and go their own ways in the "Ithaca" episode of *Ulysses*. And Bloom affirms his love for Molly and revives her love for him by permitting her to commit adultery with Blazes Boylan, just as Richard Rowan renews his love for Bertha in *Exiles* by giving her to Robert Hand. These paradoxical statements have parallels in Joyce's biography: Joyce left Ireland and broke with his parents only to return to his nation and his progenitors through art, and he was preoccupied with the idea of giving his beloved to another man.

Moreover, Stephen himself believes that the truest contact can only be achieved through separation; as he says, "There can be no reconciliation . . . if there has not been a sundering." [9] The same idea appears in Joyce's private notes for *Exiles*. In the play Richard achieves a complete union of love with his wife by giving her to Robert. This achievement is indicated in his final speech: "It is not in the darkness of belief that I desire you. But in restless living wounding doubt. To hold you by no bonds, even of love, to be

8. *A Portrait of the Artist as a Young Man* (New York, 1964), p. 250; reprinted by permission of The Viking Press, Inc. Subsequent references to pages of this text will appear in parentheses preceded by *P*.

9. *Ulysses* (New York, 1961), p. 195; reprinted by permission of Random House, Inc. Page numbers of this text will be preceded by *U*.

united with you . . . in utter nakedness—for this I longed. And now I am tired . . ." [10]

Joyce's opposition to restraint leads him here to a conception of love as something based not on certainty or obligation, but on freedom and doubt. In the notes to the play he says that "to achieve . . . union in the region of the difficult, the void and the impossible is [love's] necessary tendency" (*E* 114). In *Ulysses* Stephen defines paternity in a way that echoes this definition of love: "Fatherhood . . . is a mystical estate . . . founded, like the world, macro- and microcosm, upon the void. Upon incertitude, upon unlikelihood" (*U* 207).

These definitions of fatherhood and love are in turn echoed at the climax of *Ulysses'* action in "Ithaca," where Stephen and Bloom are described as moving "through the incertitude of the void" (*U* 697). In fact, all of "Ithaca" takes place in a cold, astronomical atmosphere of vacuity and contingency. The central action of the novel, completed in this episode, is a complex act of relationship connecting son and father, husband and wife, artist and image, subject and object, spirit and matter, man and universe. And this connection takes place in a state of freedom through separation.

This interpretation of the novel seems to me to be true to the text and to solve the difficult problem posed by the ambiguous ending; but it raises new problems of its own. For, like Goldman's thesis, it describes *Ulysses* as an embodiment of unresolved conflict, the conflict involved in the paradoxical denouement which combines connection with separation. At this point, however, the conflict is no longer one of interpretation: it is built into the works as a reflection of Joyce's intention, and therefore it lies in Joyce's mind. How can we explain it?

The idea of union through separation, reconciliation through sundering, is poetically, psychologically, and philosophically profound. It was probably an old idea when it was presented in the *Odyssey*, and it went on to become the foundation of the whole edifice of Christian eschatology.[11] It appears in some of Joyce's favorite

---

10. *Exiles* (New York, 1951), p. 112. References to this edition will be preceded by *E*. For a thorough explanation of what I believe to be going on in *Exiles*, see my "Structure and Meaning in Joyce's *Exiles*," *James Joyce Quarterly*, VI (Fall 1968), 29–52.

11. J. Mitchell Morse, *The Sympathetic Alien: James Joyce and Catholicism* (New York, 1959), pp. 19ff., emphasizes that according to Joyce's understanding of medieval Christian thought, Stephen and Bloom must part in order to profit from their relationship.

writers, such as Blake, who said, "Opposition is true friendship." Yet the idiosyncratic version of this theme which is presented in Joyce's work strikes the reader by its limitation, its oddness, its defectiveness. Why does Joyce never portray direct relationships? Are there no husbands who love their wives directly? No children who love their parents? Men who love their nations, societies, or worlds? Why does Joyce take the indirection of art and meditation as his model for life? There is an irrational, obsessive quality in Joyce's themes which suggests the usefulness of techniques designed to deal with such matters, the techniques of psychoanalysis.

II. STEPHEN OEDIPUS

"Ma mère m'a mariée." (*U* 424)

The same basic problem that leads to the use of psychoanalysis, the question of why Joyce views experience in terms of exile or relation through separation, also leads back to the *Portrait*. For the genesis of the later, more complex portrayals of relation through distance lies in Stephen's alienation from his family, his nation, and his beloved; and the question why Stephen is so alienated is a major issue of *Portrait* criticism. Moreover, if one wishes to understand the mind behind Joyce's works, it is logical to go back to the autobiographical novel that traces the development of that mind, or a version of that mind, almost from the beginning.

The action of *Portrait* consists of Stephen's sundering himself from his society, his parents, his church, his beloved E——. C——., and his nation. The novel justifies these multiple alienations by its critical portrayals of institutions and persons and by its presentation of ideas about freedom, individual development, and aesthetics. Critics have generally agreed that these ideas and criticisms have much validity, yet one wonders whether they are really at the root of Stephen's alienation. The fact is that Stephen feels alienated from the beginning, before he has formed any criticisms and intellectualizations. In the first brief section of the novel he hides under a table while Dante Riordan threatens that eagles will pull out his eyes. This scene is followed by one on a football field in which Stephen feels out of touch with his comrades and threatened by them, particularly by Wells. Throughout the novel, except for brief and essentially delusive interludes of security, Stephen's isolation is consistent, and the basis of this isolation apparently lies very early. It also seems clear that Stephen could not feel a sense of belonging in any social group for long: his alienation is built in.

Critics have had difficulty trying to define what it is that sets Stephen apart from his earliest years. They have not been able to go far beyond the main reason that Stephen gives, his poor eyesight (*P* 166–167); this is a weak explanation.[12] Another cause that the novel suggests for Stephen's alienation is preordination: he is destined to be an artist and therefore he is set apart from the first (*P* 165ff.). This may accord with Joyce's intention, but it doesn't really explain Stephen's motivation in causal terms. One critic, Robert Ryf, becomes tautological in his effort to explain Stephen's differentiation: "Stephen's isolation is patently self-induced. He would not be apart if he would conform, but he will not conform." [13] To arrive at the basis for this nonconformity, it is necessary to think psychoanalytically about both Stephen and Joyce.[14]

An examination of the first chapter of *Portrait* shows us the basic pattern of Stephen's mind, a pattern which, with modifications, controls the entire novel and all of Joyce's other works. This pattern is a variation of the standard Oedipus complex distinguished by particularly strong castration anxiety. The first section of the chapter ends with a threat which is echoed throughout the novel:

> When they were grown up he was going to marry Eileen. He hid under the table. His mother said:

12. Harry Levin, *James Joyce: A Critical Introduction* (Norfolk, 1941), pp. 51–55; Evert Sprinchorn, "A Portrait of the Artist as Achilles," *Approaches to the Twentieth-Century Novel*, ed. John Unterecker (New York, 1965), p. 13.

13. *A New Approach to Joyce: The Portrait of the Artist as Guidebook* (Berkeley, 1964), pp. 26–28.

14. Richard Ellmann, *James Joyce* (New York, 1959), pp. 302–309, suggests that Joyce's lifelong effort to be different was based upon his competition with other members of his large family for the love of his mother. A number of critics have observed that Stephen has an Oedipus complex, among them Tindall, *His Way*, p. 47; Barbara Seward, "The Artist and the Rose," *University of Toronto Quarterly*, XXVI (January 1957), 183n.; Sprinchorn, "Achilles," pp. 38, 44–46. Other significant psychoanalytic studies of Joyce are Rebecca West, *The Strange Necessity: Essays* (New York, 1928); Ruth Von Phul, "Circling the Square: A Study of Structure," *A James Joyce Miscellany*, Third Series, ed. Marvin Magalaner (Carbondale, Ill., 1962), pp. 239–277; Richard Wasson, "Stephen Dedalus and the Imagery of Sight: A Psychological Approach," *Literature and Psychology*, XV (Fall 1965), 195–209.

—O, Stephen will apologise.
Dante said:
—O, if not, the eagles will come and pull out his eyes.
   Pull out his eyes,
   Apologise,
   Apologise,
   Pull out his eyes. (P 8)

Ryf points out that this passage represents a threat of castration.[15] Injury or loss of the eyes is a symbol of castration commonly encountered in psychoanalysis. The idea of castration, according to Freud's theories, begins to play an important part in the lives of all children during the phallic or Oedipal stage of their development, which occurs at the age of four or five (Stephen is about six here). Castration anxiety generally originates in guilt for sexual desires directed at the parents. In this scene the Oedipal content is, naturally enough, disguised, but it is still clear that Stephen is being punished for showing a desire to play the role of the father: "When they were grown up he was going to marry Eileen."

Castration anxiety recurs in the ensuing scene on the football field. The pervading imagery is of an inadequacy with sexual overtones: "the greasy leather orb flew like a heavy bird . . . He kept . . . out of the reach of the rude feet . . . He felt his body small and weak amid the throng of players and his eyes were weak and watery" (P 8). The inability to rise and the sense of smallness and weakness contribute to the feeling of genital negation, but the most important image is the "rude feet," which represent a masculine or phallic threat. Fenichel says of castration anxiety, "The nature of the danger that is believed to be threatening the penis . . . varies. It might be believed that the penis is endangered by a masculine enemy, that is, by a penetrating, pointed tool, or by a feminine enemy, that is, by an encompassing instrument, depending upon whether the father or the mother appeared as the more threatening person . . ."[16] Stephen faces both types of threat throughout the

---

15. *New Approach*, p. 113. In the original early epiphany upon which this scene is based, the person voicing the threat is a man, Mr. Vance. The boy is Joyce. See Robert Scholes and Richard M. Kain, eds., *The Workshop of Daedalus: James Joyce and the Raw Materials for A Portrait of the Artist as a Young Man* (Evanston, 1965), p. 11.

16. Otto Fenichel, *The Psychoanalytic Theory of Neurosis* (New York, 1945), p. 78.

novel, but masculine threats such as the "rude feet" predominate. As the game goes on, Stephen remains sensible of a phallic threat from his peers: "fearful of the flashing eyes and muddy boots . . ." (*P* 9).

His dread of castration is a dread of reduction to femininity, and this makes him sensitive to any suggestion of homosexuality. Such a suggestion propels him into a mental flight toward the principal source of his comfort and object of his desire:

> Cantwell had answered [to another boy]:
> — . . . Give Cecil Thunder a belt. I'd like to see you. He'd give you a toe in the rump for yourself.
> That was not a nice expression. His mother had told him not to speak with the rough boys in the college. Nice mother! . . . when she had said goodbye she had put up her veil double to her nose to kiss him: and her nose and eyes were red. (*P* 9)

The sexually charged memory of the parting kiss, with its overtones of exposure, is followed on the next page by an escape into a maternal reverie. Thus, Stephen begins to show intense preoccupation with his mother. In this reverie, the novel's basic contrast between phallic threat and maternal haven is expanded and clarified. The passage begins by presenting the mother's womb as a hearth, an image that recurs (*P* 18):

> It would be nice to lie on the hearthrug before the fire, leaning his head upon his hands, and think on those sentences. He shivered as if he had cold slimy water next his skin. That was mean of Wells to shoulder him into the square ditch . . . Mother was sitting at the fire . . . She had her feet on the fender and her jewelly slippers were so hot and they had such a lovely warm smell! (*P* 10)

Wells represents a paternal, phallic threat which will be visited upon Stephen for his thoughts of the "hearth." He establishes the pattern for a lengthy series of father figures in the novel who embody the threat of castration by knocking Stephen down, striking him, degrading him, or dispossessing him. The most prominent of these are Vincent Heron (Chapter 2), Father Arnall (Chapter 3), and Cranly (Chapter 5).

It is significant that the presentation of the mother here, emphasizing her feet and "her jewelly slippers," is fetishistic—she is seen in terms of phallic symbols. Freud says of fetishes that they represent the phallus that the child imagined his mother to possess until he learned otherwise. The discovery that women are dispossessed of the penis is shocking, according to Freud, because it suggests or confirms the possibility of the child's own castration. If the shock is too great, the child may grow up a fetishist, sexually attracted to women only if they wear either a phallic symbol, such as footwear or gloves, or something that conceals the lack of a penis, such as bloomers or furs, which are thought of as genital hair. Fetishes soothe castration anxiety by denying that the female is castrated.[17] Almost all the standard fetishes recur in Joyce's works and in his letters to his wife, particularly those of 1909.[18] Descriptions of women in *Portrait* are almost always fetishistic. As the mother's feet and slippers are fetishistic in the hearth scene, so in the scene of the farewell kiss the emphasis is on her nose.

A few pages later the masculine competition of Clongowes once again forces Stephen into a yearning for the womb: "He longed to be at home and lay his head on his mother's lap" (*P* 13). Stephen is divided from the other boys because he has a sense of guilt which makes him feel threatened by them, and this threat is epitomized, at this stage of the novel, by the father-surrogate Wells. One major cause of Stephen's anxiety with men is now reiterated and clarified as Wells reminds Stephen of the root of his guilt:

> . . . Wells came over to Stephen and said:
> —Tell us, Dedalus, do you kiss your mother before you go to bed? (*P* 14)

Whether Stephen answers yes or no to the question, Wells mocks him and the other boys laugh: "Stephen blushed under their eyes . . ." We have seen that at the start of the novel, "Pull out his eyes" represented castration, and at football Stephen felt threatened by "flashing eyes" while his own eyes were weak. Throughout the novel

17. Sigmund Freud, "Fetishism," *The Standard Edition of the Complete Psychological Works*, ed. James Strachey, *et al.* (hereafter abbreviated as S.E.), 24 vols. (London, 1953–1966), XXI, 152–157; Fenichel, *Theory*, pp. 341–344.

18. *Letters of James Joyce*, II, ed. Richard Ellmann (New York, 1966), 249, 254, 257, 258, 268, 271, and passim. Joyce frequently bought Nora bloomers, gloves, furs, muffs, etc.

eyes, male or female, have phallic value. They are generally either aggressive and piercing or defeated and downcast. We note that the act of kissing the mother is given great weight. This act seems to stand for the whole idea of sexual relations with her. Reminded of his guilt, Stephen feels "hot and confused" and reduced to impotence: "he did not dare to raise his eyes . . ." (P 14). He now punishes himself by mentally going over the whole square-ditch incident in detail, but he turns again from these unpleasant images to meditate on the idea of kissing his mother (P 15).

When the characteristic combination of longing for the mother and resultant fear of castration reappears a few pages later, the womb is again represented by a hearth, the vagina by a half-door: "he had seen a woman standing at the halfdoor of a cottage with a child in her arms, as the cars had come past from Sallins. It would be lovely to sleep for one night in that cottage before the fire of smoking turf, in the dark lit by the fire, in the warm dark, breathing the smell of the peasants . . . But, O, the road there between the trees was dark! You would be lost in the dark. It made him afraid to think of how it was" (P 18). Here, as in the square-ditch passages, the threat is of more than mere castration. It is a threat of reduction to nonentity, of being sunk in a dark void, of death.

There is evidence that Stephen retains a patricidal desire on a submerged level. He is preoccupied by the ghost of a mortally wounded marshal which is supposed to have haunted the castle in which his school is housed. Stephen fears this image, yet he is fascinated by it. It appeals, as an image of wounded mature masculine authority, to his desire to kill his father. This interpretation is confirmed by the dream he has immediately after brooding on the marshal. It is the longest dream in the *Portrait,* and this is its climax: "Welcome home, Stephen! Noises of welcome. His mother kissed him. Was that right? His father was a marshal now: higher than a magistrate. Welcome home, Stephen!" (P 20). Stephen seems to be doing his father a favor in this dream, but he is actually killing him by equating him with the dying marshal.[19] We have here the classic Oedipal duality of loving the mother and killing the father. Stephen's dream of a ship bearing the corpse of Parnell may also mask patricidal tendencies. But the altered version of the Oedipus complex in which

19. Sprinchorn, "Achilles," pp. 17–18, recognizes that this dream is patricidal.

killing the father has been transformed by guilt into fear of being injured by him is much more common in Stephen's experience.

The depth of Stephen's guilt and anxiety is indicated by his reaction to the illness which is building up in him while he has his long dream. This illness may be psychoneurotically induced by guilt, for Stephen feels that its cause is not physical but emotional: "But he was not sick there. He thought that he was sick in his heart if you could be sick in that place" (*P* 13). During his illness he is preoccupied with thoughts of his own death, and he sentimentally envisions his burial: "How beautiful and sad that was!" (*P* 24). Stephen's morbidity shows the intensity of his guilt. Psychoanalysis indicates that the idea of death commonly stands for castration,[20] and throughout the novel Stephen's castration anxiety manifests itself as a fear of being lost in the void, reduced to nothingness.

The explanation that Stephen's castration anxiety springs from guilt over universal patricidal desires is incomplete because it does not account for his special masochistic anxiety. We must also consider Stephen's homosexual aspect. According to Freud, all children start out in the early Oedipal and pre-Oedipal periods with ambivalent attitudes toward both parents. Thus, for a boy, in addition to the primary or normal Oedipus complex, which consists of love for the mother and a desire to be rid of the father, there is also initially a secondary or reverse Oedipus complex which combines love for the father with a desire to be rid of the mother and to supplant her. Ordinarily, the secondary complex grows weak at an early age, but where normal heterosexual development is obstructed, the secondary complex may revive.[21] Stephen's homosexual component is first introduced when he hears a boy named Simon Moonan referred to as the prefect's "suck" (*P* 11). This means that Moonan is a sycophant, teacher's pet. But "suck" also means other things to Stephen:

> Suck was a queer word. . . . the sound was ugly. Once he
> had washed his hands in the lavatory of the Wicklow Hotel

20. Fenichel, *Theory*, p. 209.
21. Freud, *The Ego and the Id*, S.E., XIX, 31–35. Stanislaus Joyce, *My Brother's Keeper: James Joyce's Early Years* (New York, 1958), 32, 57, 59, 238, and passim, consistently refers to Joyce as a man who was extraordinarily devoted to his father and averse to his mother. This view may be superficial and biased, but it is probably not without some validity.

and his father pulled the stopper up by the chain after and the dirty water went down through the hole in the basin. And when it had all gone down slowly the hole in the basin had made a sound like that: suck. Only louder.

To remember that . . . made him feel cold and then hot. There were two cocks that you turned and water came out: cold and hot. . . . and he could see the names printed on the cocks. That was a very queer thing.

And the air in the corridor chilled him too. It was queer and wettish. (*P* 11)

Stephen's disgust with Moonan's feminine role reminds him of his disgust at his mother's castrated genitals, "the hole in the basin." According to Freud, such a traumatic horror may lead either to fetishism, as it does in Stephen's case, or, if horror of the female is insurmountable, to homosexuality.[22] The description of the father pulling the stopper out of the hole seems to constitute a screen memory for the primal scene, the child's earliest vision of sexual intercourse between his parents. Pulling the plunger out may stand for putting it in, but it also suggests castration. This vivid memory indicates that Stephen conceives of sex in terms of violence. The washbasin scene is given a dense homosexual atmosphere by the repetition of the words "queer" (three times), "suck" (three times) and "cocks" (twice). It is a vision of the primal scene laden with anxiety about being forced into the feminine role.

One indication of what lies behind Stephen's inability to develop a normal masculine attitude is seen in the Christmas dinner scene. There Stephen sees his father as essentially a weak man, rendered impotent and defeated. The Christmas dinner argument breaks down into a conflict between the sexes: on the one hand are Simon Dedalus, John Casey, and Parnell, and on the other, Dante, the old lady from Arklow who is reported to have insulted Parnell, and Stephen's mother. Mrs. Dedalus is supposed to be neutral in this scene, but she seems to be aligned with the religious Dante rather than with the men. Stephen later feels that she is betraying him by her religiousness. At the end of the Christmas dinner conflict, Dante is triumphant and the men are all crushed. Stephen is terror-stricken to look up and see his father reduced to tears (*P* 39). Boys need a

22. Freud, "Fetishism," pp. 153–154; Fenichel, *Theory*, p. 330.

strong father to identify with, and the image that Stephen has of his father as essentially weak is related to Stephen's inability to assert proper masculinity. But even while this castrated image of the father is present, there is also another, threatening aspect of the father coexistent in Stephen's mind. Because Stephen has an unconscious Oedipal desire to destroy his father, he feels guilty whenever he sees his father injured. Therefore, every evidence of weakness in the actual father causes the separate, threatening image of the father to loom more terrifying before him.

After this scene of the breaking of the father image, the remainder of the first chapter is concerned with the threats posed by acute castration anxiety manifested in masochism and homosexuality. We return to Stephen at school to find that a sprinter has knocked him down and broken his glasses—another symbolic castration. This is the period when Stephen's mind is preoccupied with thoughts of "smugging" and flogging: "And though he trembled . . . to think of . . . [Mr Gleeson's] cruel long nails and of the high whistling sound of the cane and of the chill you felt at the end of your shirt when you undressed yourself yet he felt a feeling of queer quiet pleasure inside him to think of the white fattish hands, clean and strong and gentle. . . . Mr Gleeson would not flog Corrigan hard. And Fleming had said he would not because it was best of his play not to. But that was not why" (*P* 45). Although Stephen's mind swarms with perverse fantasies for a time, when he is finally beaten by Father Dolan he experiences the pandying as a terrifyingly direct castration: "A hot burning stinging tingling blow like the loud crack of a broken stick made his trembling hand crumple together like a leaf in the fire . . ." (*P* 50). The acuteness of the sense of castration involved in the actual experience negates the pleasurable aspect of the fantasies and causes a reaction against the idea of submission. The pandying aggravates anxieties rather than placating them.

Stephen now affirms his manhood by striking out from his peers and going to stand up to the rector. His trip to the rector's office is an assertion of masculinity, and therefore it is described with emphatic repetition as an entrance into the female: "he would be in the low dark narrow corridor that led through the castle to the rector's room . . . he had entered the low dark narrow corridor . . . He passed along the narrow dark corridor . . ." (*P* 54–55). After the corridor, Stephen passes through a pair of doors to be hailed by the rector as "my little man." The chapter ends with a victory for Stephen's masculinity, but he is quickly disillusioned when he finds at the start of the second chapter that his masters were only laughing at him.

The first chapter establishes the fundamental model for all the action of the *Portrait,* a model which reappears with modifications in *Ulysses.* The desire for the mother is quite clear here, and the threat of castration is manifested in physical action. In later chapters these elements grow more and more sublimated and disguised as the original sources of Stephen's attitudes are repressed, so that eventually the issues seem to be largely intellectual, the desires aesthetic, the threat verbal. And yet longing for the distant mother and fear of the threatening father remain the basic pattern behind all of Stephen's experience.

We have seen that in the first chapter, when the threat represented by the Church's fathers grew intolerable, Stephen asserted his maleness and achieved a sort of relation to the female or mother by diverging from his fellows and going off in a new direction. In the second chapter the masculine threat is represented, paradoxically, by the collapse of Stephen's father, whose failure and aging are emphasized throughout: "There's a crack of the whip left in me yet, Stephen . . . said Mr Dedalus, poking at the dull fire with fierce energy. We're not dead yet . . ." (*P* 66). This paternal defeat stirs up guilt and anxiety in Stephen. He now wanders around Dublin aimlessly. This wandering repeats the divergence of the first chapter:

> . . . he was different from others. He did not want to play. He wanted to meet in the real world the unsubstantial image which his soul so constantly beheld. He did not know where to seek it or how: but a premonition which led him on told him that this image would, without any overt act of his, encounter him. They would meet quietly as if they had known each other and had made their tryst, perhaps at one of the gates or in some more secret place. They would be alone, surrounded by darkness and silence: and in that moment of supreme tenderness he would be transfigured. . . . Weakness and timidity and inexperience would fall from him . . . (*P* 65)

One of the most notable things about Stephen's "strange unrest" (*P* 64) is the vagueness of the "unsubstantial image" he seeks: he says that "he did not know where to seek it or how." And on the next page, when he has moved to Dublin, "A vague dissatisfaction grew up within him . . . he continued to wander up and down day after day as if he really sought someone that eluded him." If this does not seem odd to us, it may be because all adolescents are subject to such vague longings, but it is logically absurd to yearn for something without knowing what it is that one yearns for. Psychoanalysis explains such cases by showing that the object of desire has been repressed. But if Stephen does not know what he seeks, he does provide details indicating the object of his desire. He will meet it "perhaps at one of the gates or in some more secret place . . . surrounded by darkness. . . ." Thus, he associates his "image" with the womb. And he clearly associates it with tenderness and security. He also says, "They would meet as if they had known each other . . . ," and later, when he feels tempted by E——. C——., he says, "He heard what her eyes said to him . . . and knew that in some dim past, whether in life or in revery, he had heard their tale before" (*P* 69). Both in his vague state of unspecified desire and in the later stage in which he focuses his emotion on E——. C——., he senses that the object of his desire is one with which he has somehow been familiar for a long time, one he knew in the "dim past." This is obviously his mother. But the idea of mother has now been repressed and the distant goal of longing has been sublimated into a spiritual ideal associated with transfiguration. It is this maternal ideal which Stephen pursues as he wanders in ever widening circles throughout the rest of the *Portrait*.

One aspect of Stephen's pursuit of his mother is his relationship with E——. C——. (Emma Clery). In the important scene with her on the tram, Stephen's sense of having known her and her temptation before in the dim past is prominent: "He saw her urge her vanities . . . and knew that he had yielded to them a thousand times" (*P* 69). His passivity suggests the relation of son to mother: "he stood listlessly in his place, seemingly a tranquil watcher of the scene before him" (*P* 69). Stephen wants to "catch hold of" Emma, and he believes that she wants him to. Nothing of E——. C——. is described except her clothing and her eyes, the only details that Stephen is later able to recall (*P* 82). These details represent her in terms of temptation, fetishism, and phallic aggressiveness, but they also have another function. By reducing Emma to eyes and apparel, Stephen eliminates her body and thus spiritualizes her. Though he thinks of her as a calculating temptress, he cannot touch her, and when he tries to write a poem about her, the poem is set between Jesuit mottoes and colored by "the maiden lustre of the moon" (*P* 70). The poem concludes with a maternal kiss such as those we have already seen to play a prominent role in Stephen's life, and after writing it Stephen gazes at his face in the mirror of his mother's dressing table.

The two aspects of woman as temptress and virgin, which constitute a commonplace of Joyce criticism, are presented here.[23] To understand why Joyce always thought of women in terms of this dichotomy, and why Stephen thinks of Emma as a temptress and yet is unable to touch her, we must turn to Freud's essay, "On the Universal Tendency to Debasement in the Sphere of Love." [24] Here Freud describes how many children cultivate ideal, desexualized visions of their mothers. The child comes to adolescence thinking of sex as the province of whores and refusing to admit that his mother engages in it. As a man, he separates women into two aspects, one of which is idealized and loved, but cannot be defiled by sex, while the other is sexually approachable, but can never be respected. Stephen sees both sides in Emma, but the idealizing tendency is clearly dominant, for it dictates his actions toward her, while the temptress aspect only finds expression in his fantasies. For this reason Emma cannot satisfy Stephen's need for an overwhelming, transfiguring union with a mother figure.

At the end of the second chapter, after much wandering, Stephen thinks that he finds this goal in the maternal arms of a prostitute: "He wanted to be held firmly in her arms, to be caressed slowly, slowly, slowly. In her arms he felt that he had suddenly become strong and fearless and sure of himself" (*P* 101). But as he achieves contact with the mother through prostitution in the third chapter, the paternal threat begins to arise, and soon Stephen feels himself penetrated by the phallic force of the words of Father Arnall: "The preacher's knife . . . probed deeply into his diseased conscience . . . " (*P* 115); "The thought slid like a cold shining rapier into his tender flesh: confession" (*P* 126). Stephen now wanders in search of a confessional and seeks the sheltering arms of the Virgin whose name is that of his mother. But as he sets about living a

23. Tindall, *Reader's Guide*, p. 93; Kenner, *Dublin's Joyce*, p. 54; Seward, "Artist and Rose," p. 182; Irene Hendry (Chayes), "Joyce's Epiphanies," *Sewanee Review*, LIV (July 1946), 456ff.
24. *S.E.*, XI, 179–190.

religious life in the fourth chapter he comes to feel threatened because the submissive attitude he adopts toward God the Father is felt as a reduction to a feminine role, a castration: "His soul sank back deeper into depths of contrite peace, no longer able to suffer the pain of dread, and sending forth, as she sank, a faint prayer" (*P* 126); "An inaudible voice seemed to caress the soul . . . bidding her arise as for espousal and come away, bidding her look forth, a spouse . . . and the soul seemed to answer . . . surrendering herself: *Inter ubera mea commorabitur*" (*P* 152).

Stephen is feeling uneasy about his religion when the interview with the director brings things to a head. The looped cord of the blind which the director dangles before Stephen represents hanging and also castration (*P* 153–154). *Les jupes,* the skirts worn by capuchins which the director mentions to test Stephen (*P* 155), suggest that the priestly role offered to Stephen here is a castrated one.

Having left the church, Stephen wanders once more, and once more he is uncertain about what it is that he seeks: "the oils of ordination would never anoint his body. He had refused. Why? He turned seaward . . ." (*P* 165). One of the first indications of the nature of what he is looking for this time is the great value he places on words: "He drew forth a phrase from his treasure and spoke it softly to himself" (*P* 166). What value do words have for Stephen?

> Words. Was it their colours? . . . No . . . Or was it that, being as weak of sight as he was shy of mind, he drew less pleasure from the reflection of the glowing sensible world through the prism of a language manycoloured and richly storied than from the contemplation of an inner world of individual emotions mirrored perfectly in a lucid supple periodic prose? (*P* 166–167)

What he says here is that his use of words is subjective, if not solipsistic, that he writes primarily about the inner world because he draws more pleasure from within. The statement is expressed, however, in language that is circuitous and distorted. The subordination of the more important "shy of mind," itself vague, to the less important "weak of sight," the rhetorical question, the fancy, indistinct adjectives, and the general emphasis on sound over sense tend to obscure the meaning of the words. This is typical of the beach scene and of much of what has been called the purple prose of *Portrait*. This writing presents vital ideas or intense emotions in such an ornate manner that what is being said is anaesthetized and concealed by virtuosity.[25] It is not surprising that in the following chapter Stephen constructs an elaborate aesthetic theory which has as one of its main functions to deny that he uses art to express his emotions.

Stephen's use of words, then, relates to some internalized source of satisfaction. His words can be used for sexual and aggressive purposes without exposing him to the danger of physical action. In the second chapter, when Simon Dedalus and his son were sitting in a bar and Simon boasted that he was stronger and more of a man than Stephen, a friend of Simon's, "tapping his forehead," said, "But he'll beat you here" (*P* 95). And in the same chapter Stephen briefly played the role of the father and provider with money that he had won by his writing (*P* 96–98). Father Arnall's use of language clearly showed the phallic force of words, and words are Stephen's major weapon as well as his major defense. He frequently uses the "rapier point of his sensitiveness" (*P* 189) to thrust and parry in the dialogues of the last chapter, where such physical metaphors for speech often occur.

On the beach, Stephen's sense of the power of art inspires a vision of Daedalus aflight. Freud says that the common dream image of flying usually represents erection and phallic sexuality.[26] In Stephen's case the image is highly spiritualized and dissociated from its physical basis: "His soul was soaring in an air beyond the world and the body he knew was purified in a breath and delivered of incertitude and made radiant and commingled with the element of the spirit" (*P* 169). This description of flight parallels the passage describing Stephen's earlier adolescent sexual longings: "He would fade into something impalpable under her eyes and then in a moment, he would be transfigured. Weakness and timidity and inexperience would fall from him in that magic moment" (*P* 65). This central passage is echoed when Stephen meets the prostitute

---

25. "Jim is thought to be very frank about himself, but his style is such that it might be contended that he confesses in a foreign language—an easier confession than in the vulgar tongue." *The Dublin Diary of Stanislaus Joyce*, ed. George Harris Healey (Ithaca, 1962), p. 81.
26. *Leonardo Da Vinci and a Memory of His Childhood*, S.E., XI, 125–126.

(*P* 99–101), and the transfiguration described here obviously relates to religious experiences where his soul was raised and "made fair and holy" (*P* 145). The basis for this recurring idea of transfiguration is the original idea of union with the mother.

The emphatic assertion of masculinity in this scene is accompanied by an image of passage into the female which harks back to the corridor of chapter one, as Stephen's "lust for wandering" now leads him to enter a channel: "There was a long rivulet in the strand: and, as he waded slowly up its course, he wondered at the endless drift of seaweed" (*P* 170). Within this womblike setting, Stephen has his vision of a birdlike girl. His rapport with her is supposed to represent a proper mode of heterosexual relationship and also a proper relation to all of life. She stands for an acceptance of "mortal beauty" which denies the need to turn away from reality to an ideal. Stephen describes her as "without shame or wantonness" (*P* 171). Yet there are indications that the girl is significant partly because she fulfills neurotic desires. She is not free from shame, for "a faint flame" trembles on her cheek (*P* 171). Nor is she free from wantonness, for she stands before him holding her skirts up to her hips.[27] Moreover, she is described in fetishistic terms. The elaborate description of her as a bird makes her phallic, for birds are male symbols in *Portrait* (Vincent Heron, Dedalus). The emphasis on her foot stirring the water is also fetishistic. If the image of a woman is to be comforting to Stephen, she must bear a phallic symbol to ease his castration anxiety. Moreover, he cannot see an attractive woman without imagining her to be either provocative or saintly or both by turns. Stephen's intellectual realization of normal heterosexual love, "mortal youth and beauty" and "the fair courts of life" (*P* 172), may be an advance toward health and maturity, but it is clear that his relations to the opposite sex and to the world remain subject to the conditions of his neurosis. The beach scene shows us a young man who is trying to synthesize a healthy attitude in literary and intellectual terms, but finds himself limited by an injured personality.

Inspired by his vision on the beach, Stephen chooses art as his

---

27. Thomas Flanagan has suggested in conversation that the girl's position and the "noise of gently moving water . . . faint as the bells of sleep" which issues from her probably indicate that she is urinating. Her urine could constitute a phallic symbol and thus add to the scene's fetishism. See Fenichel, *Theory,* pp. 349–350.

vocation and begins to formulate his aesthetic theories. These theories attempt to fashion art into a means of protection and escape from a sense of being trapped by the past and from crippling Oedipal fixations. For this reason Stephen is anxious to prove that art can be isolated from intense personal feelings. And to this end he seizes on Aquinas' statement that art satisfies the mind, not the body, and expands it into his idea of arrest or stasis. The statement that in art "the mind is arrested and raised above desire and loathing" (*P* 205) has some truth, although, as Lynch suggests, there may be exceptions; but Stephen's explanation of this stasis is false. He claims that art operates on an entirely different level from that of kinetic emotions:

> Our flesh shrinks from what it dreads and responds to the stimulus of what it desires by a purely reflex action of the nervous system. Our eyelid closes before we are aware that the fly is about to enter our eye. . . . [But] Beauty expressed by the artist cannot awaken in us an emotion which is kinetic or a sensation which is purely physical. It awakens . . . or induces . . . an esthetic stasis, an ideal pity or an ideal terror, a stasis called forth, prolonged and at last dissolved by what I call the rhythm of beauty. (*P* 206)

It is not true, of course, that desire and loathing are purely physical reflexes. Stephen is trying to divide mental activity, which mixes reason with feeling, into two mutually exclusive levels. Even as he does so, however, his ideas are dictated by his desires, for he is attempting to construct an intellectual edifice to shelter him from neurosis and anxiety, an art to fulfill the function of his mother.

It is also untrue that art "cannot awaken . . . an emotion which is kinetic. . . ." There is probably no such thing as nonkinetic emotion, only emotion which is less strongly or less directly kinetic. Art is built upon the same drives, conscious and unconscious, which operate in daily life. But in art these drives are so manipulated by sublimation, construction, and disguise that the reader who participates in the feelings involved controls tensions and achieves gratification. This peace and gratification, which are what Stephen probably means when he refers to stasis, are arrived at either by balancing psychic forces in a pleasing or edifying manner or simply by satisfying the reader's desires vicariously. *Portrait* exemplifies this process. The book has a great appeal for many young people because it allows them to reenact their Oedipal conflicts inoffensively. The stasis that *Portrait* achieves is an imperfect one that balances desire for the mother against fear of the father. The novel gratifies the reader by presenting a solution to the Oedipal problem in sublimation: Stephen relinquishes his real mother and constructs an artificial mother in the stasis of art.[28]

Other aspects of Stephen's aesthetic theory, such as the explanation of beauty in terms of three stages of perception, elevate formal considerations at the expense of content. Again, Stephen is trying to deny the deepest feelings behind art because such feelings are associated with anxiety. Yet, formalistic as it is, the aesthetic theory contains hints that art is essentially a sexual activity for Stephen. The aesthetic object that he uses as his main example in the discussion with Lynch is a beautiful woman. And the final stage of the process of apprehension, *claritas* or radiance, is described as a luminous state of mind and compared to a fading coal (*P* 213). This description suggests the idea of orgasm, and Joyce describes orgasm in terms of fading fireworks in the "Nausikaa" episode of *Ulysses*. The phases following this aesthetic consummation are described as "artistic conception, artistic gestation and artistic reproduction . . ." (*P* 209). We may reasonably surmise that the sexual union involved in Stephen's conception of art is a sexual union with the mother. The villanelle he composes in the next section is addressed to a female figure who combines elements of the Blessed Virgin with the idea of the temptress and whose heart is "wilful from before the beginning of the world" (*P* 217). These are the earmarks of Stephen's maternal fixation.

While Stephen is preparing to strive for union with an idealization of the mother through art, in the last third of the novel he is renouncing and rejecting his real mother and her surrogates in life. In the fourth chapter he began to have a growing feeling that his mother was betraying him by her devotion to the Church: "A dim antagonism gathered force within him and darkened his mind as a cloud against her disloyalty: and when it passed, cloudlike, leaving his mind serene and dutiful towards her again, he was made aware dimly and without regret of a first noiseless sundering of their lives" (*P* 164–165). Stephen's "dim" and cloudy feeling that his mother

---

28. Sprinchorn, "Achilles," pp. 38, 44–46, presents a similar interpretation of the ending of *Portrait*.

has betrayed him is based on a universal tendency of adolescents to blame their mothers for infidelity because their mothers have given themselves to their fathers sexually.[29] His vision of a defiled, treacherous mother expands in the last chapter to include all of Ireland. Stephen here thinks of his country as a "venal" woman who has given herself over to domination by England and Rome, usurpers. He sees images of decay, corruption, and foreign power all about him as he walks the streets:

> . . . he went . . . slowly, choosing his steps amid heaps of wet rubbish . . . stumbling through the mouldering offal . . . (*P* 175)

> . . . whether he looked around the little class of students or out of the window across the desolate gardens of the green an odour assailed him of cheerless cellardamp and decay. (*P* 178)

> . . . he walked on in a lane among heaps of dead language (*P* 179)

> . . . sloth of the body and of the soul crept over it [statue of "the national poet of Ireland," Moore] like unseen vermin . . . (*P* 180)

> The soul of the gallant venal city which his elders had told him of had shrunk with time to a faint mortal odour rising from the earth and he knew that in a moment when he entered the sombre college he would be conscious of a corruption . . . (*P* 184)

And he is preoccupied by thoughts of low, promiscuous women, such as the flower girl he meets (*P* 183), a factory girl who calls to him (*P* 220), and the peasant woman who offered herself to his friend Davin: the woman "stood forth . . . as a type of her race and his own, a batlike soul waking to the consciousness of itself in darkness and secrecy and loneliness and, through the eyes and voice and gesture of a woman without guile, calling the stranger to her bed" (*P* 183). Just as Irish womanhood gives itself away basely, so

---

29. Freud, "A Special Type of Choice of Object Made by Men," S.E., XI, 165–175.

does the nation as a whole: "My ancestors threw off their language and took another, Stephen said. They allowed a handful of foreigners to subject them. Do you fancy I am going to pay in my own life . . . debts they made?" (*P* 203). He sees Ireland as a maternal betrayer, "the old sow that eats her farrow" (*P* 203).

Stephen's obsession with the idea of the unfaithful mother extends itself to include E——. C——., who has all along been an obvious mother-surrogate. He imagines that E——. C——. is unfaithful to him with two father-figures, Father Moran (*P* 220–221) and Cranly (*P* 232–233). Stephen's best friend Cranly, like Lynch and Davin, his two other close friends, is described in terms of aggressive masculinity. It is this masculinity, rather than any intellectual trait, that constitutes their common attraction for Stephen. The men he dislikes, such as McCann and Temple, are described in feminine terms (*P* 196–198). All Stephen's friends play the role of father-figures to whom he confesses: Cranly calls him "my child" (*P* 247). Because they are father-figures, Stephen's friends must all eventually come to threaten him, and he must abandon them:

> His [Cranly's] hat had come down on his forehead. He shoved it back: and in the shadow of the trees Stephen saw his pale face, framed by the dark, and his large dark eyes. Yes. His face was handsome: and his body was strong and hard. He had spoken of a mother's love. He felt then the sufferings of women, the weaknesses of their bodies and souls: and would shield them with a strong and resolute arm and bow his mind to them.
>
> Away then: it is time to go. A voice spoke softly to Stephen's lonely heart, bidding him go and telling him that his friendship was coming to an end. Yes; he would go. He could not strive against another. He knew his part. (*P* 245)

Stephen's decision to leave Ireland represents the latest cycle in an expanding spiral of action that repeats itself again and again in *Portrait*. In each cycle he wanders off in search of some version of his mother. But whenever he establishes himself in a satisfying position with regard to some mother-surrogate, whether it be his Alma Mater, a prostitute, the Blessed Virgin, E——. C——., or Ireland, he begins to become aware of a paternal threat and he feels the need to wander off again in search of another substitute. "The usual restlessness in wanderers is rooted in the fact that for the most part the protection they seek once more becomes a danger, because . . . their longing is felt as a dangerous instinct." [30] Stephen will always be a wanderer, as Joyce himself was. Even Joyce's writing habits, in fact, reflected this pattern of the compulsively renewed action of setting forth. It is reported of him that while engaged in the writing of each new literary work, he would dismiss all his previous works as being of no interest to him. Thus, when he was working on *Finnegans Wake* he shrugged off *Ulysses* with contempt: "Ulysses! Who wrote it? I've forgotten it." [31]

It is clear that Stephen is not resolving his problems by running away from Ireland at the end of *Portrait;* he is merely repeating the same play of Oedipal conflicts in which he has been engaged all through the novel. In order to find a resolution for these problems, we must turn to *Ulysses,* which carries on Stephen's story and deals with the psychological conflicts of the *Portrait* in greater depth and detail.

III. THE UNQUIET FATHER

> I fear him. I fear his redrimmed horny eyes. It is with him I must struggle all through this night till day come, till he or I lie dead, gripping him by the sinewy throat till . . . Till what? Till he yield to me? No. I mean him no harm. (*P* 252)

It is known that Joyce originally planned to have the action of *Portrait* extend up to June 16, 1904, and manuscript fragments of *Portrait* (then *Stephen Hero*) material exist which represent the scene in the Martello tower that begins *Ulysses.*[32] In view of the fact that *Ulysses* is partly an extension of material which originally was to have been included in *Portrait,* it is not surprising that there is a great deal of thematic continuity between the two works. In fact I will be obliged, in my examination of the problems of Stephen

30. Fenichel, *Theory,* p. 370.
31. Ellmann, *Joyce,* p. 603n.
32. A. Walton Litz, *The Art of James Joyce: Method and Design in Ulysses and Finnegans Wake* (New York, 1964), pp. 132–137.

Dedalus in *Ulysses,* to deal with the closely related problems of Leopold Bloom.

In the early part of *Ulysses* Buck Mulligan has replaced Cranly as Stephen's friend and as a representative of the paternal threat: "Cranly's arm. His [Mulligan's] arm" (*U* 7). Fear of castration emerges plainly as Stephen imagines Mulligan and his friends "ragging" Clive Kempthorpe: "he hops and hobbles round the table, with trousers down at heels, chased . . . with the tailor's shears. . . . I don't want to be debagged! Don't you play the giddy ox with me!" (*U* 7). At the beginning of the episode Mulligan takes Stephen's handkerchief to wipe his razor (*U* 4); at the end Stephen is preoccupied by the fact that Mulligan wants to take his key and finally does so. Stephen's defense against the phallic threat that he feels to emanate from all men with whom he comes in contact is his art, which, as we have seen, is invested with symbolic sexual powers. Stephen invokes this defense here: "Parried again. He fears the lancet of my art as I fear that of his. The cold steelpen" (*U* 7). But this defense is not adequate: on the next page we see that Mulligan's words leave "gaping wounds" in Stephen's heart.

Mulligan pierces Stephen in this manner by reminding him that his mother is "beastly dead." The major event of Stephen's life since the end of *Portrait* is the death of May Dedalus. This loss has exacerbated Stephen's anxieties and weakened his defenses. It haunts him throughout *Ulysses.* The ideas of castration and death are interchangeable in the unconscious, and Stephen apprehends his mother's death as a castration. This feeling augments in him a profound revulsion from the female genitals which is related to his castration anxiety: "he saw the sea hailed as a great sweet mother by the wellfed voice beside him. The ring of bay and skyline held a dull green mass of liquid. A bowl of white china had stood beside her deathbed holding the green sluggish bile which she had torn up from her rotting liver by fits of loud groaning vomiting" (*U* 5). A little later he thinks of "woman's unclean loins . . . the serpent's prey" in death (*U* 14).

Mulligan verbally castrates Stephen as he recalls the death-castration of Stephen's mother by repeated references. Because of his cold, brutal, scientific reduction of her death ("I see them pop off every day"), Mulligan aligns himself in Stephen's mind with the paternal power that has effected that death: God. Mulligan's opening line is

"Introibo ad altare Dei," and he invokes God on the first page. In the following ten pages he has these lines: "God, isn't he dreadful?" (*U* 4); "God, . . . Isn't the sea what Algy calls it: a grey sweet mother?" (*U* 5); "God knows" (*U* 6); "God knows . . . God, Kinch" (*U* 7); "What happened, in the name of God?" (*U* 8); "Do, for Jesus' sake" (*U* 10); "Bless us, O Lord . . . O jay . . . The blessings of God on you . . . *In nomine Patris et Filii et Spiritus Sancti*" (*U* 12). Later in the chapter Mulligan presents himself as the embodiment of God by singing "The Ballad of Joking Jesus" (*U* 19).

Although Mulligan's references to God are all blasphemies, from Stephen's point of view Mulligan is indeed on the side of God. Throughout *Ulysses*, Stephen is preoccupied with the idea of God as "*dio boia*, hangman god" (*U* 213).[33] The *dio boia*, essentially a paternal castration threat, is a monster or vampire who destroys life through the media of time and circumstance. God has taken Stephen's mother and she, religious woman, has submitted to him as she earlier submitted to Simon Dedalus. Early in *Ulysses* Stephen tells Mulligan that he is not concerned with the offense to his mother involved in Mulligan's reference to her being "beastly dead," but with the offense to himself (*U* 9). She has left him to go over to the side of the *dio boia*, of the malignant aspect of the father and of Buck Mulligan's empirical world of medicine. Her death is a final confirmation of her falseness, and the virginal aspect of the mother, which was prominent in *Portrait*, hardly ever appears in *Ulysses* except as a mockery, such as Gerty MacDowell.[34]

In *Ulysses*, as in *Portrait*, the idea of the fallen mother has expanded to become a view of politics: Ireland is the old lady who has given herself to usurpers. This pattern is seen in the old milk woman who is patronized by Mulligan: "Silk of the kine and poor old woman, names given her [Ireland] in old times. A wandering crone, lowly form of an immortal serving her conqueror and her gay betrayer, their common cuckquean" (*U* 14). Another instance of this image of Ireland as fallen mother is "A Pisgah Sight of Palestine

33. William M. Schutte examines Stephen's conception of God as *dio boia* in *Joyce and Shakespeare: A Study of the Meaning of Ulysses* (New Haven, 1957), pp. 104–120.
34. Mark Shechner, in an unpublished paper, points out that Bloom's beach scene with Gerty in "Nausikaa" is an ironic undercutting of Stephen's scene with the bird girl in *Portrait*.

or the Parable of the Plums" (*U* 145–150), Stephen's story for the
pressmen. This bitter sketch shows two sterile Dublin crones labor-
ing to climb Nelson's pillar, obviously under the phallic domination
of the "onehandled adulterer."

Just as Stephen experiences his mother's death with a sense of his
own castration, so he feels his motherland's subjugation as his own.
He expresses these feelings quite directly in "Oxen of the Sun":

> Remember, Erin, thy generations and thy days of old, how
> thou settedst little by me and by my word and broughtest in a
> stranger to my gates to commit fornication in my sight and to
> wax fat and kick like Jeshurum. Therefore hast thou sinned
> against the light and hast made me, thy lord, to be the slave
> of servants. (*U* 393)

The conception of the mother's death as a sexual violation by the
father appears forcefully in "Proteus," where Stephen broods upon
the sexual relationship of his parents: "Wombed in sin darkness I
was . . . By them, the man with my voice and my eyes and a
ghostwoman with ashes on her breath. They clasped and sundered,
did the coupler's will. From before the ages He willed me . . ."
(*U* 38). Later in the episode Stephen sees a couple whom he believes to be gypsy cocklepickers and imagines them making love to
each other (*U* 46–47). Then he thinks of the woman in terms that
represent his principal conception of his mother—subjugated, oppressed, and destroyed by a phallic threat:

> Across the sands of all the world, followed by the sun's flam-
> ing sword, to the west, trekking to evening lands. She trudges,
> schlepps, trains, drags, trascines her load. . . . Behold the
> handmaid of the moon. In sleep the wet sign calls her hour,
> bids her rise. Bridebed, childbed, bed of death, ghostcandled.
> *Omnis caro ad te veniet.* He comes, pale vampire, through
> storm his eyes, his bat sails bloodying the sea, mouth to her
> mouth's kiss. (*U* 47–48)

The final lines, which form the basis of a poem that Stephen composes, are a distorted vision of parental intercourse, conceived in
terms of the father castrating the mother, of the *dio boia* killing her
with a kiss. We recall that the idea of kissing the mother had heavy

sexual connotations in *Portrait*. This image cluster, the horrifying idea of the castrated mother accompanied by the paternal phallic threat, haunts Stephen throughout *Ulysses*. It is a version of the *Portrait's* combination of a longing for the mother and an accompanying fear of castration, now transformed by the injury of the mother's death.

These elements appear, for example, when the text dips into Stephen's mind for a few seconds during "Wandering Rocks." We find Stephen at first thinking of a female figure with great revulsion and then thinking of a nearby dynamo as the threatening *dio boia:*

> She dances in a foul gloom where gum burns with garlic. A sailorman, rustbearded, sips from a beaker rum and eyes her. . . . She dances, capers, wagging her sowish haunches and her hips, on her gross belly flapping a ruby egg. . . . hum of dynamos from the powerhouse urged Stephen to be on. Beingless beings. Stop! Throb always without you and the throb always within. . . . I between them. Where? Between two roaring worlds where they swirl, I. Shatter them, one and both. But stun myself too in the blow. Shatter me you who can. Bawd and butcher, were the words. I say! Not yet awhile. A look around.
>
> Yes, quite true. Very large and wonderful and keeps famous time. You say right, sir. A Monday morning, 'twas so, indeed. (*U* 241–242)

Stephen is thinking of the *dio boia* in the latter part of this passage. "Bawd and butcher" were attributes he gave to the hangman god earlier (*U* 213). The god is seen in the dynamos because he is the power behind the world and the Newtonian universe: "Very large and wonderful and keeps famous time." God runs the temporal system of mutability which has killed May Dedalus. Stephen thinks of shattering the two (inner and outer) worlds, but he abruptly halts the tendency of his thoughts toward patricide and blasphemy because he fears the presence of the castrating father, whom, indeed, he bears within himself: "Not yet awhile. A look around." Frightened, he retracts his aggression and turns to praising the universe. The key to this process is the reference to *Hamlet* in the final line. Hamlet is mocking Polonius to Rosencrantz and Guildenstern when Polonius himself approaches. The prince suddenly switches his discourse when the old man comes within hearing, saying, "You say right sir, o' Monday morning, 'twas so indeed." [35]

Whenever the thought of patricide enters Stephen's head, as it frequently does, the crime must be denied and reversed because of the castration anxiety that it calls forth: "Shoot him to bloody bits with a bang shotgun, bits man spattered walls all brass buttons. Bits all khrrrklak in place clack back. Not hurt? O, that's all right. Shake hands. See what I meant, see? O, that's all right. Shake a shake. O, that's all only all right" (*U* 42). The essential point is that while Stephen broods over his dead mother, her castration, and her act of betrayal, he feels constantly threatened by the phallic father.

Stephen's most intense and terrifying vision of castrated mother and threatening father occurs, as one might expect, during the climaxes of "Circe." It is brought on by the dance of the hours. Stephen is asserting his masculinity and independence in this dance, and the assertion is represented by height imagery. Flying, birds, and elevation are all common symbols of potency with which Stephen has been trying to associate himself since adolescence. Throughout "Proteus," for example, he thinks of himself as trying to fly and being pushed or pulled down: "Get down, bald poll!" (*U* 40). In the dance of the hours, Stephen is frantically trying to raise himself and to deny the threats he feels. He cries "Pas seul!" and is described in these terms: *"leaping spurn soil foot and fall again"* (*U* 578). In the midst of Stephen's attempt to fly, his father appears and says, "Think of your mother's people!" (*U* 579). Then his mother appears, and she is described with extremely violent images of castration:

> *(Stephen's mother, emaciated, rises stark through the floor in leper grey with a wreath of faded orange blossoms and a torn bridal veil, her face worn and noseless, green with grave mould. Her hair is scant and lank. She fixes her bluecircled hollow eyesockets on Stephen and opens her toothless mouth uttering a silent word. . . .)* (*U* 579)

There are five images of castration here: torn veil, hair, eyes, nose, and teeth. The mother is accompanied by Buck Mulligan, who mocks her and calls her "beastly dead." She comes not on her own authority, but in the service of the *dio boia,* and in his name she

---

35. *Hamlet,* II.ii.405–406; cited in Schutte, *Joyce and Shakespeare,* p. 111.

threatens her son with phallic castration, extending her arm: "Beware! God's hand!" (*U* 582). The scene ends with Stephen striking the lamp. The image of shattering the world, seen here, first appears in "Nestor" and recurs frequently (*U* 24, 42, 43, 242, 432, and passim). It represents killing the father or destroying what the father has made. But this attempt at patricide doesn't change anything. Stephen is inevitably knocked down (castrated) by the soldiers afterward. The entire sequence of events is only a stronger version of what has been going on in his mind all day.

In this afflicted state Stephen projects conditions of life that would satisfy his desires and ease his anxieties. He creates a fictional person structured by his own mental conflicts—the Shakespeare of "Scylla and Charybdis." The Shakespeare discussion in the library, in which Stephen sets forth his ideas about parenthood and art at some length, is the most extensive theoretical statement in *Ulysses*. It has often seemed to critics that this section constitutes the theoretical core of the novel and that it somehow explains the mysterious relationship of Stephen to Bloom. This theoretical centrality of "Scylla and Charybdis" may be explained in psychoanalytical terms.

A major factor operating in the construction of Stephen's Shakespeare is fetishism. Fetishism has been characteristic of Stephen's mind since the first chapter of *Portrait,* but at this point it is particularly necessary because the death-castration of the mother has aggravated castration anxiety. Freud says of fetishism, "It remains a token of triumph over the threat of castration and a protection against it. It also saves the fetishist from becoming a homosexual, by endowing women with the characteristic which makes them tolerable as sexual objects." [36] The fetishist, then, might be a potential homosexual because of his "aversion from the real female genitals," but he avoids homosexuality by attributing a phallus to the female.

In "Scylla and Charybdis" this pattern is modified. Stephen transfers the phallus from the father to the mother here, so that the phallic threat is felt to originate with her. By making the paternal threat maternal, Stephen alleviates it, for sexual submission to the mother is not as abhorrent as to the father. In our examination of the *Portrait* we observed that Stephen was a masochist. His masochism is played down in *Ulysses,* but he continues incessantly to think of himself as being attacked. In discussing male masochists,

36. "Fetishism," p. 154.

Freud points out that it is common for them to desire to be beaten by women, but that deep analysis shows their basic fantasy to be that of being sexually assaulted by the father—a fantasy disguised by the idea of the aggressive woman.[37] The compulsive masochist acts out fantasies of castration under conditions that alleviate castration anxiety. Disguise of the paternal threat as maternal is one of the most common of these conditions. In accordance with this strategy Stephen, in "Scylla and Charybdis," reverses the prevailing image of the primal scene—not father castrating mother but mother castrating father: "You are the dispossessed son: I am the murdered father: your mother is the guilty queen" (*U* 189).

The mother referred to here is Shakespeare's wife, Ann Hathaway. Though she is his wife, she is described in terms suggesting his mother, and she is also associated with Stephen's mother:

> —She saw him into and out of the world. She took his first embraces. She bore his children and she laid pennies on his eyes to keep his eyelids closed . . . on his deathbed.
> Mother's deathbed. Candle. . . . Who brought me into this world lies there, bronzelidded, under few cheap flowers. (*U* 190)

Shakespeare fulfills a basic Oedipal desire by marrying his mother, but not before he fulfills more individualized masochistic desires of Stephen's by being raped by her:

> —He was chosen, it seems to me. If others have their will Ann hath a way. By cock, she was to blame. She put the comether on him, sweet and twentysix. The greyeyed goddess who bends over the boy Adonis, stooping to conquer . . .
> And my turn? When? (*U* 191)

The last line, which, unlike the others, is not spoken but thought by Stephen, seems to indicate the gratifying nature of this fantasy to him. The fetishistic idea of the woman bearing a penis implied

37. " 'A Child Is Being Beaten': A Contribution to the Study of the Origins of Sexual Perversions," *S.E.*, XVII, 179–204. Freud's findings are confirmed by Edward D. Joseph, ed., "Beating Fantasies," *The Kris Study Group of the New York Psychoanalytic Institute: Monograph I* (New York, 1965), pp. 30–66.

in "by cock, she was to blame" is expanded in another description
of this scene: "He was overborne in a cornfield . . . The tusk of the
boar has wounded him . . . woman's invisible weapon" (*U* 196).
The threat remains a paternal one—this is indicated by its phallic
nature—but it is disguised as maternal. By shifting the phallic threat
to the mother, Stephen avoids the appalling idea of sexual submission to the father:

> —Who is the father of any son that any son should love him
> or he any son? . . .
> —They are sundered by a bodily shame so steadfast that the
> criminal annals of the world, stained with all other incests and
> bestialities, hardly record its breach. . . . The son unborn
> mars beauty: born, he brings pain, divides affection, increases
> care. He is a male: his growth is his father's decline, his youth
> his father's envy, his friend his father's enemy. (*U* 207–208)

Stephen protests too much in his intense reaction against the idea
of loving the father. He has Shakespeare solve the father problem
by killing John Shakespeare and becoming his own father. The
relish with which this is carried out is reflected in the exultant tone
of Stephen's discourse and in the emotional casuistry of his argument:

> —The corpse of John Shakespeare does not walk the night.
> From hour to hour it rots and rots. He rests, disarmed of father-
> hood [castrated], having devised that mystical estate upon his
> son. . . .
> —Well: if the father who has not a son be not a father can
> the son who has not a father be a son? When . . . [Shake-
> speare] . . . wrote *Hamlet* he was not the father of his own
> son merely but, being no more a son, he was and felt himself
> the father of all his race, the father of his own grandfather . . .
> —Himself his own father, Sonmulligan told himself. (*U* 207–
> 208)

Shakespeare, according to Stephen, succeeds in becoming his own
father in his works (*U* 212–213), as Joyce may also wish to; but in
life Shakespeare is finally incapable of this narcissistic self-suffi-

ciency. He has a tragic flaw: "the theme of the false or the usurping or the adulterous brother . . . is . . . always with him. . . . it
was the original sin that darkened his understanding, weakened his
will and left in him a strong inclination to evil. . . . an original sin
and, like original sin, committed by another in whose sin he too
has sinned" (*U* 212). The original sin is cuckoldry, and his wife is
the other "in whose sin he too has sinned." Psychoanalysis tells us
that a man who seeks or permits his own cuckoldry is recreating in
his wife conditions of love in which he originally related to his
mother: the necessary competitor serves as a father.[38] Stephen has
already shown this tendency in relation to Cranly and others. In the
present passage the competitor appears to be a brother, but it is
the father and not the brother who ultimately threatens Stephen. In
the midst of his theorizing Stephen says to himself, "Where is your
brother? Apothecaries' hall. My whetstone" (*U* 211).

Stephen's Shakespeare tries to escape his father, to replace him,
but guilt makes it necessary that he be punished by the return of
the father, and the paternal threat comes back to cuckold him. The
blame for this phallic threat, however, is placed with the mother,
for it is Ann who is guilty of the "original sin," as Eve was. In
"Scylla and Charybdis" Stephen presents an escape from the masculine threat through fetishism into an environment of feminine authority: "She saw him into and out of the world." By submitting to
the female, one supposedly escapes the terrible possibility of submitting to the male. This process of escape is essential to *Ulysses*,
for the ideal that Stephen envisions in Shakespeare is substantially
embodied by Leopold Bloom.

William Schutte points out in *Joyce and Shakespeare* that
Stephen's Shakespeare corresponds closely to Bloom. He lists many
characteristics that the two men have in common:

> As Shakespeare was overborne in a rye field by Ann Hath-
> away, so Leopold Bloom was overborne by Marion Tweedy on
> Ben Howth. Marriage for each is made necessary by the im-
> pending arrival of a girl-child. The physical intimacy of each
> couple is broken off after the second labor of the woman. To
> each is born a son; each loses his son. . . . Each is thereby
> left without either father or son. Of Bloom one may say, as

38. Freud, "Special Object Choice," pp. 168–172.

Stephen says of Shakespeare: "Belief in himself has been untimely killed. . . ."

Both "Shakespeare" and Bloom are cuckolds; neither seeks . . . redress. . . . Bloom, like Shakespeare, cannot rid his mind either of the broken "bedvow" or of the "dullbrained yokel on whom [his wife's] favour has declined" (200). Each man returns home after the adultery. . . .[39]

The details mentioned by Schutte demonstrate that "Shakespeare" is a sketch of Bloom, though he is, as we have seen, shaped by Stephen's desires. Here is the point of linkage between Stephen and Bloom in Joyce's imagination.

Bloom's sexual life is identical in all significant respects with that of "Shakespeare." In the courtship scene with Molly on Howth hill in which she "got him to propose" (*U* 782), as she puts it, Molly played the role of a nursing mother. Bloom, as his memory indicates, was "ravished," and Molly was larger than life:

Ravished over her I lay, full lips full open, kissed her mouth. Yum. Softly she gave me in my mouth the seedcake warm and chewed. . . . Joy: I ate it: joy. Young life, her lips that gave me pouting. Soft, warm, sticky gumjelly lips. Flowers her eyes were, take me, willing eyes. . . . Screened under ferns she laughed warmfolded. Wildly I lay on her, kissed her; eyes, her lips, her stretched neck, beating, woman's breasts full in her blouse of nun's veiling, fat nipples upright. Hot I tongued her. She kissed me. I was kissed. All yielding she tossed my hair. Kissed, she kissed me. (*U* 176)

This scene, with its infantile orality, is clearly a recreation of the original situation of nursing at the mother's breast. It is associated in Bloom's mind with an image of woman as a deity who rules the world. Later, in "Sirens," when Bloom is titillated by the sight of a barmaid's hand on a beerpull (a fetishistic image) he has the following thoughts: "Beerpull. Her hand that rocks the cradle rules the. Ben Howth. That rules the world" (*U* 288). The Molly of Howth hill now reappears as a phallic mother goddess.

39. Pp. 127–128. Schutte also mentions, among other points, that Stephen's Shakespeare and Bloom are both avaricious, incestuous, and Jewish, three qualities that Stephen links together.

Bloom continues to play a submissive, filial role with Molly. As with many of his sexual attitudes, this one, while present all through the day, emerges most clearly in "Circe." Near the beginning of the episode Bloom has a brief vision of his mother which abruptly changes to a vision of Molly:

ELLEN BLOOM

(. . . appears over the staircase banisters, a slanted candle-stick in her hand [phallic mother] *and cries out in shrill alarm.)* . . . Sacred Heart of Mary, where were you at all, at all?

(Bloom, mumbling, his eyes downcast, begins to bestow his parcels in his filled pockets but desists, muttering.)

A VOICE

(Sharply.) Poldy!

BLOOM

Who? *(He ducks and wards off a blow clumsily.)* At your service.

(He looks up. Beside her mirage of datepalms a handsome woman in Turkish costume stands before him. Opulent curves fill out her scarlet trousers and jacket slashed with gold. . . .)

BLOOM

Molly!

MARION

Welly? Mrs Marion from this out, my dear man, when you speak to me. *(Satirically.)* Has poor little hubby cold feet waiting so long?

BLOOM

(Shifts from foot to foot.) No, no. Not the least little bit.

(He breathes in deep agitation, swallowing gulps of air, questions, hopes, crubeens for her supper, things to tell her, excuses, desire, spellbound. A coin gleams on her forehead. On her feet are jewelled toerings.) (U 438–439)

Bloom's attempt to have an adulterous affair with Martha Clifford reveals the same tendencies of masochistic submission to the mother. Here are the phrases of Martha's letter that excite him: "I am awfully angry with you. I do wish I could punish you for that. . . . naughty boy" (*U* 77). Later in the day, after masturbating in "Nausikaa," Bloom thinks, "Damned glad I didn't do it in the bath this morning over her silly I will punish you letter" (*U* 368). Clearly, this letter is sufficiently exciting to Bloom to serve as a medium for masturbation.

Bloom's masochism is fetishistic in that it arms the woman with phallic, punishing, castrating powers. But what of the father, from whom the phallus may be said, in a sense, to have been taken? As with Shakespeare (but not Stephen or Joyce), Bloom's father has been conveniently eliminated. Because Rudolph Bloom has committed suicide, the question of patricide is avoided. Yet, as with Shakespeare, the paternal threat returns in Bloom's persistent need to be cuckolded, to be punished, to be symbolically castrated by a phallic threat.

Insofar as Stephen creates Shakespeare, it may be said that in a sense he creates Bloom. But Joyce's biography and letters show that Bloom has a great deal in common with Joyce, psychologically and in other respects.[40] It may be said that Bloom and Stephen represent different stages or aspects of Joyce's life. What this suggests is that Joyce's life style of middle age represented a fulfillment of the wishes of his youth, the child being father to the man: "He found in the world without as actual what was in his world within as possible. Maeterlinck says: *If Socrates leave his house today he will find the sage seated on his doorstep. If Judas go forth tonight it is to Judas his steps will tend*" (*U* 213).

Bloom seems to have the potential for fulfilling Stephen's need through fetishistic submission to the mother. Moreover, Bloom is, paradoxically, a father-figure who is castrated, and so Stephen can relate to him with a minimum of anxiety. In the climactic "Ithaca" episode Bloom makes an offer to Stephen which would satisfy Stephen's utmost desires and fantasies. Here Bloom, the father ren-

---

40. Ellmann, *Joyce*, pp. 288–293, 327–328, describes Joyce's preoccupation with the idea of his wife's infidelity. Letters which Joyce wrote to Nora in 1909 address her as a mother and show jealousy, masochism, fetishism, coprophilia, and other characteristics of Bloom again and again. *Letters*, II, 232–233, 242–243, 248–249, 254, 268–274, 281.

dered harmless, offers the mother, Molly, to Stephen. This offer has been in preparation all through *Ulysses*. Stephen dreamed of it the night before the action of the novel (*U* 47) and it is on Molly's mind as the book concludes (*U* 781). It is, in fact, implicit in the juxtaposition of Stephen, Bloom, and Molly which is *Ulysses*, and its presence as a possibility is increasingly felt by the reader throughout the latter half of the novel. As he makes the offer, Bloom also presents to Stephen the idea of submitting to the mother as a phallic deity:

> What visible luminous sign attracted Bloom's, who attracted Stephen's gaze?
> In the second storey (rere) of his (Bloom's) house the light of a paraffin oil lamp with oblique shade . . .
>
> How did he elucidate the mystery of an invisible person, his wife . . . denoted by a visible splendid sign, a lamp?
> With indirect and direct verbal allusions or affirmations . . . (*U* 702)

Thus, Bloom presents to Stephen a mode of reconciliation to the parents by the use of fetishism as a defense. Moreover, each man would supply the other's need to share his beloved with a male competitor. As Joyce points out in the notes to *Exiles*, "the bodily possession" of the same woman "would certainly bring into almost carnal contact the two men" (*E* 123).[41] Thus, a *ménage à trois* involving Stephen, Molly, and Bloom would result in sexual union not only between son and mother but also between son and father.

The relationship among Stephen, Bloom, and Molly is intended to constitute a self-sufficient totality. According to Joyce's schematic chart for *Ulysses*, Stephen is the brain, Bloom the organs, and Molly the flesh of a complete human being.[42] The two men are designed to complement each other in this "at onement"; Stephen's intellectualism and spirituality will correct and be corrected by Bloom's

---

41. Joyce said that Richard Rowan and Bloom were "of the same family," according to Frank Budgen, *James Joyce and the Making of Ulysses* (Bloomington, 1960), p. 315.
42. The chart is reproduced in Kenner, *Dublin's Joyce*, pp. 226–227, in Stuart Gilbert, *James Joyce's Ulysses: A Study* (New York, 1955), p. 30, and elsewhere. Tindall supports the idea of the three uniting to form one ideal person in *His Way*, p. 38.

physicality and materialism; Stephen's independence opposes Bloom's submissiveness; Stephen's selfishness, Bloom's selflessness. In many other repects the two characters, father looking for son and son looking for father, set each other off, fulfill each other's wishes, serve as reciprocal defenses. They are conflicting aspects of one man, the man whose mind created them in its image. Joyce's object is to be "all in all" through his work as Stephen's Shakespeare is, to contain within himself father and son, narcissistically to be his own father.

These relationships make up the central fantasy of *Ulysses*, the purpose around which the entire work is organized. But Joyce's inhibitions cannot allow the fulfillment of this fantasy to be directly presented. Instead, he has Stephen and Bloom part, leaving it highly doubtful that they will ever meet again. The result for the reader is an impression of tough irony, a realization of the sorrow of failed human communication. Yet many details suggest that a meaningful relationship between Stephen and Bloom is intended to take place. Stephen's description of Shakespeare is a foreshadowing of Bloom, as is Stephen's dream; both men look in a mirror in "Circe" to see the face of Shakespeare (*U* 567); and the Homeric parallels, the symbolic celestial sign in "Ithaca" (*U* 703), and the pairing and interweaving of the two characters' thoughts are all portentous.

The combination of connection and separation in the ending of *Ulysses* reflects two separate intentions, corresponding to Bloom, who accepts and desires the union without reservation, and to Stephen, who rejects it as false. These positions represent a conflict within Joyce: he wants "at onement" at the same time that he realizes it to be a delusion. Let us consider the ironic way in which *Ulysses* undermines its own basic project and shows the impossibility of the union of Stephen, Molly, and Bloom.

The principal difficulty is that Bloom, who is supposed to be a paternal figure, is not really a father. His relation to his wife, as I have indicated, is essentially that of son to mother. He has a daughter, but Milly never actually appears, and Bloom's thoughts about her are mainly elegiac. He is preoccupied by the fact that he is losing her, that she is being taken away from him and corrupted. She tends to appear to him as another Molly. He confuses the two, and his preoccupation with Milly's seduction in Mullingar is parallel to his concern over the adultery of his wife-mother (see, for example, U 67, 542). Moreover, Bloom's paternity is questioned:

> —Do you call that a man? says the citizen.
> —I wonder did he ever put it out of sight, says Joe.
> —Well, there were two children born anyhow, says Jack Power.
> —And who does he suspect? says the citizen.
> Gob, there's many a true word spoken in jest. One of those mixed middlings he is. Lying up in the hotel . . . once a month with headache like a totty with her courses. (U 338)

In "Sirens" Bloom reflects on the fact that his daughter doesn't have any interest in good music: "Milly no taste. Queer because we both I mean" (U 278). The idea that he may not be her father trails away here, but he revives it in "Ithaca": "blond, born of two dark, she had blond ancestry, remote, a violation, Herr Hauptmann Hainau, Austrian army, proximate, a hallucination, lieutenant Mulvey, British navy" (U 693).

Bloom has also had a son, but the baby died after eleven days. After Rudy's death, Bloom lost the ability to have normal sexual intercourse with his wife: "Could never like it again after Rudy" (U 168). This inhibition has lasted almost eleven years (U 736). Why should the baby's death have had such an extraordinary effect? Fenichel says, "The ego renounces sexual pleasure if this pleasure is believed to be connected with an intense danger. As a rule, the basic danger implied is castration, the unconscious idea being that the penis might be injured while in the vagina." [43] According to one of the standard formulations of psychoanalysis, an infant may often be a symbol for the phallus.[44] For the already neurotic Bloom, Rudy's death evidently symbolized the destruction of the penis that could be "put out of sight." Here again we can appreciate Bloom's need for fetishes. Elsewhere we find that his mother has given him a potato which he carries in his pocket at all times. He lets a woman, Zoe, take his potato from him in Nighttown, but then he regrets having

43. Fenichel, *Theory,* p. 170.
44. Freud, "On Transformations of Instinct as Exemplified in Anal Erotism," *S.E.,* XVII, 127–133.

given it away when the threats around him, particularly Bella-Bello Cohen, become unbearable, and he asks for it back (*U* 476, 555).

Freud, as we have noted, found that male masochism is generally based on a fantasy of homosexual submission to the father, a fantasy which is concealed by the idea of submission to forceful women. In "Circe" we find when Bella changes to Bello that the aggressive, horsey women that Bloom prefers are really men in disguise. The basic fantasy emerges when Bloom himself is transformed into a female, ridden by Bello, and told that "she" will be offered to Bello's male friends (*U* 528–554). Even Zoe appeals to Bloom for perverse reasons: she is an aggressive, maternal figure, and Bloom is attracted to her by the thought of the "male brutes" who have had her (*U* 500–501). Bloom's sexual attitudes tend to be female. We have already seen that he has menstrual pains; he also gives birth to eight fantasy children in "Circe" (*U* 494). In "Penelope," which is itself a monument to the ability of a man to associate himself with woman, Molly reveals that Bloom often dwells on her relations with other men, actually encouraging her interest in competitors:

> . . . who is in your mind now tell me who are you thinking of who is it tell me his name who tell me who the German Emperor is it yes imagine Im him think of him can you feel him trying to make a whore of me what he never will he ought to give it up now at this age of his life simply ruination for any woman and no satisfaction in it pretending to like it till he comes and then finish it off myself anyway . . . (*U* 740)

Stanley Sultan, in his large recent study of *Ulysses*, emphasizes that Bloom actively arranges to give Molly away.[45] He needs to have her commit adultery not only so that he can see her as mother, but also so that he can see Blazes Boylan as father. Blazes is the masculine element he is constantly trying to evade during the day: "Today. Today. Not think" (*U* 180). "Wish they'd sing more. Keep my mind off" (*U* 280). Whenever Bloom thinks of or sees Boylan, as he does quite often in the course of the day, he energetically turns his thoughts to his business or his daydreams, to time and objective, material reality, which distract him: "Is it [Blazes]? Al-

---

45. "Argument," pp. 132–133, 331, 407.

most certain. Won't look. Wine in my face. Why did I? Too heady.
Yes, it is. The walk. Not see. Not see. Get on" (*U* 183).

Here Bloom reverts in effect to anality, relinquishing the genital
sexual problem and busying his mind with the accumulation of time
and material goods. His plans and dreams culminate in his "ultimate ambition" in "Ithaca," a seven-page daydream of wealth and
property in which he envisions himself as "Bloom of Flowerville."
When the daydream is over, the text asks,

> For what reason did he meditate on schemes so difficult of
> realisation?
>
> It was one of his axioms that similar meditations or the
> automatic relation to himself of a narrative concerning himself
> or tranquil recollection of the past when practised habitually
> before retiring for the night alleviated fatigue and produced
> as a result sound repose and renovated vitality.
>
> His justifications?
>
> As a physicist he had learned that of the 70 years of com-
> plete human life at least 2/7ths . . . passed in sleep. As a
> philosopher he knew that at the termination of any allotted
> life only an infinitesimal part of any person's desires has been
> realised. As a physiologist he believed in the artificial placa-
> tion of malignant agencies chiefly operative during somnolence.
>
> What did he fear?
>
> The committal of homicide or suicide during sleep by an
> aberration of the light of reason . . . (*U* 719–720)

This passage is immensely significant. It suggests that all of
Bloom's materialism and daydreaming, which is to say almost all
of his life, are an effort to repress "malignant agencies chiefly operative during somnolence." This parallels his continual attempt to
avoid the thought of Boylan by going about his business. One of the
material things in which Bloom takes an interest in order to placate
these agencies is Molly; for, as I have shown in an earlier essay,
there is a fundamental equation between Bloom's interest in matter
and his interest in Molly.[46] Both attract him because of their tendency to change, and Bloom is finally reconciled to his wife in

46. "Time, Sexuality and Identity in *Ulysses*," *James Joyce Quarterly*, VII
(Fall 1969), 30–51.

"Ithaca" because her infidelity is as "natural" as any other change in the material world (*U* 733). As Joyce notes in the manuscript, "M B = spinning earth." [47]

But what are the malignant agencies that are placated by Bloom's pursuit of Molly and of matter? The text, in saying that they emerge in sleep and threaten to overcome reason, suggests that they are unconscious. They threaten "homicide or suicide." Of these, homicide doesn't seem to carry any weight: Bloom doesn't seem capable of it.

Suicide, however, is another matter. Bloom shows definite suicidal tendencies. At the chemist's, he thinks, "Poisons the only cures" (*U* 84); on O'Connell bridge, "If I threw myself down?" (*U* 152). In "Circe," where Bloom has several fantasies of being killed, he says, "All insanity. Patriotism, sorrow for the dead, music, future of the race. To be or not to be. Life's dream is o'er. End it peacefully. They can live on. . . . I am ruined. A few pastilles of aconite. The blinds drawn. A letter. Then lie back to rest. (*He breathes softly.*) No more. I have lived" (*U* 499). Bello says, "Die and be damned . . . if you have any sense of decency . . . We'll bury you in our shrubbery jakes . . ." (*U* 543–544). In other passages a curious interest in death mingles masochism and suicidal tendencies, as in Bloom's observation of his cat: "Cruel. Her nature. Curious mice never squeal. Seem to like it" (*U* 55). Bloom's suicidal urge would seem to be a guilty reaction to aggressive feelings going back to early childhood. Fenichel suggests that any person who could commit suicide must first have been contemplating homicide, suicide being a turning inward of aggressive forces.[48] This may illuminate the reference to homicide in the quoted passage of "Ithaca." The patricidal fantasies obliquely entertained by Stephen are deflected to masochism in Bloom.

Although it is sometimes difficult to gauge the extent of Joyce's awareness of his psychological material, it seems incontrovertible that the passage on Bloom's bedtime meditations shows a penetrating insight into Bloom's psyche. It is the ironic detachment of Stephen that allows Joyce to go below the surface play of compulsion and evasion in Bloom's mind, just as it is the recognition of human needs and limits shown in Bloom that allows Joyce to see Stephen's ego-

47. Litz, *Art of Joyce*, p. 46.
48. *Theory*, p. 400.

tism. As a result of the complexity of Joyce's perspective, both are characterized with great depth and richness. The stature of Joyce's work seems to me to rest primarily on the depth of his psychological vision. We understand the minds of Stephen and Bloom with a fullness that is almost unparalleled.[49]

Joyce's understanding is nevertheless limited, and this limitation is nowhere more seriously reflected than in his portrayal of Bloom. Because Bloom is unable to think of himself as a parent and is himself bound to parental authorities, he is less a father than a son, and this is a major failure of *Ulysses*. Bloom and Stephen are both sons, confused with each other, and therefore the theme of paternity in *Ulysses* loses much of its force. We may guess that if Bloom and Stephen were to unite with Molly they would soon find themselves in need of a third man to act as a father figure to them. The novel can only describe fatherhood as a failure, whatever symbolic success may be intended.

Moreover, Joyce's attempt to differentiate the two protagonists founders on the fact that they have essentially identical psychological complexes. Both men are centrally preoccupied by the idea of the father taking the mother away from them and castrating or violating her (God taking May Dedalus, Blazes taking Molly). Both consider the mother to have betrayed them; both view sex as a castrating violence; both are horrified at the thought of the woman's castrated genitals and tend to associate themselves with the mother; both feel strongly threatened and tempted by father figures; both are inclined toward fetishism and other strategies of perversion, although only Bloom has submitted to the authoritarian mother so as to placate the threat of the father.

It might be said that in certain respects Stephen is a healthier character than Bloom, for Stephen realizes that the essential conflict is with the father and he refuses to live, as Bloom does, in a world of delusion and subterfuge. But Stephen's position in *Ulysses* does not allow for any human relations at all. He finds all contact with people painful and all interpersonal sensuality disgusting: women are repugnant to him and men are threatening. Insofar as he has any sexual objectives, they are those of infantile narcissism.

49. "He [Joyce] regarded psychology, which he was then [1902] studying, as the basis of philosophy, and words in the hands of an artist as the medium of paramount importance for the right understanding of the inmost life of the soul." Stanislaus Joyce, *Keeper*, p. 181.

This essay began with the idea that Joyce's works can be described in terms of one central problem of relationship. In these terms, movement from Stephen to Bloom is movement from hopeless conflict to a reconciliation based on delusion. In the earlier phase, the criminal act that the father or Father has committed with the mother is an absolute one that cannot be forgiven: murder. In the later phase, it is not the father but the mother who is supposedly responsible for the crime, and that crime is just another "natural phenomenon," "neither first nor last nor only nor alone in a series originating in and repeated to infinity" (*U* 731). The early phase is apocalyptic: Stephen, student rebel, predicates the "ruin of all space . . . and time one livid final flame" (*U* 24). The later phase is cyclical: Bloom says, "The year returns. History repeats itself" (*U* 377). The work in which the Stephen phase predominates is the *Portrait*. The ultimate expression of the Bloom phase is *Finnegans Wake*. *Ulysses*, which stands between these two works, moves from Stephen to Bloom, from anxious rebellion against the father to fetishistic submission to the mother. While working on *Ulysses*, Joyce remarked that he was no longer as interested in Stephen as he was in Bloom,[50] and Stephen progressively fades from the novel as it proceeds. The book ends with the ascendancy of Molly as earth mother. As Tindall says, "By her existence and her position at the end Mrs. Bloom resolves the tensions of the book."[51] And this resolution leads to the world of *Finnegans Wake*, which attempts to vest ultimate authority in the mother deity A. L. P.:[52] "In the name of Annah the Allmaziful, the Everliving, the Bringer of Plurabilities, haloed be her eve, her singtime sung, her rill be run, unhemmed as it is uneven!"

50. Cited in Budgen, *Making of Ulysses*, p. 105.
51. *His Way*, p. 36.
52. Northrop Frye says of the *Wake*, "the central figure is female because the containing form is ironic and cyclical." "Quest and Cycle in *Finnegans Wake*," *Fables of Identity: Studies in Poetic Mythology* (New York, 1963), p. 263.

FIVE ⌒ THE PRIVATE THEMES
OF PATER'S *RENAISSANCE*

RICHARD L. STEIN

> *Some of those whom the gods love die young. This man, because the gods loved him, lingered on to be of immense, patriarchal age, till the sweetness it had taken so long to secrete in him was found at last.*
> —*"The Poetry of Michaelangelo"*

I.

Since its first appearance in 1873, *Studies in the History of the Renaissance* rarely has been read as "mere history." Its power is well documented. Immediately controversial despite a drab, academic title, the volume continued to excite a literary avant-garde for at least a generation. Reading the book today, we find it easy to sympathize with its earliest admirers and almost as easy to understand the shock of its critics. Walter Pater's first, best-known, and probably finest book, it is, in fact, a semifictional work. *The Renaissance* reads like a novel, far more than Pater's laborious historical novel *Marius the Epicurean*, written mainly to apologize for the excesses of the earlier book. Composed separately over a period of six years, the essays of *The Renaissance* nevertheless convey a compelling sense of unity. Although confining itself to actual historical figures, real events, and existing works of art, Pater's book manages to engross us in what appears to be a world of its own making. This is the power we expect from any successful novel. In

Pater's essays, biography is polished into romance as history becomes mythical, engaging, intimate. This fragile balance of real and imaginary worlds made the book a classic for writers of the nineties, men like Yeats or, more famously, Oscar Wilde, who cherished it as "my golden book . . . the very flower of decadence." [1]

The Renaissance is a difficult book for critics who wish to go beyond Wilde's hyperbole. Its strength is a matter of charm, an elusive freshness that remains through many readings but does not yield to the ordinary tools of literary analysis. This quality is in itself appealing, especially for modern readers, and there is reason to believe that Pater created it intentionally. *The Renaissance* is varied, uneven, and eccentric. Pater's concerns constantly shift. Historical and biographical narrative alternate with occasional discussions of aesthetic theory and with Pater's celebrated prose-poems. The mosaic effect that results is calculated to please, but by whetting rather than satisfying the reader's appetites. Pater is consciously making a protean book.

Pater supplies several theoretical explanations for his variety, notably in the "Preface" and "Conclusion." His goal is to demonstrate the value and necessity of a flexible, critical mind. Impressionism, the main technique of thought to emerge from the book, applies this attitude at once to life and to art, justifying it in terms of Heraclitean "flux," the constant dissolution and reformation of the external world. Since life is composed of disconnected moments, Pater asserts, we must appreciate them individually, for their own sakes. Pater's clearest application of this notion to his task as writer appears in the "Preface":

> What is this song or picture, this engaging personality presented in life or in a book, to *me*? What effect does it really produce on me? Does it give me pleasure? and if so, what sort or degree of pleasure? How is my nature modified by its presence, and under its influence? The answers to these questions are the original facts with which the aesthetic critic has to do; and, as in the study of light, of morals, of number, one must realise such primary data for one's self, or not at all. (viii)[2]

1. *The Autobiography of William Butler Yeats* (New York, 1958), p. 87.
2. References to *The Renaissance* are given in parentheses after quotations; they refer to the Library Edition (London, 1910).

Here Pater deliberately obscures the boundary between aesthetics and morals; the inclusion of the latter in a list of sciences is calculated to startle his readers.

Impressionism even justifies the type of history presented in *The Renaissance*. As an "aesthetic critic," Pater's first responsibility is to himself: even historical lives must be evaluated as impressions. If this produces uneven results (in terms of historical accuracy, for example), they at least will be honest. Pater's text will express his responses to his subjects. If fictional qualities are present, this merely attests to the uniqueness of the observer.

But Pater's defense of subjectivity shows a yearning toward more absolute and authoritative disciplines. As in the "Conclusion," where scientific language is converted into an ethical-aesthetic creed, there are strong hints here that Pater would like to give his internal discoveries the status of scientific experiments. His impressions are "data" and "facts." Their results are compared to optics and mathematics. As much as he identifies himself with a fragmented world, exploded by the new sciences of the nineteenth century, Pater is uncomfortable in his solipsism, and longs for a solid reality he can trust. In this sense, his "aesthetic critic" has a dual role. Not only does this approach to the Renaissance prove that history can be interpreted impressionistically; it also asserts, implicitly, that impressionism has historical truth. It seems that one dimension of Pater's mixed style is ambivalence about his task in *The Renaissance* and about the meaning of the book.

This dilemma is illustrated vividly in Pater's change of the book's title. His alteration turns on the place of the word "history," thus confirming the hint in the Preface that he felt deeply the conflict of objective and subjective views of experience. *Studies in the History of the Renaissance* became, in the second edition of 1877, *The Renaissance: Studies in Art and Poetry*. There could then be no objection, as there was in 1873, that the book was less historical than advertised. Now it was a collection of "studies" only, and the volume was made to sound fragmentary and less unified in subject or theme. Pater even suggested to Alexander Macmillan, his publisher, that they call the second edition "A Series of Studies . . ."[3] This modesty conceals a deep defensiveness about the book.

Most contemporary criticism of the first edition attacked sup-

3. Lawrence Gove Evans, "Some Letters of Walter Pater" (unpublished Ph.D. dissertation, Harvard University, 1961), p. 20.

posedly immoral passages rather than historical inaccuracy, but I suspect that Pater linked these objections in his own mind. Some additional pieces of textual history support this identification. When Pater issued the second edition, with its new title, he removed the "Conclusion," against which most of the moral outrage over the book was directed. He restored it in the third edition (1888) with an apologetic and guilty footnote relating his fears that "it might possibly mislead some of those young men into whose hands it might fall" (233). Pater's conditional verbs in the note dramatize the persistence of his nervousness fifteen years after the initial controversy over "this brief conclusion," as the footnote rather self-disparagingly calls it. At the same time that he returned the "Conclusion" to its original place, Pater added a tenth section to the volume, "The School of Giorgione." [4] Not surprisingly, the essay is an extended display of ambivalence. In fact, Pater's nervousness hinges on his use of history and on the morality of art.

The Giorgione essay contains the most famous assertion from *The Renaissance*, that "*All art constantly aspires towards the condition of music*" (135). But that statement is part of an opening section on aesthetics which Pater divides from the rest of the study by a large gap on the printed page. Only half of the chapter is theoretical, the other half historical, with the result that for once Pater seems undecided about what his aesthetic critic is up to. Even within the aesthetics section itself, Pater's theory argues against itself as he discusses the "responsibility" of art. He begins by defending art's "sensuous" element: "Each art . . . has its own special mode of reaching the imagination, its own special responsibilities to its material" (130–131). Later on, however, he adds that "Art . . . is . . . always striving to be independent of the mere intelligence, to become a matter of pure perception, to get rid of its responsibilities to its subject or material . . ." (138). Not until his essay on "Style" (1888) was Pater to resolve this conflict between the formal determinants of art and its universal symbolism. Here Pater risks self-contradiction in order to stress what art is *not*. He is insisting that all art is self-contained, that it has no moral responsibilities, however much its form is shaped by the demands of material. Applied to criticism, this argument becomes a defense of his own work and, specifically, of the Conclusion to *The Renaissance*. Criticism

4. It was, however, written earlier, perhaps for the first edition of *The Renaissance;* see Evans, "Letters," pp. xix, 7.

is an abstract science, the passage implies; it is not immoral but amoral, deriving its terms from art and not from a vocabulary of ethical "responsibilities." Despite the claim in that famous footnote that the "Conclusion" had been explained adequately by *Marius the Epicurean,* Pater continues to apologize for its contents.

Furthermore, the essay on Giorgione alters the impact of the entire book. If *The Renaissance* is passionate in its first edition, Pater's addition of "The School of Giorgione" breaks the spell of its most extended display of prose energy. "Joachim du Bellay," Pater's second French study, follows smoothly in the first edition from Leonardo's death at Amboise. "Giorgione," placed between the two essays, severs their connection abruptly, just as its aesthetic theory disturbs the continuity of history as the central, dominant mode of the book. Pater had confined aesthetics in the first edition to the "Preface" and "Conclusion," leaving in the body of the book what he calls at one point "the enchanted region of the Renaissance" (26). "Giorgione," then, is a defensive essay, but its role goes beyond merely vindicating Pater in the face of moral and historical controversy. Pater uses it to mar the tranquility of *The Renaissance,* making it hard not to conclude that his elaborate defenses fend off internal pressures as well as public criticism. Pater's discomfort with his book, his attacks on its strengths, and his revisions demand an explanation that would account for his feelings about the very writing of history.

At the beginning of his first study, entitled in the second and subsequent editions "Two Early French Stories," Pater compares the Renaissance to a river. According to his metaphor, history-writing becomes a kind of mythical journey. "The history of the Renaissance ends in France, and carries us away from Italy to the beautiful cities of the country of the Loire. But it was in France also, in a very important sense, that the Renaissance had begun" (1). The passive luxuriance of this language reveals Pater in the midst of a brief but pronounced imaginative regression as he first considers his topic. The "history" that carries him passively away on its damp stream becomes a nurturing mother. This suggestion is supported by the rich vowel sounds of "Loire" and by the fairy-tale rhythm of the phrase that surrounds it ("the beautiful cities of the country of the Loire"). For an instant, at least, study becomes the path of the "beautiful cities" of an idealized childhood.

Placed in the first lines of Pater's first Renaissance "study," this brief reverie seems to have an almost accidental quality. Its charm, the magic of an initiatory formula that permits graver secrets to be divulged, is of an ephemeral type. What is striking, then, is that it betrays one of Pater's central themes, one, in fact, around which he organizes his essays. Here, as throughout *The Renaissance*, Pater assumes that an order is inherent in his material. Structure, by analogy from the meaning of history, is defined as a natural occurrence, and one of its consequences is to make the history-writer a passive spectator of this continuous process.

At an early stage of his book, Pater defines this process in more detail. In the "Preface," one of four essays published in the volume for the first time, he explains that he added two of the other original pieces to facilitate organization. He included the "two little compositions in early French" at the beginning, he explains, to "help the unity of my series" (xii). Pater then goes on to mention France's dual role in Renaissance history. The terms of the following sentence reveal strong unconscious components of his sense of structure. As Pater expands upon his metaphor of historical development, it becomes clear from his tone and elegant language that his imagination is fully engaged:

> The Renaissance, in truth, put forth in France an aftermath, a wonderful later growth, the products of which have to the full that subtle and delicate sweetness which belongs to a refined and comely decadence, just as its earliest phases have the freshness which belongs to all periods of growth in art, the charm of *ascêsis*, of the austere and serious girding of the loins in youth. (xii–xiii)

Here the passage of time is an organic process. By the end of the sentence, in fact, history mirrors the "growth" of man. Pater's metaphor implies that the unity of his studies will derive from the pattern of human development itself. Potentially, the past can represent for Pater all the complex associations he attaches to childhood and growth. The inevitability of historical fact becomes, in this way, a vehicle for neutralizing the images of personal history and giving them meaning.

In its context, of course, the analogy has a more specific reference. Pater is speaking of his first and last studies of Renaissance subjects— "Two Early French Stories," in the first edition titled "Aucassin and Nicolette," and "Joachim du Bellay." Both give the analogy of growth from "ascesis" to "decadence" definite meanings, and they demonstrate the ease with which Pater personalizes history, in these cases literary history, making biography and criticism serve private goals. Each essay develops a particular vocabulary of praise for the literary products of changing civilizations, France in the early thirteenth and mid-sixteenth centuries. Pater arranges the essays to progress toward consummate examples of these literatures, the conclusion of *Li Amitiez de Ami et Amile* and du Bellay's *D'un Vanneur de Blé aux Vents*. Emotionally, however, the studies move in opposite directions. In the final "morsel" from the first story, "the harmony of human interests is still entire" (27). Not only are the two friends "more than faithful unto death" (27), but the story itself seems to anticipate a unified society, one in which "liberty of heart" conflicts with no "system" in the external world. At the end of the essay Pater points out that the story belongs to the tradition of saints' lives and probably was written by a monk, a representative of such an integral world. But Amis and Amile were "excluded from the martyrology" at the end of the Renaissance (27), as if, in Pater's view, they lost their popular appeal once removed from that "enchanted region." Their inseparability, then, stands for a general condition of the environment, where dedication is rewarded.

Du Bellay's poetry, on the other hand, possesses a more fragile charm, with little moral or social effect outside itself. This results from the poet's living at odds with his age. Born in 1525, "the disastrous year" as Pater calls it (164), du Bellay quickly sympathizes, as a member of the Pleiad, with "the catholic side, the losing side, the forlorn hope" (166). His affiliation is not caused by birth, however, as Pater makes clear by failing to mention du Bellay's birth until halfway through the essay. A more suggestive cause of the poet's alienation is presented in the opening sentence:

> In the middle of the sixteenth century, when the spirit of the Renaissance was everywhere, and people had begun to look back with distaste on the works of the middle age, the old Gothic manner had still one chance more, in borrowing something from the rival which was about to supplant it. (155)

Joachim du Bellay, along with the entire school of poets surrounding Ronsard, is involved in a revolution. Pater, following the example of numerous historians and even revolutionaries, describes this as a generational struggle, son against father. In psychological terms, of course, this is an Oedipal conflict, and Pater's sentence betrays some uneasiness in the face of this theme. His syntax obscures the nature of the "rivalry"—it is the new style of du Bellay and the Pleiad that is "about to supplant" both Gothic and Italian influences in France by "borrowing something" from both. But this historical displacement has a psychological meaning, suggesting the serious fear of a paternal figure "borrowing something from the rival . . . about to supplant it." His immediate unconscious allusion to the threat of castration indicates that Pater's sympathies in the historical contest are clearly with the rebelling son.

As the essay develops, Pater's language suggests with increasing strength the familial connotations of du Bellay's literary radicalism. Pater makes him, even before the explicit announcement late in the essay, the "true child of his age" (172). As with all Oedipal children, the object of his efforts is a maternal figure. Hence, as Pater discusses the ennoblement of sixteenth-century French through du Bellay's efforts to restore its purity, the historical events become a screen for the deeper fantasy of recovering the honor of a defiled woman.[5] The poet, Pater explains, "is really pleading for . . . his mother-tongue" (163). The most genuinely French products of the past, in the works of Villon and Clouet, have an equivalent in vernacular speech, which Pater describes as if it were a legacy of virginity and gentility that must be saved from being debased. "It is the higher touch making itself felt here and there, betraying itself, like nobler blood in a lower stock, by a fine line or gesture or expression, the turn of a wrist, the tapering of a finger. In Ronsard's time that rougher element seemed likely to predominate." (157–158). Family romance and the Oedipal dream converge in this portrait of language as a neglected princess: the avenging son proves his own "nobler blood" by banishing "that rougher element" from the scene.

In the second half of the essay, du Bellay's work is defined against a background of hostility, as if to balance the catalog of his achievements in the early pages. As in much of Pater's fiction, the defensive

5. This fantasy is familiar from Freud's essay, "A Special Type of Choice of Object Made by Men (Contributions to the Psychology of Love, I)," in *The Standard Edition of the Complete Psychological Works of Sigmund Freud*, ed. James Strachey, *et al.* (hereafter abbreviated as *S.E.*), 24 vols. (London, 1953–1966), XI, 165–175.

role of his own ego and superego is assumed by the cultural environment of a represented age. Seemingly culture or history itself
punishes or at least harasses psychic offenders. Pater explains that
the poet finds freedom in the language which is also "the medium
of what he calls, in one of his great phrases, *le discours fatal des
choses mondaines*," a phrase Pater significantly translates as "that
discourse about affairs which decides men's fates" (163). It is from
this point that he goes on to mention du Bellay's birth in that "disastrous year," then his "cruel sufferings" (164), and at last his death
"at the early age of thirty-five" (165).

One of Pater's principal points in the essay is that du Bellay's
refinement, the "decadence" mentioned in the "Preface," grows out of
a consciousness of death. Pater compares du Bellay to the story-
tellers of the *Decameron.* Admitting that all their pleasure is
doomed, Pater still must add that "they amuse themselves with
wonderful elegance" (169). It is natural to him that a fated man
like the French poet could produce verse which "made much of
manner, and carried it to a high degree of perfection" (166). And
if this description seems remarkably appropriate to Pater's own
mannered style, that is merely a reflection of the modernity of
sixteenth-century "decadence." Like the nineteenth-century figure
Pater outlines in his "Conclusion," du Bellay lives, in Victor Hugo's
phrase, "under sentence of death" (238). Pater's account of the
gaiety of the Pleiad provides a sober analysis of the denials implicit
in Victorian aestheticism, a movement which was to claim *The
Renaissance* as a crucial inspiration.

Death comes to du Bellay after a journey from Rome back to the
Loire. This sequence is a central image of the book. Du Bellay's
tragic journey, imitating the progress of Renaissance history, mirrors
similar fatal trips in the lives of Leonardo and Winckelmann, narrated in the studies next to "Joachim du Bellay" in the first edition.
As Pater approaches the end of the essay, the psychological significance of travel becomes clear in his discussions of the countryside to which the "homesick" French poet longs to return. These
passages, which grow increasingly intense after the center of the
essay, culminate in Pater's description of du Bellay's greatest poem.

In Rome, du Bellay "continually" dreams of France, of "the soft
climate of Anjou—*la douceur Angevine*" (174). As usual, Pater's
translation is a clue to his thought: such Angevine softness is not
necessarily climatic. Earlier, Pater had used the locale in a descrip-

tion of Ronsard's ideal maiden, "a rare and peculiar type of beauty, *la petite pucelle Angevine*" (167); that French phrase, in turn, is echoed when Pater speaks of the "domesticity" and a "homeliness" that is "true to its country" in "du Bellay's *Olive*, a collection of sonnets in praise of a half-imaginary lady" (171). On a psychic level, Pater senses feminine, even erotic, qualities in du Bellay's landscapes. The women praised in the Pleiad's poetry merge with their native countryside, making the poets "true" to both simultaneously. This association appears most strikingly when Pater discusses du Bellay's homesickness in Rome. The poet's thoughts go

> not so much to the real France . . . with its dark streets and roofs of rough-hewn slate, as to that other country, with slenderer towers, and more winding rivers, and trees like flowers, and with softer sunshine on more gracefully-proportioned fields and ways, which the fancy of the exile, and the pilgrim, and of the schoolboy far from home, and of those kept at home unwillingly, everywhere builds up before or behind them. (174)

There are clear sensuous proportions to this imaginary country—and the converging of "slenderer towers" with "more winding rivers" suggests a childish dream of magical potency rewarded. The dreamer's identity is hardly a mystery, for the developing sentence outlines a character far more like Pater than du Bellay. That final reference to a frustrated, uneventful life is surely an unconscious slip in the explanation of the poet's attitude in Rome. Pater is thinking instead of himself. It is, in fact, a passive dream much like the one that introduces "Two Early French Stories," where history carries Pater windingly on a visit to "that other country."

Pater identifies du Bellay's return with the composition of his greatest poem. As he describes it, the erotic quality of the poet's achievement is still more pronounced: "in the cooler air of his own country, under its skies of milkier blue, the sweetest flower of his genius sprang up" (174). Unconsciously, this is a fantasy of possession with a well-defined goal: oral gratification at the fertile mother's "milkier" breast. The image of phallic excitement, Pater's flower metaphor, extends the passive implications of his wish, for it "sprang up" after being watered under native skies.

Only pleasant associations, then, attach to the sources and motives of du Bellay's masterpiece, "The Winnower of Wheat to the

Winds." When Pater describes the poem's "incident" itself, however, his language suggests another unconscious meaning. His rhythms become faster, he refers explicitly to speed and violence, and we sense an undercurrent of anxiety:

> The sweetness of it is by no means to be got at by crushing, as you crush wild herbs to get at their perfume. One seems to hear the measured motion of the fans, with a child's pleasure on coming across the incident for the first time, in one of those great barns of du Bellay's own country, *La Beauce*, the granary of France. A sudden light transfigures some trivial thing, a weather-vane, a windmill, a winnowing fan, the dust in the barn door. A moment—and the thing has vanished, because it was pure effect; but it leaves a relish behind it, a longing that the accident may happen again. (176)

The order of Pater's thoughts is the best clue to their psychological meaning: crushing, sounds of motion, a sudden light, "the thing has vanished," finally an accident. This "incident," observed "for the first time," is described as a primal scene, the child's discovery of his parents having intercourse. From the infantile perspective, violence is the only explanation of what is taking place, so that Pater's first sentence has the force of a strong denial, as does, indeed, his reference to "a child's pleasure," which is somewhat out of place in the manifest content of the passage. Children believe that fathers do "crush wild herbs to get at their perfume," and this vision is hardly pleasurable. Seeing is implied by the "sudden light," a common psychological displacement. It is also familiar to find Pater attaching a wide range of associations to the phallic image. At first, the "trivial thing" is a weather vane; here the symbolism is simple. The "windmill" and "winnowing-fan," however, suggest violence both belonging to and directed at the phallus, a violence confirmed when "the thing has vanished." It is typical in such a fantasy (or memory) to take the disappearance of the penis inside the female as castration, and Pater responds to his psychic confusion with appropriate fear, appropriately masked. His "longing" at the conclusion both denies the actual emotion and expresses a wish that the male organ will reappear, so that "the accident may happen again."

There is another connotation to that last phrase. Filling out

Pater's version of the poem is a further familiar detail of infantile fears about such events. The child can cause an "accident" to terminate the primal scene. After the more violent, active imagery at the center of the passage, "the dust in the barn door" (still slang for the opening in a pair of pants) symbolizes the genesis of the attempted interruption. Dust, a Victorian euphemism for feces, confirms that this child's "accident" is the most primitive response to fear. Sexual aspiration, then, has led Pater unconsciously to visualize a most fundamental type of sexual rebuff, the parents' active proof that the child's fantasied powers are insignificant after all. The progress of the passage not only suggests that the incident produces a loss of sphincter control; it also dramatizes Pater's psychological retreat from genital ambition to a more primitive level of sexual pleasure, that of anal eroticism. By the end of the description, "longing" and "relish" are directed toward this substitute activity, to represent a wish that not the scene but "the accident may happen again."

Earlier in the essay on du Bellay, Pater placed this concluding view of the world in a philosophical perspective. He alluded to the reassuring effect of Roman ruins when introducing the poet's homesickness and fear of death. There, Pater explains, "he is consoled by the thought that all must one day end, by the sentiment of the grandeur of nothingness—*la grandeur du rien*. With a strange touch of far-off mysticism, he thinks that the great whole—*le grand tout*—into which all other things pass and lose themselves, ought itself sometimes to perish and pass away. Nothing less can relieve his weariness" (174). These sentences condense the entire range of analerotic defenses against the threats implied by du Bellay's sexual longing for home. The primary process work begins and ends with ruins, first as symbols of the danger of castration, then as symbols of a safer activity. Similarly, the thought that things "lose themselves" is countered by the pleasing consideration that everything can be made "to perish and pass away."

On a manifest, philosophical level, Pater is referring to the Heraclitean concept of flux, the idea that everything flows and passes away in an ongoing universe. The conclusion of his imitation of *D'un Vanneur de Blé aux Vents* involves the same reference. Through that passage, then, we can explain one psychological component of the "Conclusion" to *The Renaissance*, where flux is the precondition for enjoying "art for art's sake." When all things flow, a sense of personal control over experience is available through mastery of this process on an individual level, biologically and psychologically. Pater's affection for "accidents" at the end of "Joachim du Bellay" and in the book's conclusion, then, involves a forceful metaphor of double significance. By insisting on the random quality of natural phenomena, Pater can deny that any universal or personal threats are directed against himself; by creating "accidents" of his own, he can represent a pleasure to substitute for those fate has denied him. In these respects, the eclecticism of Pater's aesthetic creed is deeply defensive.

Pater contrasts the "decadence" of "Joachim du Bellay" with a more "austere" and youthful condition, presented in the first study of the book. If we consider the second and subsequent editions of *The Renaissance*, there can be little question that this austerity consists in an absence of heterosexual love. The second of the "Two Early French Stories," the tale of Amis and Amile, is an openly homosexual romance. It is likely that this story added to the lurid appearance of the book for Victorian readers after 1877, although it seems that Pater added it as a moderating force in the book's total structure, a denial of his fascination with sex. Undoubtedly the section also raised open questions about Pater's own homosexuality, which became a well-known secret as his fame increased. Today the story is interesting as a homosexual's version of homosexuality. In any direct examination of the nature of Pater's sexual inversion, it should be a prime document.

Li Amitiez de Ami et Amile describes the lives of two childhood friends who, after being separated, rediscover one another late in life and abandon wives and children to resume their presexual companionship. Pater's treatment of the story emphasizes the narcissistic quality of their relationship; this will play an important role in "Leonardo da Vinci." He introduces the tale by remarking on "the romantic circumstance of an entire personal resemblance between the two heroes" (9), and this twinship is symbolized throughout the story by ornate wooden cups, "adorned with gold and precious stones," that the children received at baptism from the Pope. The story "turns" on these cups, which produce the reunion when the two heroes expose them to each other in a psychologically loaded scene. More significantly, Pater indicates that he is attracted to the tale by the pleasures of vision and touch represented in the cups. The cups "cross and recross very strangely in the narrative, serving the two heroes almost like living things, and with that well-known effect of a beautiful object, kept constantly before the eye in a story or poem, of keeping sensation well awake . . ." (9). By merging the effects of the cups on characters and readers, Pater suggests that the gratifying power of this story stems from the ease of identifying with its homosexual "heroes."

The first-edition version of this essay, "Aucassin and Nicolette," was named for one of the heterosexual love stories it narrates. Alongside that story, Pater describes and translates details from the romance of Abélard and Héloïse. His treatment of both suggests the motive for balancing them, in later editions, with the homosexual tale that concludes "Two Early French Stories." In his presentation, heterosexual love inevitably implies grave potential dangers, threats of castration, as a result of its incestuous connotations. This unconscious implication explains an omission which might otherwise be puzzling, Pater's failure to translate the portion of "Aucassin and Nicolette" where "mutual fidelity is rewarded." Instead, he praises isolated "details" for supplying the narrative's "charm." "These adventures are of the simplest sort, adventures which seem to be chosen for the happy occasion they afford of keeping the eye of the fancy, perhaps the outward eye, fixed on pleasant objects, a garden, a ruined tower, the little hut of flowers which Nicolette constructs in the forest whither she escapes from her enemies . . ." (19–20). Concentration on images like these represents an escape for Pater too; his attention to beauty here, as in much of the fastidiousness of aestheticism, is based on the denial of a less pleasing world.

Even these details, however, as much as Pater takes them as distractions from the love plot, indicate what he feels to be the content of the tale. Heterosexual love implies failure (as in the "ruined tower" above) and, more important to the essay's manifest meaning, environmental hostility. "Enemies," that is, are necessary components in a world of love between the sexes.

In "Two Early French Stories," history itself facilitates the denial of these hostilities. With the addition of "Amis and Amile," Pater sharpens his definition of the Middle Ages as a childhood for society, an unfallen world not yet destroyed by passion. Concluding the study, Pater is far less engaged in his description of Abélard than in portraying the harmonies implicit in the lives of the two martyrs, and he reminds us that their story was probably written by a monk (27). There is, in fact, a faint but unmistakable idealization of the authoritarian, restrictive, desexualized medieval social order. Pater, comparing Abélard's life to the Tannhäuser legend, declares that both represent a "sinister claim for liberty of heart and thought" and complains that "care for beauty" and "worship of the body . . . impelled" people "beyond the bounds of the Christian ideal" (24–25). If his language contains some irony, on the deepest level his ambivalence is genuine. Writing for the edition of 1877, Pater is, of course, disavowing once again the implications of his "Conclusion." His attraction to monastic controls, as an alternative to the antinomian tendencies of aestheticism, reminds us of the escapist quality of much Victorian medievalism.

Early in the essay Pater illustrates the beauty of *Li Amitiez de Ami et Amile* through the parallel of another "classical" friendship. He quotes Chaucer's *Knight's Tale,* in which, he says, "one knows not whether the love of both Palamon and Arcite for Emelya, or of those two for each other, is the chiefer subject" (8). When he discusses the description of Palamon's first-sight love from the prison window, however, it is clear which kind of love Pater finds most important in Chaucer's story. "What reader," Pater asks, "does not refer something of the bitterness of that cry to the spoiling, already foreseen, of the fair friendship, which had made the prison of the two lads sweet hitherto with its daily offices?" (8–9). That final phrase can refer only to homosexuality; Pater's preference is stated with remarkable openness. It is possible for him to be so direct here, and to ignore Abélard for the more satisfying, narcissistic story, because this is a world in which the "spoiling" of such "fair" relationships is only "foreseen." The "daily offices" of homosexual love are based on the insular prison world of a child's life before external objects have entered his consciousness. Pater, then, uses this historical period as a screen-symbol for a highly personal kind of nostalgia. His tone betrays the longing for a world into which women have not yet entered.

This narcissistic, homoerotic fantasy gives the fullest meaning to Pater's prefatory remarks about "the girding of the loins in youth." It also exposes the sexual content of his famous description of the modern mind in the "Conclusion," where he links impressionism to the isolation of the individual. "Experience," he says, "is ringed round for each one of us by [a] thick wall of personality . . . each mind keeping as a solitary prisoner its own dream of a world" (235). Pater repeatedly seeks a psychic return to a world of self-gratification. Both history and criticism become symbolic of this flight.

Pater's last words in "Two Early French Stories," before his quotation of the burial scene from "Amis and Amile," directly forecasts the progress of *The Renaissance*. The contrast between the two kinds of thirteenth-century story reflects a general problem in Renaissance history, he explains, since antagonism and conflict exist in every age. But in "the enchanted region of the Renaissance," to which I have referred already, "one needs not be for ever on one's guard" (26–27). There, he says, "all breathes of . . . unity of culture." Pater goes on to suggest that the rest of his book will steer a middle course between conflicting parties in an attempt to remain within this magic circle:

> The wicked popes, and the loveless tyrants, who from time to time became its patrons, or mere speculators in its fortunes, lend themselves easily to disputations, and, from this side or that, the spirit of controversy lays just hold upon them. But the painter of the *Last Supper*, with his kindred, lives in a land where controversy has no breathing-place. They refuse to be classified. (27)

Pater's adjectives in the first sentence refer to the Renaissance and its arts interchangeably, a central assumption throughout the volume. It is in keeping with the mood of this initial study that here Pater furtively reasserts Oedipal desire as part of a fantasy implying its complete success. The cruel fathers of the Renaissance, "wicked" and "loveless," will suffocate in the world where Leonardo "breathes" freely, along with his "kindred" artists whom those "tyrants" tried to patronize and control. In psychic terms, this is a fantasy in which the mother aids her filial lover by allowing him alone to find gratification at her breast (the first "breathing-place"). Pater openly identifies with the figure of the artist, who is somehow immune to the world's threats; he develops this theme at greater length in "Leonardo da Vinci." This is another sense in which Pater sees his first essay as depicting an ideal, prehistorical world, offering a "harmony of interests" to which the art of later ages will aspire to return.

The opening essay also previews one of the book's central sexual themes, one implicit in the passivity of the description just quoted. The homosexuality of Amis and Amile reappears twice, in the figures of Leonardo da Vinci and Winckelmann. Pater explicitly refers to sexual inversion in discussing each, notably in the artist's love for Andrea Salaino and in Winckelmann's admiration for sculpted male nudes. These are, in fact, the best essays in the book; it is hard not to suspect that their intensity and polish betrays Pater's personal affinity for both men. Leonardo's homosexuality even dominates the volume visually. Pater made his famous drawing of the "face of doubtful sex" (115) the frontispiece to *The Renaissance;* elsewhere he calls it his "favourite drawing by L. da V." [6] It suggests an image he might have had in mind when he kept the "Conclusion" from "young men," or what he may have meant by ending lists of experiences to be cultivated with references to "a fair personality in life or in a book" (ix) and "the face of one's friend" (237). Even for Victorian readers, there is overwhelming evidence of the author's interest in inverted sexual lives.

Still, although the first essay organizes the book historically and psychologically, its narcissism is only one extreme of the unconscious range of *The Renaissance.* This may provide an index of the book's literary power. In *Marius the Epicurean,* a tamer and more controlled book, self-consciously moralistic, Pater's last scene echoes the end of "Two Early French Stories." But Marius' beautiful death points to one of the novel's principal flaws: Pater seems to stop only when he has nowhere to go. Martyrdom hardly forms a viable social ideal, and even Marius' conversion remains ambiguous. The novel's insularity is unsatisfying, and Pater ends by retreating from most of the intellectual and moral issues he has raised earlier. As with his compulsively symmetrical form, Pater's plot proves, in the end, his defensiveness in 1885. *The Renaissance,* on the other hand, accepts the fact of a changing cultural environment and points ultimately toward the emergence of the nineteenth century. Retreat into the self is consummated, not in the book's conclusion, but in its initial essay, after which the complex external world receives its due.

In this sense, the development of *The Renaissance* can be seen as an experiment in the relation of regression to culture. Even if Pater would have frowned upon such terms, he clearly sensed that his essays mediated between the desire for an idealized past and the conditions of the modern world. In "Winckelmann," which discusses a modern critic of art like Pater, this concern is stated directly in

6. Evans, "Letters," p. 29. The subject was probably Andrea Salaino. See p. 199 below.

connection with the Greek society studied by the German. "Breadth, centrality, with blitheness and repose, are the marks of Hellenic culture. Is such culture a lost art?" (227). In the studies leading to the Winckelmann chapter, which in turn introduces the language of the "Conclusion," this question is always implicit. Those essays, focusing on the fifteenth century—Pater's "enchanted region" in *The Renaissance*—use history, criticism, and biography to define a lasting value in the creation, and more particularly in the study, of art.

II.

Pater describes du˙ Bellay as being "almost . . . the poet of one poem" (175), and the phrase applies equally to himself. For most readers he is known as the author of the "poem" on the *Mona Lisa,* perhaps as the inventor of the "hard, gemlike flame," and probably as little else. In the view of Graham Hough, Pater's essays on art "tend to split up in the mind of the reader into a few famous purple patches." [7] Pater consciously directs his essays toward the effects of single passages, self-contained pieces of rhythmic prose, highly charged with meaning and emotive power, and he emphasizes the creation of striking impressions by other artists. He most admires works that resolve into a few suggestive, consummate images. Du Bellay's famous poem, Botticelli's madonnas, Michelangelo's "sweetness" or his command of the "sentiment of profound pity" (94), most notably the *Mona Lisa* itself—all become symbols behind which the larger artistic and personal careers of their makers recede. By focusing on particular art objects, Pater allows the general progress of a period or even an artist's life to disappear from view. In *The Renaissance* as a whole, this technique represents an escape from history into Pater's impressionistic, fictional world.

Even the specific instances of Pater's most lavish writing tend toward this distilled effect. He delights in using prose for its own sake. His soothing rhythms, exotic vocabulary, and ornate constructions have a plainly erotic quality, one which ultimately dominates the meaning and attraction of any subject. Indeed, Pater's "decadence," which he acknowledged far less readily than did Wilde, amounts to precisely this—morbid absorption in a personalized at-

7. *The Last Romantics* (New York, 1961), p. 165.

mosphere of style. Nowhere is the character of this verbal narcissism more visible than in his description of *La Gioconda*, a passage Wilde and his fellow aesthetes chanted religiously on visits to the Louvre, as if to keep from substituting a direct response for Pater's artificial portrait-of-a-portrait. And this is exactly Pater's intent. His description becomes a ritual, effacing any traces of the acts of painting or viewing the picture. The result, in which the images of Leonardo and Pater himself are only faintly visible, is a magnificent symphony of allusions whose references are impossible to untangle completely.

As I have suggested, *Mona Lisa's* obscurity is deliberate. Pater emphasizes the independence of his prose from its subject through a vocabulary stressing mystery, ineffability. She becomes a *"presence that rose thus so strangely* beside the waters . . . It is a beauty wrought out from within upon the flesh, the deposit, little cell by cell, of *strange* thoughts and *fantastic* reveries and *exquisite* passions" (124–125; italics mine). Even the painting has an independent life, as Pater suggests with his metaphors of spontaneous birth. Self-generation implies a constellation of psychic imagery I will discuss at length in connection with "Winckelmann." Here it is important to notice that Pater's references to growth are in the past, at a distance; even the long periods of his separate sentences help make the beauty of the passage inert. Pater's treatment of *La Gioconda* describes neither the painting nor his response to it, but rather the memory of an emotion itself only vaguely associated with viewing the picture. Max Beerbohm, with perceptive wit, beautifully caricatured the tendency of such prose literally to "deaden" the objects and experiences it seems to illuminate. Pater, he said, wrote English as a "dead language," in a "sedulous ritual wherewith he laid out every sentence as in a shroud . . ."[8] Beerbohm was suggesting that Pater's best-known writing has an underlying morbidity, and that is a quality with widespread significance in *The Renaissance* and throughout Pater's career.

Much of Pater's morbidity takes the overt form of concentration on the theme of death. His earliest biographer, in terms that apply to *The Renaissance* as well, speaks of the "macabre, the decadent element" implicit in the doomed heroes of *Imaginary Portraits.*[9]

8. *Works* (London, 1895), p. 150.
9. A. C. Benson, *Walter Pater* (New York, 1906), p. 131. For other references to morbidity, see pp. 36, 81, 138, and 164.

Fatality forms the background of a number of Pater's Renaissance essays, notably the "Conclusion" and "Joachim du Bellay." At the end of "Two Early French Stories," Pater seems to elevate past over present and death over life by offering as his culminating image of medieval beauty the burial of Amis and Amile. Michelangelo's greatest sculpture is based, similarly, on the contemplation of death; his pietàs belong to a tradition in Florentine art whose masters, Pater says, often "leaned over the lifeless body" and so learned "to see death in its distinction" (93). The trace of necrophilia here reappears in the autobiographical "imaginary portrait" called "The Child in the House," when the hero scrutinizes with aesthetic detachment corpses in the Paris morgue. Pater's *Mona Lisa* herself, "like the vampire, . . . has been dead many times, and learned the secrets of the grave" (125). In Pater's view, all great art has been redeemed from death.

Not surprisingly, there is a basic psychological link between Pater's morbid taste and his elaborate, "decadent" style. His most mannered style attempts, as we have seen for the "Conclusion," to master fatality. And confronted with death, he tames it with artificial language, a stylistic ritual. Death is always accompanied by some sort of ceremony in Pater; his response to it is fearful, defensive. When Amis and Amile die, Pater focuses our attention on the miracle of their inseparable coffins, followed by a month of "offices" at the church of St. Oseige (28–29). "Two Early French Stories" ends with a page of ritual. Similarly, while insisting that such details are of "little importance," Pater concludes "Leonardo da Vinci" by recording "the thirty masses and great candles for the church of Saint Florentin" prescribed in the artist's will (128).

Even the ending of the du Bellay essay hints at ritualized death. Pater introduces *D'un Vanneur de Blé aux Vents* by narrating for a second time the poet's final journey home. By the parallel of the first description, we are meant to read Pater's version of the poem as an end point in du Bellay's life, a verbal equivalent of his death. Style, then, becomes explicitly morbid in this overdetermined scene. Equally morbid is Pater's reference, in the last lines of his "impression," to possible recurrence, the chance "that the accident may happen again." Repetition, as I have mentioned, is a technique for denying the traumatic quality of this moment; Pater is undoing death. Through all these scenes, in fact, his response to death is obsessive-compulsive. He controls such threats by reenactment, and this suggests the double morbidity of his most highly charged passages. Pater's lushness at the end of "Joachim du Bellay," as was the case for the *Mona Lisa,* represents a ceremony built around a fatal image.

There is an important biographical analogue to this compulsive and ceremonial treatment of death. Pater's father, described by the son's biographers as a benevolent physician,[10] died when the writer was just five years old, leaving him in the care of his mother, his grandmother, and a maiden aunt. The four moved to a new country home, where Pater first began a game that all his biographers have recognized as an early sign of seriousness and piety:

> Pater's favourite amusement . . . was playing at being a clergyman, and getting . . . other lads to form a procession. There was a tiny, darkish, and almost useless room at the back of the house, and here, arrayed in a nightgown for a surplice, he preached regularly and with unction to his mother, grandmother, and admiring Aunt Bessie.[11]

This pastime has an obsessional quality hinted at in the phrase "regularly and with unction." Later in his life, Pater revived these theatrics in his intense involvement in church ritual. Most of his biographers attribute to him a sudden religious reconversion, one that caused him, among other things, to attend two services each Sunday, unnecessarily kneeling through both sermons. At this time he took great pride in his record of church attendance.[12]

More important, this youthful ritual was renewed in Pater's books. *Marius the Epicurean,* which ascribes the game to its hero, best suggests the complex range of associations Pater found in ceremonies of death. Marius first recalls his acting after the death of Flavian, an Epicurean friend whose role in the novel is plainly paternal. The memory appears as the product of a long "reverie" on Heraclitus, during which Marius projects himself out of "the actual present . . . with a delightful sense of escape in replacing the outer world of other people by an inward world as himself

---

10. Benson, *Pater,* p. 3.
11. Thomas Wright, *The Life of Walter Pater,* 2 vols. (London, 1907), I, 21.
12. See Wright, *Life,* II, 201, and Germaine d'Hangest, *Walter Pater: l'homme et l'œuvre,* 2 vols. (Paris, 1961), II, 243ff.

really cared to have it." [13] Such a retreat to self-contained dreaming is already familiar in Pater, although its psychological significance here is larger than a return to infantile narcissism. "Escape" from a doomed world is facilitated by a symbolic ritual. As the culmination of an extended exercise in the imagery of flux and decay, the ceremony gains control over fatality by imitating, implicitly, their periodic rhythms. This is the same brand of magic operating at the end of "Joachim du Bellay," although its appearance has changed. As in that essay, consciousness of a decaying world is, in reality, the projection of deep internal anxiety. Similarly, the manner of denying and undoing that anxiety betrays its actual source. The masquerade as preacher, among whose commonest functions is attendance on the dead and dying, reflects Pater's Oedipal guilt over a death in his own past history. In *Marius*, this is clearly linked to the death of a fatherly friend, which in turn echoes the death of Marius' father in the first pages of the book.

Playing at priests, as it is called in *Marius*, was not an unfamiliar Victorian pastime. Ruskin recounts a similar episode from his own life in *Praeterita* (his message: "People, be good!").[14] A different set of social values motivates modern children to play "doctor," to which the Victorian game is a rough equivalent—without, that is, the sex. For Pater, in fact, the two social roles seem to have merged in his consideration of death, for the dead man in his life was a doctor. Both physicians and priests attend his literary deathbeds, and in *Marius* they are symbolized together as a way of undoing Oepidal guilt. As Marius lies dying, he is nursed, washed, baptized, and fed sacraments by "early Christians," who, half-mistakenly, take him for a martyr. Religious symbolism and the plot of the novel leave no doubt that Marius *is* dying as a substitute for someone else, although his Christianity is accidental. His death, then, reverses the biographical truth of Pater's life: the child dies comforted and beloved by his parents. The scene strongly denies that Marius' father, or Pater's, ever died; the hero is like his father, is comforted by a symbol for his father, and takes on the redemptive qualities of the Son. The last scene relieves the book's first memory as a way of

13. *Marius the Epicurean*, Library Edition, 2 vols. (London, 1910), I, 132–133.
14. John Ruskin, *Works*, Library Edition, 39 vols. (London, 1903–1912), XXXV (1908), 25–26.

undoing it. The ending of "Joachim du Bellay" is overdetermined in precisely the same way.

Pater's studies of the past always involve such reconciliations with historical fathers. One of the sources of the personal, fictional quality of *The Renaissance* is Pater's desire to "rescue" his subjects from the oblivion of the past, just as du Bellay "rescued" his "mother-tongue." Botticelli, when Pater studied him, was "a comparatively unknown artist" (51), and Luca della Robbia remains a minor figure today. When dealing with more important men, Pater carefully limits his treatment to lesser-known aspects of their careers or environments—hence Michelangelo's *poetry*, or "The *School* of Giorgione," or even Leonardo considered as a scientist. It might be argued that all history-writing involves incestuous impulses; in Pater's case the desire to discover historical kinship is present throughout both his essays and his fiction. Most notably, in the first of his *Imaginary Portraits*, Pater studies Jean Antoine Watteau through the invented sister of that painter's actual apprentice, Jean-Baptiste Pater, an artist he claimed as a distant relation. After the story was published, Arthur Symons inquired if the kinship was real, and Pater's reply was surprisingly passionate. "I think so, I believe so, I always say so." [15] But the striking fact about the Watteau story, "A Prince of Court Painters," is that it is narrated by a woman, so that the medium for this historical love is feminine and maternal. This is the pattern for "rescue" in *The Renaissance*.

The critic's relation to the past is defined in the essay on Botticelli, perhaps the only genuine discovery Pater made.[16] Minor figures, he explains at the end of his essay, eventually become absorbed into the works of great successors, and this process establishes a set of common accomplishments. Beyond this, painters like Botticelli "convey to us a peculiar quality of pleasure which we cannot get elsewhere." Without explicitly defining this "quality," Pater's next statement offers its unconscious meaning. Such artists, he says, "have their place in general culture, and must be interpreted to it by those

---

15. Arthur Symons, *A Study of Walter Pater* (London, 1932), p. 104.
16. Ruskin was working on *Mornings in Florence,* a book often credited with introducing Botticelli to England, at about the time he might have read the first edition of *The Renaissance.* He seems to echo Pater in a reference to Botticelli's "weary" madonnas. *Works,* XXIII, 334. See also d'Hangest, *Pater,* I, 355, 356.

who have felt their charm strongly, and are often the object of a special diligence and a consideration wholly affectionate, just because there is not about them the stress of a great name and authority" (61). Here, as critic, Pater fantasies himself administering maternal care. Obscurity implies the absence of the interfering father, whose "great name and authority" might bring "stress" to the relationship of nurturing mother and passive child. But, as in the identically "affectionate" ending of *Marius,* paternal love too is secured by this image of the "aesthetic critic." By imagining himself in a feminine role, Pater can bestow unrestrained love on a historical father—for Pico della Mirandola, della Robbia, and Botticelli were the artistic ancestors of accomplished lines of descendants. Pater's use of such intellectual lineage, however, involves a constellation of psychic imagery that is fully developed only toward the end of *The Renaissance.*

As the book progresses, in fact, we become aware not only of the growing intensity and complexity of unconscious themes, but of their increasing relation to Pater's manifest concerns. Even the "aesthetic critic" is a changing image. In the Preface, his is a narcissistic act. " 'To see the object as in itself it really is,' " says Pater quoting Arnold, one must "know one's own impression as it really is, . . . discriminate it, . . . realise it distinctly" (viii). By the end of the book, Pater seems concerned most with bringing history to bear upon the present, recommending art study as a way of life, one which prepares us to deal with society and fate. I have already quoted Pater's question making this point in "Winckelmann," where he introduces a rare pun to suggest the urgency of applying past to present. "Breadth, centrality, with blitheness and repose, are the marks of Hellenic culture. Is such culture a lost art?" Both "art" and "culture" have double meanings in the last half of *The Renaissance,* as Pater tries to "cultivate" an ideal modern temperament. His final essays deal largely with personality, and this provides an important explanation for their remarkable unity. Pater's discussions of the art of life seem to give him increased access to his own unconscious themes. Furthermore, the common manifest themes of the last essays —discovery, journey, and death—suggest that all historical lives enact fundamental, universal human experiences. Beginning with the essay on Michelangelo, then, Pater searches on many levels for historic conditions to resolve his psychic tensions.

"The Poetry of Michaelangelo" represents an extreme of Pater's personalizing critical technique. Probably the best-known artist Pater treats, Michelangelo is not readily transmuted into the author's own creature. In one sense, the study shows Pater at his most decadent, substituting an artificial, literary atmosphere for the reality of what he admits was a passionate and eventful life. Throughout the essay we are overwhelmed by Michelangelo's "sweetness"—and the word appears dozens of times. It is Pater's way of insisting upon his own version of Michelangelo, making him a man of adjectives instead of verbs. At times the essay is cloyingly persistent in its stress on Pater's role. As I have mentioned, his concentration on Michelangelo's poetry serves the same goal.

When he summarizes the value of Michelangelo's sonnets, in a discussion of the artist's old age, Pater invokes metaphors familiar from his other allusions to the rescue theme. Michelangelo writes love sonnets, but, like Dante, "his true mistress is death,—death at first as the worst of all sorrows and disgraces, with a clod of the field for its brain; afterwards, death in its high distinction, its detachment from vulgar needs, the angry stains of life and action escaping fast" (88). Pater finds in Michelangelo a pleasing taste for death over passion. But curiously, death's second meaning, its "high distinction" as a kind of escape, is described in images of birth. "Death in its distinction" is offered in opposition to "the worst of all sorrows and disgraces" and to "vulgar needs," both suggesting the sexual activity from which life originates. Thus the purification of death and birth is their common release from sexuality and its products, the "stains of life and action." The anal quality of this "detachment," the willfulness suggested in "angry stains," emerges from the common infantile fantasy that birth itself is a type of defecation.

As this passage indicates, and as we might expect from Pater's insistence on "sweet" Michelangelo, the entire essay denies the artist's sexuality, as if this were an unpleasant, "vulgar" association to be avoided scrupulously. The generally reserved atmosphere of the study seems to be in direct contrast to the immediacy, even passionateness, of "Leonardo da Vinci." "The Poetry of Michaelangelo" is a defensive essay, its principal psychic mechanism being denial; and this accounts for Pater's emphasis on his subject's age and consequent sedateness. The poems to Vittoria Colonna were written during a "charmed and temperate space in Michaelangelo's life, without which its excessive strength would have been so imperfect"

(85). The power of the sonnets, in Pater's view, consists in a type of sublimation, for in them "the lifelong effort to tranquillise his vehement emotions by withdrawing them into the region of ideal sentiment, becomes successful" (86). As poet, Michelangelo symbolizes control.

At the beginning of his discussion of the sonnets, Pater takes pains to dispel a popular misconception that they "were a mere cry of distress, a lover's complaint" (83). In fact, he insists, their emotions are subdued. Michelangelo wrote them when he was "nearly seventy years old. Vittoria herself . . . vowed to perpetual widowhood . . . was then no longer an object of great passion" (83–84). Furthermore, these poems describe no action, contain only one actual event —a "doubtful allusion to a journey" (87). This understated reference is, in fact, to the kind of journey present in images throughout *The Renaissance*—birth. But Pater's attitude is guarded, and although there are numerous allusions to the primal quality of this relationship, Pater dwells on them only briefly, often leaving untranslated telling lines from the original verse:

> And this gives the impression in him of something flitting and unfixed, of the houseless and complaining spirit, almost clairvoyant through the frail and yielding flesh. He accounts for love at first sight by a previous state of existence—*la dove io t'amai prima.* (87)

"The place where I loved you first" follows from the rest of the passage because it refers, on an unconscious level, to life in the womb. An earlier mistranslation, or at least a shift from the original emphasis, indicates how strongly this fantasy occupies Pater as he considers Michelangelo's "sweet" love: "Is it carnal affection, or, *del suo prestino stato* (of Plato's ante-natal state) *il raggio ardente?*" (84). The "natal" reference is, of course, Pater's own. In the passage previous to this, his language shows preoccupation with the same fantasy: "unfixed . . . houseless . . . the frail and yielding flesh."

Pater's discussion of Michelangelo as a sculptor places birth in a context common to the constellation of fantasies associated with Oedipal rescue. Freud explains this form of "gratitude" as the boy's wish "to have by his mother a son who is like himself: in other words, in the rescue phantasy, he is completely identifying himself with his father. All his instincts, those of tenderness, gratitude, lustfulness, defiance and independence, find satisfaction in the single wish *to be his own father.*" [17] Michelangelo's "genius" is defined as a "concern . . . almost exclusively with the making of man," and Pater's expansion of the phrase emphasizes that such creation is sudden and independent. The "making of man . . . is not, as in the story itself, the last and crowning act of a series of developments, but the first and unique act, the creation of life itself in its supreme form, off-hand and immediately, in the cold and lifeless stone. With him the beginning of life has all the characteristics of resurrection . . ." (75). Michelangelo's art contains all the constituents of birth within itself; it has the magical power of spontaneous self-creation. As a *"master of live stone"* (76; italics in original), the sculptor plays at being God the Father, giving life where and when he wishes. In fact, this potency subsumes both paternal and maternal principles within itself. The phrase Pater repeatedly offers as the theme of Michelangelo's life, *ex forti dulcedo,* implies a combination of passive and active powers, and even stipulates that sweetness is "born" out of strength.

Pater's cautiousness in this essay derives from the full psychic meaning of *ex forti dulcedo.* He avoids discussing Michelangelo's "strength," which the essay identifies with art rather than poetry, because this belongs to an atmosphere of violence in the artist's life. "He knew too," Pater quickly reminds us in discussing the sonnets, "how to excite strong hatreds . . . in a quarrel with a fellow-student he received a blow on the face which deprived him for ever of the comeliness of outward form" (78). The masterpieces for which Michelangelo is known—the Sistine ceiling, the tomb of Julius II, and the Sacristy of St. Lorenzo—are ignored by Pater precisely because they suggest emotional turbulence: "a thousand hesitations, a thousand disappointments, quarrels with his patrons, quarrels with his family, quarrels perhaps most of all with himself" (80). The contrast is drawn deliberately between these youthful works and his poetry, where "his genius is in harmony with itself" (81).

Both harmony and hostility are defined in terms of familial relationships, as is suggested in Pater's list of quarrels. When he offers an example of the "discordant note" in Michelangelo's life, Pater immediately turns to Raphael's statement that he "treats the Pope

17. Freud, "Special Type," p. 173.

as the King of France himself would not dare to treat him," walking through Rome "like an executioner" (80). The aspect of the sculptor's temper Pater persistently resists is his filial hostility. At every approach to this theme, the increased intensity of his prose betrays the cause of Pater's resistence. He is deeply attracted as well as alarmed by Michelangelo's rebelliousness; he identifies with both the placid and the murderous moods in the artist's life. By focusing on poetry instead of sculpture, Pater attempts to control his disturbing ambivalence.

Pater's fullest concentration on the artist's Oedipal possibilities appears in a long passage introducing the discussion of Michelangelo's sonnets. Most of the imagery is open enough to require no commentary, but it is interesting to note that Pater's own language becomes calmer as he moves from active to passive aspects of Michelangelo's life. He begins by referring to the half-concealed self-portrait in the Sistine Chapel, which takes on paternal connotations in the syntax of the sentence. But by the end of the long discussion, the paternal artist (who superintends his own birthplace) gives way to a passive, childish observer:

> What passionate weeping in that mysterious figure which, in the *Creation of Adam,* crouches below the image of the Almighty, as he comes with the forms of things to be, woman and her progeny, in the fold of his garment! What a sense of wrong in those two captive youths, who feel the chains like scalding water on their proud and delicate flesh! The idealist who became a reformer with Savonarola, and a republican superintending the fortification of Florence—the nest where he was born, *il nido ove naqqu'io,* as he calls it once, in a sudden throb of affection—in its last struggle for liberty, yet believed always that he had imperial blood in his veins and was of the kindred of ˌthe great Matilda, had within the depths of his nature some secret spring of indignation or sorrow. We know little of his youth, but all tends to make one believe in the vehemence of its passions. . . . But his genius is in harmony with itself . . . The interest of Michaelangelo's poems is that they make us spectators of this struggle; the struggle of a strong nature to adorn and attune itself; the struggle of a desolating passion, which yearns to be resigned and sweet and pensive, as Dante's was. (80–82)

The value of Michelangelo's poetry, then, is that it puts conflicts at a distance, making us only "spectators" of hostility. Ultimately, this yearning "to be resigned" is connected with the role Pater finds for himself as critic. That role, as in the case of the female narrator of "A Prince of Court Painters," is womanly and passive. By making the sculptor an aged, idealistic poet, Pater succeeds in taming his own tone, modifying his stance from intensive involvement to calm observation. *Ex forti dulcedo*, the essay's theme, speaks as much for Pater as for its ostensible subject: Michelangelo becomes a rhetorical device for defining the critic's image.

The subdued tone of "The Poetry of Michaelangelo" prepares us for the omission of a central event: the artist's death is never represented. This results in part from the difficulty of terminating a life of such "sweetness." On a psychic level, it constitutes a refusal to punish a figure defined in terms of innocence and lack of desire. Michelangelo, in fact, "lingers on; a *revenant*, . . . a ghost out of another age . . ." (90); that is, Pater hints that he never dies. As is plain in the lines beginning my essay, his "immense, patriarchal age" proves that the paternal "gods" love him. At the same time, Michelangelo becomes a father himself. Pater uses this essay to make the same affirmation involved in the expiatory, substitutive deaths of his young heroes. The artist's interminable life, read as a symbolic statement, asserts that such a good child never harbored undesirable thoughts toward his father, and that such accusations are unwarranted because his father never died.

But Pater cannot completely avoid the theme of death, any more than he can ignore Michelangelo's sculpture for his entire essay. In the last pages, the subjects appear together in the description of the growth of Florentine death-studies leading to Michelangelo's *Pietà*. Most of this passage has been quoted, but its conclusion shows that Pater's necrophilia is given a specific meaning in "The Poetry of Michaelangelo":

> Of all this sentiment Michaelangelo is the achievement; and, first of all, of pity. *Pietà*, pity, the pity of the Virgin Mother over the dead body of Christ, expanded into the pity of all mothers over all dead sons . . . (94)

Pater's style and subject here dramatize the psychological frailty of the tranquility in "The Poetry of Michaelangelo." The essay is closer to "Leonardo da Vinci" than its surface suggests. Pater's conservative and passionate studies emerge from identical psychological themes, differing only in treatment. The date for the Michelangelo essay, two years after the appearance of "Leonardo da Vinci" in 1869, suggests, indeed, that Pater's defensiveness may have derived from doubts about the flamboyancy of the earlier work. Hence the ending of the essay on the sculptor-poet reveals Pater succumbing to a return of the repressed.

Even the language in which his defenses crumble relates to the more open essay on Leonardo. Pater concludes the study by placing Michelangelo in the history of art. The sculptor's fifteenth-century followers, Pater explains, exaggerated his strength and neglected the sweetness, separating themselves from his genuine legacy. Only Blake and Hugo, modern figures, deserve to be linked to the name of Michelangelo. They, although "not of his school, and unaware, are his true sons, and help us to understand him, as he in turn interprets and justifies them" (97). Pater himself uses *The Renaissance* as a filial search for justification by intellectual or artistic fathers. The arrangement of *The Renaissance* makes it hard for us to miss echoes of these terms in the opening of "Leonardo da Vinci," which immediately follows. Leonardo too is an interpreter; Pater's epigraph for the essay is "Homo minister et interpres naturae." Furthermore, the question of justification of sons by fathers is central to the study.

Pater begins by referring to a familiar filial task, biography. Vasari, like Pater with *The Renaissance*, modified the first edition of Leonardo's biography to make the artist less "a bold speculator, holding lightly by other men's beliefs, setting philosophy above Christianity" (98). "Winckelmann," strongly anti-Christian when published in 1867, was altered in precisely the same way. Here, Pater praises such changes on the grounds of historical accuracy. No statements by Leonardo "justify" Vasari's first version, and this is because of the tendency of his "genius . . . to lose itself in a refined and graceful mystery" (98). Clearly, the obscurity of Leonardo's life has aesthetic value for Pater, whose own life had the same, seemingly self-chosen, quality. Leonardo's life and work, "enigmatical" and "exotic" (98, 99), offer a test of devotion for his modern student, the "lover of strange souls" (100). To discover the truths of such a shadowy life brings the biographer into a pleasing relationship with his subject. If Pater's "impression" is accurate, then "The *legend* . . . may now and then intervene to support the results of this analysis" (100; italics in original).   ,,

As at the end of "The Poetry of Michaelangelo," Pater hopes to identify the "true sons" of a great Renaissance artist. In Leonardo's lifetime, this problem takes on a more specific meaning:

> The dishonour of illegitimacy hangs over his birth. Piero Antonio, his father, was of a noble Florentine house, of Vinci in the *Val d' Arno*, and Leonardo, brought up delicately among the true children of that house, was the love-child of his youth, with the keen, puissant nature such children often have. We se him in his boyhood fascinating all men by his beauty . . . (100)

Pater uses the artist's birth to indulge in his own family romance, as he did by reporting Michelangelo's confidence in the "imperial blood in his veins." Illegitimacy obliquely refers to the *minister et interpres naturae* as well. Leonardo "serves" nature insofar as he is the product of natural passion; in the Elizabethan sense of the word, he is a "natural." Pater's language shows that this quality has special attraction for him, implying close family ties. Contrasted with Piero's legal children, Leonardo is a "love-child," itself a complex pun on illegitimacy. One meaning is that he was the result of youthful excess, the child of love. The ambiguous reference of "youth," however, suggests other connotations of the phrase. Leonardo is also compared to a love-child *from* his father's "youth," an image reviving a former affection. Beyond this, he is a Cupid (the mythological love-child), to whom his father, still young himself, must respond. This meaning is echoed by his "keen, puissant nature . . . fascinating *all men* by his beauty."

All these possibilities coalesce to indicate an irresistible charm that Pater assigns Leonardo as a result of his birth. The painter enjoys ideal filial relationships; his father loves him after an idyllic fashion that Pater believes to be characteristic of youthful feelings. In the psychological order of his thoughts, Pater imagines that being a love-child results in being "brought up delicately." Somehow, then, Leonardo becomes for him the "true child" of the household. In this sense he stands for a rather striking "justification" of nature. Its ambiguity is the key to such charm. Leonardo is "true" because he is illegitimate; or, to put it another way, Pater uses him to represent a homosexual wish for a love affair with paternal figures because simultaneously he is and he is not a "true" son. The father is, after all, the ambiguous figure behind "natural" births. Incestuous homosexual possibilities can be obscured by this uncertainty.

This complex sexual identity corresponds to Leonardo's dual roles throughout Pater's essay. As the Latin caption suggests, he is both a servant and an active interpreter of nature, spectator and participant in the emotions of the world. His life, furthermore, was divided between science and art, and this dual calling embodies one of Leonardo's central meanings for Pater. A recent study has shown that the figure of the artist-scientist was popularized for Pater and his age through the life of Goethe.[18] Leonardo's double role thus links him to the essay on "Winckelmann," where Goethe becomes a crucial figure and science is a theme at the end. Pater's treatment of all three men is a means of enlarging the meaning of "aesthetic criticism," a term which itself implies alternate responses to experience. Goethe, Winckelmann, and Leonardo combine the virtues of art and criticism. While indulging in the most forbidden pleasures suggested in the images of art, they maintain immunity from punishment or guilt through a simultaneous critical detachment. As Pater remarks at the end of "Two Early French Stories," such figures "refuse to be classified" (27).

Pater's essay contains frequent allusions to taboos violated by Leonardo. Such references partake of the primitive response to art as a "forbidden . . . activity," as one writer has called it, a belief implying "the artist's magical power." [19] The description of the *Mona Lisa* is, perhaps, Pater's most primitive version of Leonardo. "Was it," he asks just before the start of his incantation, "by stroke of magic, that the image was projected?" (124). Such fears are echoed in Pater's references to Leonardo's central image, which becomes the pivotal symbol in this essay as well: the smile of women, "the unfathomable smile, always with a touch of something sinister in it . . ." (124). Even the term "unfathomable" defines smiling as a symbol of the prohibitions the artist violates, but Pater's idea is precisely that Leonardo explores those depths unthreatened; this is the "magic" of his life and work. Leonardo's created fantasies of erotic beauty are removed from his life, just as Pater's own writing

18. Antony Ward, *Walter Pater: The Idea in Nature* (Worcester, Mass., and London, 1965), pp. 27ff.
19. Ernst Kris, *Psychoanalytic Explorations in Art* (New York, 1952), p. 78.

constantly places its subjects at a distance. Pater's decadence, then, simultaneously evoking and "deadening" highly charged imagery, attempts to imitate the charmed double vision of figures like Leonardo.

Indeed, as Pater interprets the artist's response to Milanese society, his language shifts to the highly personal terms of ritual. He sets his description apart from its subject by placing Leonardo at the top of the Duomo. "Below, in the streets . . . moved a people . . . fantastic, changeful, and dreamlike. To Leonardo least of all men could there be anything poisonous in the exotic flowers of sentiment which grew there. It was a life of brilliant sins and exquisite amusements: Leonardo became a celebrated designer of pageants . . ." (109). We are meant to parallel that final remark with the stylistic pageant Pater has just presented. As an artist, Pater suggests, Leonardo refines poison plants into "exotic flowers of sentiment." The last lines of the paragraph explicitly attribute this ethereal, artistic distance to double vision; pageants "suited the quality of his genius, composed, in almost equal parts, of curiosity and the desire of beauty. . . ." Devoted equally to science and art, Leonardo tames the dangerous force of "desire" by sublimating it into "curiosity." Even the artist's death is abstracted into a "last curiosity," as Pater uses the symbol of Leonardo's detachment to transform his own most highly charged theme into a delicate, graceful scene.

There was also a negative side of Leonardo's science, its distracting role in the artist's life. Knowing this, Pater senses the "infantilism" that Freud ascribed to many of Leonardo's inventions and investigations.[20] Pater frequently shows the painter "making strange toys" (127), or, in more loaded terms, as "he trifles with his genius" (99). A similar connotation appears at the beginning of a long passage on Leonardo's scientific work. "He wasted many days in curious tricks of design, seeming to lose himself in the spinning of intricate devices of line and colour. He was smitten with a love of the impossible . . ." (104). If, like many of Leonardo's biographers, Pater seems uncomfortable with his subject's "losing himself" in "tricks" of his own making, he also participates, unconsciously, in the artist's self-absorption. The "spinning" image makes Pater's fantasy of onanism plain, for thread is a common dream symbol for semen. And

20. "Leonardo da Vinci and a Memory of His Childhood" (1910), *S.E.*, XI, 125–129 and 74–81 (hereafter referred to as "Leonardo").

as the passage continues, his delight in Leonardo's speculations becomes more open:

> He was smitten with a love of the impossible—the perforation
> of mountains, changing the course of rivers, raising great build-
> ings, such as the church of *San Giovanni*, in the air; all those
> feats for the performance of which natural magic professed
> to have the key. . . . Two ideas were especially confirmed in
> him, as reflexes of things that had touched his brain in child-
> hood beyond the depth of other impressions—the smiling of
> women and the motion of great waters. (104)

Clearly, the fantasies of childish sexual power here are directed
toward the penetration of a great female image. Leonardo's scientific
notebooks arouse Pater's Oedipal desire—indeed, he seems to be
responding in kind to the artist's own Oedipal dreams. The order of
the imagery suggests that, for Pater, masturbation and its associated
fantasies, which introduce this passage, represent an attempt to recover the sense of being fondled; maternal smiles, after all, "had
touched his brain in childhood." Pater, then, imagines science as
simultaneously a substitute and a primary gratification.

Pater's description of Leonardo's apprenticeship, and of his growing scientific interests, gives these fantasies a biographical source.
On one level the account concerns an Oedipal revolt. In Verrocchio's
studio, Leonardo perfects his teacher's techniques to the point of
disenchantment, when he decides instead to seek new methods in
nature, "the true mistress of higher intelligences" (Leonardo's words)
(103). Rejecting the paternal "master" seems to lead him directly
to a mother: "He plunged, then, into the study of nature" (103).
Science, at this point, clearly stands for sexual desire.

But Pater's sense of Leonardo's development is more complex
than this, for his description shows some signs of anxiety. If Verrocchio's "discouragement and decrease" are offered as conditions
for better future art and humanity's "final success," Pater's language
mitigates this triumph. The crucial episode is famous. Leonardo
is allowed to complete an angel in the corner of Verrocchio's *Baptism
of Christ;* it is a minor masterpiece. Yet Pater sympathizes with the
master's response to the accomplishment, as the energy of his description makes clear: "Verrocchio turned away as one stunned, and as
if his sweet earlier work must thereafter be distasteful to him, from
the bright animated angel of Leonardo's hand" (102). Two kinds

of discovery and shock are implied in this scene. Not only painting, but another act is interrupted; the "bright animated angel of Leonardo's hand" adds to connotations here of a father's discovery of a masturbating son. Verrocchio's response, in this sense, also constitutes a rejection of his filial apprentice, so that the "sweet earlier work" which becomes distasteful refers both to art and to the son he has created.

These overtones explain Pater's later anxiety as he insists that the rupture was not total. "To the last Leonardo recalls the studio of Verrocchio, in the love of beautiful toys, such as the vessel of water for a mirror, and lovely needle-work about the implicated hands in the *Modesty and Vanity* . . ." (102). If filial revolt implied a traumatic discovery, this can be resolved through Pater's familiar technique of reviving the traumatic scene. Masturbation, then, becomes in Pater's imagery a ritual, a symbolic effort to woo and placate the paternal figure. "Implicated hands," such "toys" as a "vessel of water for a mirror," suggest onanistic acts, and "recall" Leonardo's artistic home in a wishful, erotic sense. Similarly, Pater notes that his pursuit of Mother Nature was, finally, in "the manner of the older students" (103). Even in his most narcissistic act (for the phallic "vessel of water" is a "mirror"), Leonardo models himself after a father and seeks maternal comfort following his revolt.

It is curious that Pater's conclusion to this episode becomes the history of a homosexual development. In fact, "Leonardo da Vinci" tells more about Pater's sexuality than any essay in *The Renaissance*. One of the best explanations of the growth of homosexual feeling appears in Freud's essay on Leonardo. Oedipal love, he says, after "the discovery . . . that women do not have a penis . . . often turns into its opposite and gives place to a feeling of disgust which in the years of puberty can become the cause of psychical impotence, misogyny and permanent homosexuality." [21] In Pater's famous phrase, "the way to perfection is through a series of disgusts" (103). Leonardo, he explains, first revolted from Verrocchio's style in a painting of Paradise that is no longer extant; Pater's description of Eden, then, must be his own. "It was the perfection of the older Florentine style of miniature-painting, with patient putting of each leaf upon the trees and each flower in the grass, where the first man and woman were standing" (103). From this opportunity

21. "Leonardo," p. 96.

to inspect the facts of sexual life, and indeed to embellish them with leaves and flowers, Leonardo, in Pater's view, must have recoiled. "Because it was the perfection of that style," Pater suggests, "it awoke in Leonardo some seed of discontent which lay in the secret places of his nature. For the way to perfection is through a series of disgusts. . . ." In Pater's mind, the object of aversion is the condition of heterosexuality itself, the human organs that painters cover with leaves because they make sexuality possible. It is not accidental that the "seed" which this arouses "lay in the secret places of his nature." Pater's psychic response is masturbatory, a retreat into narcissistic pleasure from a disappointment at the unpleasant facts of human sexual history, represented in the Fall.

Science, then, is overdetermined in "Leonardo da Vinci." A desire to possess feminine nature, it also connotes the wish to escape to a prelapsarian, presexual condition of life. Furthermore, the "disgust" with which Leonardo is said to flee from art pointedly echoes Verrocchio's "distaste" earlier in Leonardo's life. This is another of Pater's compulsive dramatizations of a traumatic event: through Leonardo's imitation of his "master," Pater hopes to restore infantile dreams of paternal love. Even the *Mona Lisa* description, although female-oriented, involves this homosexual constellation. "It is hard," Pater insists, "not to connect with these designs of the elder, by-past master, as with its germinal principle, the unfathomable smile, always with a touch of something sinister in it . . ." (124). The hint is unmistakable that even in his masterpiece Leonardo is the passive recipient of a paternal gift. It also seems clear that one source of the smile's "sinister" quality is the fact that its "master" is "by-past." By discovering science, Leonardo abandons his master forever. Pater's Oedipal anxiety results from this reminder that his own murderous wishes were fulfilled in his father's death.

Leonardo's naturalism implies the blended "extremes of beauty and terror," for, Pater asks, "has not nature too her grotesques?" (104–105). Consequently, as an artistic image of the painter's science and nature studies, Pater selects the Medusa, present in numerous works besides the vampire-like *Mona Lisa*. Freud explained the Medusa theme as a product of the castration complex, denying through its multitude of snakes the fear of genital loss which arises from seeing female sexual organs.[22] Pater's description becomes

22. "Medusa's Head" (1940 [1922]), S.E., XVIII, 273–274.

intense when he alludes to these phallic qualities in one painting: "The delicate snakes seem literally strangling each other in terrified struggle to escape from the Medusa brain" (106). Here, terror is clearly displaced from the observer. But the subject also implies masculine rebuffs for Pater, producing the suggestive reference to the Medusa of the *Uffizii*, where "all those swarming fancies unite." There, science produces an accurate Tuscan landscape, in which "The lizards and glow-worms and other strange small creatures . . . are as true to nature as the pretended astonishment of the father for whom the boy has prepared a surprise" (105–106).

Masculine relationships are discussed openly when Pater considers Leonardo as a teacher. Snake imagery reappears in the image of the artist's lover and student, Andrea Salaino, "beloved of Leonardo for his curled and waving hair . . . and afterwards his favourite pupil and servant" (116). Salaino is depicted in a portrait that "Love chooses for its own," making him, like Leonardo in his father's house, a Cupid. This pupil, in fact, "identified himself so entirely with Leonardo, that the picture of *Saint Anne* . . . has been attributed to him" (116). Pater makes it clear that, for Leonardo, Salaino was a self-referential symbol; he taught his pupil in order to bestow love upon an image of himself. Freud's study of Leonardo gives this a definite meaning:

> The boy represses his love for his mother: he puts himself in her place, identifies himself with her, and takes his own person as a model in whose likeness he chooses the new objects of his love. In this way he has become a homosexual. What he has in fact done is to slip back to auto-erotism: for the boys whom he now loves as he grows up are after all only substitutive figures and revivals of himself in childhood—boys whom he loves in the way in which his mother loved *him* when he was a child.[23]

In Pater's treatment, as I have mentioned, this love also involves Leonardo's paternal identifications.

Salaino's mistaken connection with *Saint Anne* (or *The Holy Family*) is a crucial symbol for these psychological connotations. Freud pointed out that the painting is explicitly a fable of the

23. Leonardo," p. 100.

artist's own childhood.[24] Like the young Christ, Leonardo had two maternal protectors, and this became a determinative factor in his adult psychosexual character. More recent biographers of the artist question this account of his first five years,[25] but Pater clearly relied on identical information. Furthermore, Freud's history of Leonardo applies to Pater even more than it did to the painter himself. After Pater's father died, as I have mentioned, he was raised by a maternal pair. He could easily feel strong identifications with the youthful situation depicted in *Christ with Saint Anne and the Virgin*, as with Leonardo's own life. *The Holy Family* thus becomes an idealization of his own childhood relations with the females in his life. As a psychic statement about Salaino, Pater's repetition of the traditional confusion has an additional significance. The allusion restores an ideal triangle in an art-historical family romance. Pater's discussion asserts that the master-pupil relationship, unsatisfactory in the case of Leonardo and Verrocchio, finally achieves unrestrained love. Furthermore, this relationship coexists with the child's total devotion to the maternal objects in his life. Salaino, then, becomes a symbol of idealized childhood, in which parental love is bestowed freely from all sides at once.[26]

Leonardo chose his pupils, Pater explains, for their birth, for their personal charm, or because they had "just enough genius to be capable of initiation into his secret" (117). His language suggests a final aspect of his homosexuality. Otto Fenichel notes that many homosexuals consider themselves "students" of their partners. These "regard the condition of being a masculine man's 'feminine' partner as learning the secrets of masculinity from the 'master,' or as depriving him of those secrets."[27] Pater's manifest and unconscious meanings are in conflict: sexually, it is Leonardo who is given "initiation" by his "pupils." Another passage confirms Pater's sense that Leonardo, as a teacher, served his own passions. Leonardo, with his students at a country villa,

24. "Leonardo," pp. 112ff.
25. Brian Farrell, "On Freud's Study of Leonardo," in *Leonardo da Vinci: Aspects of the Renaissance Genius,* ed. Morris Philipson (New York, 1966), p. 234.
26. These connotations of studentship suggest one of the underlying erotic fantasies in "The School of Giorgione," an essay filled with ambiguous scenes of seduction and with allusions to infantile love. Unfortunately, limitations of space prevent my discussing this essay here.
27. Otto Fenichel, *The Psychoanalytic Theory of Neurosis* (New York, 1945), p. 334.

worked at his fugitive manuscripts and sketches, working for the present hour, and for a few only, perhaps chiefly for himself. Other artists have been as careless of present or future applause, in self-forgetfulness, or because they set moral or political ends above the ends of art; but in him this solitary culture of beauty seems to have hung upon a kind of self-love, and a carelessness in the work of art of all but art itself. Out of the secret places of a unique temperament he brought strange blossoms and fruits hitherto unknown; and for him, the novel impression conveyed, the exquisite effect woven, counted as an end in itself—a perfect end. (117)

Pater sees Leonardo's version of art for its own sake as a homosexual devotion to the youthful image of himself. Characteristically, the passage culminates in a fantasy of sexual gratification; not only "blossoms and fruits" from the "secret places" within Leonardo, but the weaving symbol for semen, suggest phallic pleasure. The luxuriance of this prose corresponds to Pater's unconscious participation in the images. The rhythmic, pleasurable intensity of his language—here as throughout "Leonardo da Vinci"—is Pater's own exercise in "self-love."

This lack of restraint is encouraged by the manifest conditions of the artist's life: Leonardo manages to pursue a "solitary culture of beauty" and still win a prominent place in the world by creating great art. But at the end of the essay, for an instant only, Leonardo's magical immunity cracks. Pater's treatment of his banishment from Italy is significant, psychologically, as a return of the repressed anxieties Leonardo's remarkable life seemed to have overcome. His exile is introduced by a scene resembling the fantasy preceding his rejection of Verrocchio's studio. "We catch a glimpse of Leonardo again, at Rome in 1514, surrounded by his mirrors and vials and furnaces, making strange toys that seemed alive of wax and quicksilver" (127). When, in the next lines, he is accused of treason, it becomes a revival of that traumatic masturbatory scene in which the father rejects the son he catches in the act. Leonardo is "suspected of secret French sympathies. It paralysed him to find himself among enemies; and he turned wholly to France, which had long courted him" (128). Pater unconsciously seeks a maternal figure—a clear connotation of France throughout *The Renaissance*—in the face of such hostility. But, as I have noted, Pater is uncomfortable in conventional Oedipal flight, so he quickly goes on to deny implicitly that the separation amounts to much. "France was about to become an Italy more Italian than Italy itself. Francis the First, like Lewis the Twelfth before him, was attracted by the *finesse* of Leonardo's work; *La Gioconda* was already in his cabinet . . ." (128). Pater is insisting that Leonardo's escape leads to a substitute father, with whom he can enjoy blissful possession of his "ideal lady" as well.

The progress of this final section, from masturbation to suspicion, exile, and death, adds another detail to our understanding of Pater's filial guilt. Death is connected with a paternal rejection of a childish, homosexual attempt at seduction through masturbation. Such an advance is behind the "surprise" prepared by the son in Pater's Medusa description. Leonardo's final, substitutive death, then, is "caused" by the suspicions of "the political society of Rome," which are merely the projection of his own desires. Psychologically, it is clear in what sense Leonardo is "paralysed . . . to find himself among enemies." Rejected by the world he had "courted," he turns to a society Pater represents as totally denying this possibility, having "long courted him."

At Leonardo's death, Pater cannot refrain from repeating the fantasy that introduced this brief, final cycle of anxiety. Leonardo returns to an ideal household, becoming *peinteur du Roy*. If the details of his last moments are uncertain, Pater still can speculate on them to hint that the central conditions of death scenes in *The Renaissance* were fulfilled. "Two questions remain, after much busy antiquarianism, concerning Leonardo's death—the question of the exact form of his religion, and the question whether Francis the First was present at the time" (128). For Pater, the solutions to these are identical, since both symbolize his filial guilt. Without answering them, for he is limited by the facts of history, Pater fulfills their terms by using the vocabularies of art and science, attaching to the scene the psychological connotations of sublimated gratification.

Finally, Pater says, questions of religion or of Leonardo's last companion are insignificant. Leonardo's request for elaborate masses was "immediate and practical; and on no theory of religion could these hurried offices be of much consequence" (128). (This statement offers a suggestive measure for Pater's religious revival, begun at the gloomy conclusion of his brief "experiment" in London living.[28]) Leonardo, like Winckelmann, is valued for his sublimation of religion to art; the latter's insincere Catholicism, Pater writes later, "was only one incident of a culture in which the moral instinct, like the religious or political, was merged in the artistic" (187). This fusion makes Leonardo's "last curiosity" a symbolic "proof" of the resolutions of filial conflict dramatized elsewhere in religion or in relations with art patrons. Curiosity, his most modern quality, represents loyalty to both parents and the reciprocation of this love from outside. In France, Pater concludes, questions of a father's presence or of religion become unimportant. Indeed, "We forget them in speculating how one who had been always so desirous of beauty, but desired it always in such precise and definite forms, as hands or flowers or hair, looked forward now into the vague land, and experienced the last curiosity" (128–129). This moment invokes the erotic pleasure associated with Leonardo's natural investigations through the symbolic "curiosity." Looking and experiencing, the artist is active and passive for one last time. It is the finest scene in *The Renaissance.*

III.

If "Leonardo da Vinci" contains Pater's best writing, "Winckelmann" still is the crucial chapter in *The Renaissance.* His subject, for the first time, is a critic-historian studying the past through its arts, a modern writer who is, quite plainly, an image of Pater himself. Winckelmann's passion for Greece, not to mention the intensity of his entire life, realizes in actual history all the emotional attitudes urged by Pater's style. One can even speculate that this essay, Pater's second published work and the first part of *The Renaissance* to be written, inspired his construction of an entire book after the model of a critic's romance with the past.

28. R. V. Osborn suggests that Pater's attempt to live in society, an abrupt shift from his retired life-style before 1885, represented an effort to carry out the principles of *Marius,* to accept social and moral responsibilities. One might also say that his London life reenacted the failures of his heroes to blend with their environments. Pater's choice of a dull, unresponsive society and his subsequent chastened return to Oxford appear to have been masochistically designed to furnish additional excuses for isolation and compulsive piety. See Osbourn, "Marius the Epicurean," *Essays in Criticism,* I (1951), 387–403, esp. 402–403.

In *The Renaissance,* of course, the hero as spectator refers to Pater himself. He becomes his own leading character, leaving a supporting role open for his audience, which he hopes to involve in his most ecstatic responses to history and art. For beyond the level of self-indulgence, as Richard Ellmann has observed, *The Renaissance* consists of "exercises in the seduction of young men by the wiles of culture." [29] "Winckelmann," with whose conquest this affair begins, suggests Pater's uneasiness at dramatizing this appeal. The essay develops fitfully, nervously, as Pater's discussion moves from Winckelmann's work to Hellenic culture, then to Goethe, and finally to the subject of modern life. This progression, leading directly to the overdetermined language of the "Conclusion," shows how much is at stake as Pater defines his own role.

Even putting chronology aside, it is easy to understand why Pater reserved this study for the end of his book. It sums up all his major themes; Winckelmann's life reenacts the vital episodes from Pater's other biographies. Winckelmann's travels, like his education, provide an escape from the "dark poverty" of his father's home, where he first felt "a wistful sense of something lost to be regained" (179). Following the sun, he journeys south, and Pater quotes Madame de Staël's explanatory remark that "A fine sky brings to birth sentiments not unlike the love of one's Fatherland" (179). The German's pursuit of art, leading finally to Rome, is part of a family romance, the search for an ideal "lost" father among the products of classical Greece; it is also a search to "regain" his own sexuality. In an important sense, Pater shares this fantasy. Echoing Madame de Staël's terms, he ascribes a heroic "birth" to Winckelmann's Hellenism. "The key to the understanding of the Greek spirit, Winckelmann possessed in his own nature, itself like a relic of classical antiquity, laid open by accident to our alien, modern atmosphere" (220). Pater's metaphor reveals an infantile confusion of birth and defecation. Winckelmann's birth "by accident" makes him the offspring of "antiquity" and all history, which is governed by accidental flux. He is, consequently, Pater's child as well as an

---

29. "Overtures to Wilde's *Salome,*" *Yearbook of Comparative Literature,* XVII (1968), 24. Ellmann also suggests that Pater's description of Leonardo's painting of John the Baptist—"whose treacherous smile would have us understand something far beyond the outward gesture or circumstance" (118)—"may be Victorian hinting at the heresy, a specially homosexual one, that Christ and John (not to mention Leonardo and his model) were lovers." See Ellmann, p. 23.

intellectual father, and later in the essay this fantasy becomes the
key to a new critical ideal.

Goethe is assigned another vision of Winckelmann's miraculous
birth. Significantly, the language remains Pater's in a situation that
frequently leads him to quotation. Winckelmann "imprints" his
character on Goethe's imagination, "at the beginning of life, in its
original and simplest form, as in a fragment of Greek art itself,
stranded on that littered, indeterminate shore of Germany in the
eighteenth century" (227–228). The connotations of this sentence
substantiate the hints of the earlier one. Pater unconsciously connects
birth with a "littered" anal mess, of which Winckelmann represents
one "fragment . . . stranded." The context even enables us to re-
construct the meaning of this primary-process work. Pater's syntax
is ambiguous, so that both Winckelmann and Goethe are identified
as the products of the birth alluded to. Each is characterized "at the
beginning of life . . ." It is, of course, one of Pater's most explicit
points that Goethe discovers in his predecessor a spiritual father,
whose character, then, is "imprinted" on his son through some sort
of bio-literary transmission. Winckelmann, Pater says earlier, "became to him something like what Virgil was to Dante" (197).

But if Winckelmann, too, is being "born" here, then he is both
father and son. Insofar as he represents a model for Goethe and
Pater, they become identified with his double role. These dual meanings finally explain the mixed imagery of birth and defecation in
the reference to Winckelmann's discovery by modern criticism.
The ideal critic, according to these terms, symbolizes self-creation
and self-detachment. He can be both bearer and born, producer and
product, author, actor and observer in the drama of his own writing.
In the moments when Pater most strongly points out the identification of Greece-Winckelmann-Goethe-himself, his language becomes
colored by the infantile fantasy of a birth anyone can effect. Ultimately, Winckelmann's complex role generates the anal language
of flux in the "Conclusion," Pater's most famous statement of the application of critical attitudes to life.

Winckelmann's autonomy as father of himself, active and passive
figure, derives from Greece itself. Greek artists were self-born,
Pater says, and he describes them as having "grown up on the soil
of their own individuality, creating themselves out of themselves,
and moulding themselves to what they were, and willed to be. . . .
They are ideal artists of themselves" (219). The implication of this

language is that lives, like statues, can be shaped, and that the
critical intelligence makes this possible. Pater's birth imagery repeatedly treats Winckelmann himself as a kind of artifact. Early in
the essay he reports that Goethe "classes him with certain works
of art" (177). Similarly, Winckelmann's intuitive grasp of Hellenic
culture affects the way he lives. "In morals, as in criticism, he followed the clue of instinct, of an unerring instinct" (220). Thus, as
Winckelmann "reproduces" the "earlier sentiment of the Renaissance" in his "*finding* of Greek art," he creates a work in his own
life, a model for modern living. Goethe comments that "One learns
nothing from him . . . but one becomes something." And Pater
translates the "secret of this influence" as "wholeness, unity with
one's self, intellectual integrity" (184–185). These are precisely the
qualities of Hellenic life which Pater, particularly in the "Conclusion," refuses to consider a "lost art."

Winckelmann's contact with the past is described as a sexual
encounter. "That world in which others had moved with so much
embarrassment, seems to call out in Winckelmann new senses fitted
to deal with it. He is in touch with it; it penetrates him, and becomes part of his temperament" (194). Here the critic is both active
and passive; that "touch" only alters his "temperament," implying
a solely aesthetic response, detached from any social "embarrassment." Once again, Pater is describing a figure whose dabbling in
forbidden arts is immune to external threats. Pater's primary assertion, throughout the essay, is that Winckelmann is "in touch" with
the past in a literal way. The German's achievement is "to lay open
a new sense, to initiate a new organ for the human spirit" (188).
One psychic meaning of this language relates to Winckelmann as a
symbol of self-birth, a fantasy based on childish wishes for a "new
organ." More generally, the critic stands for the simultaneous revival,
in history, of visual and tactile powers, a recovery of natural human
capacities. Through the examination of art, Winckelmann has rediscovered his own sexuality. Clearly, Pater finds it important to
deny the sexual quality of such criticism by insisting on its status as
a purely aesthetic act.

There is a basic psychological connection of vision and touch
underlying Winckelmann's critical contact with Greece. Neurotic
compulsions to see, scoptophilia, take vision as a substitute for
touching, a fact with clear implications for Pater's own interest in
art. He too discovers a "new organ" through symbolic perceptions.
Furthermore, the defenses common to voyeurs are conspicuous in

Pater's life. Shyness and shame protect the self against a return of the visual aggression it directs outward against others.[30] Pater's personal reserve, then, can be linked to his intense visual energies. His personality offers an important account for the language used to praise Winckelmann's greatest Hellenic inheritance. His "temperament" results in a "serenity . . . which characterises Winckelmann's handling of the sensuous side of Greek art. This serenity is, perhaps, in great measure a negative quality: it is the absence of any sense of want, or corruption, or shame. With the sensuous element in Greek art he deals in the pagan manner . . ." (221). The German critic represents freedom from guilt, and specifically from the anxiety which for Pater arises from the aggressive, erotic connotations of viewing art. Like Leonardo, Winckelmann enjoys intense sublimated sexual gratifications with immunity.

Winckelmann is a Renaissance figure for the same reason his work is said to be "in the pagan manner." Like the other inhabitants of that "enchanted region" of history, he returns to a way of life submerged at the advent of the Christian Middle Ages; he is "simple, primeval, Greek" (189). Pater accepts the Romantic convention of modern society's detachment from a purer human childhood, destroyed by cultural repression. Crossing this gap, Winckelmann finds fundamental human pleasures in the arts of ancient Greece. Through him Pater suggests the possibility of merging physical and intellectual gratifications into a single unified consciousness, which is a central idea in Romantic literature from Blake to the twentieth century.[31] At the heart of Winckelmann's Hellenism is freedom. To the extent that he avoids the repressions of other critics of Greek sculpture he becomes, in Pater's view, a Greek himself, freed from the false moral restraints of modern society. In this process, Winckelmann becomes the fused artist-critic I have already discussed. Pater takes some pains to classify the German critic with Hellenic artists and to explain that the serenity of Greek beauty does not preclude the "sensuous" involvement of Winckelmann or its creators. To produce his subdued results, the Greek artist "has gradually sunk his intellectual and spiritual ideas in sensuous form," merging the two. Like the Greek sculptors, Winckelmann directly confronts the "fire of colour" latent in the forms of Hellenic art, "steeps his thought" in it "again and again":

30. Fenichel, *Psychoanalytic Theory,* pp. 70–72, 139.
31. See Frank Kermode, *The Romantic Image* (New York, 1964).

To the Greek this immersion in the sensuous was, religiously, at least, indifferent. Greek sensuousness, therefore, does not fever the conscience: it is shameless and childlike. Christian asceticism, on the other hand, discrediting the slightest touch of sense, has from time to time provoked into strong emphasis the contrast or antagonism to itself, of the artistic life, with its inevitable sensuousness.—*I did but taste a little honey with the end of the rod that was in my hand, and lo! I must die.*— It has sometimes seemed hard to pursue that life without something of conscious disavowal of a spiritual world; and this imparts to genuine artistic interests a kind of intoxication. From this intoxication Winckelmann is free: he fingers those pagan marbles with unsinged hands, with no sense of shame or loss. That is to deal with the sensuous side of art in the pagan manner. (221–222; italics in original)

As a self-creator, a latter-day Greek artist, Winckelmann enjoys the erotic content of "the sensuous side of art" while avoiding "intoxication." His life in the historical middle ground of criticism protects him from a "provoked . . . antagonism" to Christianity. Pater's understanding of Christian guilt, in fact, explains why such "fingering" might be opposed by rigid societies. If Winckelmann's vision amounts to tasting "a little honey with the end of the rod that was in my hand," it represents, through the Biblical imagery, intense homoerotic gratification. Phallic and oral symbols merge into a homosexual fantasy of the penis as breast, a vision quickly subsumed by a masturbatory image. Later on, Pater explains Winckelmann's "instinct of self-culture," which carries its own overtones of onanism, in terms vividly suggesting masturbation. "The demand of the intellect is to feel itself alive. . . . It struggles with those forms till its secret is won from each, and then lets each fall back into its place, in the supreme artistic view of life" (229). Secrets are sexual, as we saw in "Leonardo da Vinci." [32] Criticism here becomes a series of self-initiated orgasms.

32. "Poring over his crucibles, making experiments with colour, trying, by a strange variation of the alchemist's dream, to discover the secret, not of an elixir to make man's natural life immortal, but of giving immortality to the subtlest and most delicate effects of painting, he seemed . . . rather the sorcerer or the magician, possessed of curious secrets and a hidden knowledge, living in a world of which he alone possessed the key" (107). Leonardo's secretiveness evokes sexual pleasures here through the art-science of masturbation.

In fact, the psychological imagery of Pater's famous line in the "Conclusion" amounts to the same wish: "To burn always with this hard, gemlike flame, to maintain this ecstasy, is success in life" (236). The concept of historical flux involves a belief in timelessness which is also implicit in calling Winckelmann a Greek or making him part of the Renaissance. Both contain hidden pleas for what Pater calls in the *Mona Lisa* passage "the fancy of a perpetual life, sweeping together ten thousand experiences" (125). Both represent wishes for endless youth, with uninterrupted sexual potency. Hence the "new organ" Pater credits Winckelmann with discovering is phallic.

The erotic connotations of Hellenism do not end here. Winckelmann's "supreme, artistic view of life" is a homosexual one. Like John Addington Symonds after him, Pater identifies Greek, or "pagan," living with sexual habits, and he makes open references in this essay to the quality of Winckelmann's friendships. Pater emphasizes at several points the avoidance of heterosexuality in Greek subjects, which is what he means by their "sexlessness." Hellenic art "keeps passion always below that degree of intensity at which it must necessarily be transitory, never winding up the features to one note of anger, or desire, or surprise." (216). And, in a passage echoing "The Poetry of Michaelangelo," Pater praises the "unchanging characteristics" of Greek sculpture: "That white light, purged from the angry, bloodlike stains of action and passion, reveals, not what is accidental in man, but the tranquil godship in him, as opposed to the restless accidents of life" (213). Sexual connotations are "purged" from art in an anal sense. Pater's defense against the "restless accidents of life" takes its form from his psychic perception of the nature of "action and passion."

The alternative to a world of sexual conflict is one in which the sexes do not mix at all. Hence, when Pater quotes the German critic on Greek beauty, it is a long passage extolling its male ideals, statues of Narcissus placed by women's bedsides in the hope of producing ideal children, or the contests held by the King of Arcadia, where "a prize was offered to the youths for the deftest kiss" (208). "Winckelmann" is based on an all-male world. Pater even records some of the critic's letters to "friends," in which Winckelmann celebrates finding "in a beautiful body a soul created for nobleness," and so forth (192). Winckelmann's sexual taste becomes the essay's most compelling image of the merger of aesthetics with life through the pursuit of beauty. In this sense, Pater's version of

210 Psychoanalysis and Literary Process

Hellenism is just as subversive as his critics feared. At its extreme, friendship becomes an art form itself, a medium for developing critical perception. "These friendships, bringing him into contact with the pride of human form, and staining the thoughts with its bloom, perfected his reconciliation to the spirit of Greek sculpture" (191). The metaphoric "stains" of "contact" leave little doubt that Pater understood the sexual activities implied in these relationships.

The most intense homosexual episode in the essay occurs in Pater's description of Winckelmann's death. It provides a release for his prose; for, after this scene, Pater first considers the Greek ideals out of which he develops a vocabulary of praise for Winckelmann's "sexlessness" and his "uncorrupted" admiration of beauty. As a homosexual atonement, the scene repeats that familiar fantasy of expiating for a paternal death "caused" by filial homoerotic desire. Mario Praz considers Winckelmann's actual death an explosion of the myth concerning his "pure" life: his murder reveals "the black sediment of neurasthenia . . . at the bottom of the soul of the worshipper of Greek beauty."[33] Pater uses the sordidness of the episode to enforce his own sense of it as a symbolic punishment.

Conveniently, the murderer is named Arcangeli. Pater's language makes his a rather passive role, so that, in fact, no killer is ever perceived causing the critic's death. Winckelmann begins his fatal journey in order "to revisit the country of his birth" (195), a phrase suggestive of erotic wishes that might demand punishment. He befriends his future killer, Pater hints, in a homosexual gesture, "with characteristic openness" (196). Although the murder is inspired by the critic's gold medals, Pater insists that Arcangeli's greed itself is a reflex, so that his "avarice was aroused." Then the act itself is divided into two sentences, to further separate the killer from the scene, making Winckelmann's final moments almost solitary. "Arcangeli begged to see the medals once more. As Winckelmann stooped down to take them from the chest, a cord was thrown round his neck" (196). The fantasy of self-birth, here illustrated with vivid anal characteristics as the German stoops for his gold, concludes in umbilical strangulation.

It is characteristic of Pater's permissive defense that the repression symbolized by this violence is only half-effective. There are

33. *The Romantic Agony*, 2nd ed. (London, 1951), p. 473.

three further results of Winckelmann's death, three symbolic rewards attached to this scene, each suggesting that it was, in fact,
a consummation. On an unconscious level Pater feels that Winckelmann and his last male friend perfected their relationship through
murder. Dying, of course, has sexual connotations in much of literature, but Pater attaches specific consequences to this scene. First,
the discovery of the body is described in some detail. "Some time
afterwards, a child with whose companionship Winckelmann had
beguiled his delay, knocked at the door, and receiving no answer,
gave the alarm" (196). As an unconscious assertion, this suggests
both that the paternal figure himself made the desired advances
before dying and that the son actually survived the trauma innocent
and unharmed; someone else is responsible. Second, Pater provides
an epitaph for the critic that is particularly striking in its seeming
contradiction to the violence of his last appearance. It is, in fact, an
inversion of the famous statement about Michelangelo: "It seemed
as if the gods, in reward for his devotion to them, had given him a
death which, for its swiftness and its opportunity, he might well
have desired" (196). Death, as we have seen, actually cements relationships with the masculine, heavenly authorities. Its "swiftness" is
an infantile image of sexual power. Once again, Pater is resolving
his chief obsession through drama.

The third conclusion to Winckelmann's career provides the most
tangible gratification of all, in terms of his position in *The Renaissance*. His death implies the possibility of close attachments through
history, making Pater himself a potential recipient of his favors as
well as those of other figures in the book. Pater quotes Goethe on
Winckelmann's influence: "He has . . . the advantage of figuring in
the memory of posterity, as one eternally able and strong; for the
image in which one leaves the world is that in which one moves
among the shadows" (196). As Winckelmann died, Goethe, a young
student, awaited his arrival at Leipzig. It is the last of the series
of encounters of young luminaries and their older, less brilliant predecessors in *The Renaissance*, all containing homosexual implications.[34] Since this meeting never took place, Pater can refer to it in
terms of his most intensely cherished fantasies: it is his event to
create.

34. The first instance of this relationship, which I shall not discuss in this
    essay, is in the friendship of Pico della Mirandola and his biographer,
    Ficino.

> Goethe, then in all the pregnancy of his wonderful youth, still unruffled by the "press and storm" of his earlier manhood, was awaiting Winckelmann with a curiosity of the worthiest kind. As it was, Winckelmann became to him something like what Virgil was to Dante. And Winckelmann, with his fiery friendships, had reached that age and that period of culture at which emotions hitherto fitful, sometimes concentrate themselves in a vital, unchangeable relationship. (197)

Ironically, Pater can enjoy such relationships only across history. It remains a matter of speculation whether he ever dared to form homosexual friendships outside literature.[35]

Goethe's role indicates a final quality of the fantasy life in "Winckelmann." His "pregnancy" in this imagined encounter is caused by the "fire" of Winckelmann's friendship, and the erotic character of this term is plain if only from literary tradition. Psychologically, fire symbolizes the erotic gratifications atatched to urethral functions, a source of water which can extinguish fires of many kinds.[36] In this near-meeting, Winckelmann's sexual potency is fantasied on a urethral level of psychic development. Other "births" he causes contain the same implication—as when he "reproduces" the feelings of early Renaissance scholars when "the buried fire of ancient art rose up from under the soil" (184). As a young man, his passion is not "a vague, romantic longing . . . Within its severe limits his enthusiasm burns like lava" (185). These connotations are focused on Goethe in the passage I have quoted, and he responds with a sublimated sexual energy symbolized by the central term of "Leo-

---

35. Ellmann concludes his remark on the seductions of *The Renaissance* for young men by stating that "Pater may not have seduced them in any way except stylistically . . ." (24). George Moore's last words on Pater suggest the same judgment, although he is not addressing the question of homosexuality: "Behind the mask . . . that he did not lift, that he could not lift, was a shy sentimental man, all powerful in written word, impotent in life." *Avowals* (New York, 1926), p. 233. Yet Thomas Wright claims to have identified Pater's homosexual friend, one Richard Jackson. Wright prints poems from Jackson to Pater, discusses their relationship at great length, and even suggests that Jackson's residence at St. Austin's Anglican "monastery" in London inspired Pater's late religious revival. However, there is more evidence to suggest that Wright, rather than Pater, was the lover of Jackson, to whom the biography is dedicated. See Wright, *Life*, II, 21, 38, 41, 45, 90, 142, 271–272.
36. See Freud, "The Acquisition and Control of Fire" (1932), S.E., XXII, 187–193.

nardo da Vinci," "curiosity." His gain from the near-meeting, and from his study of the older critic, is sexual knowledge, for which infantile "curiosity" often stands.

Pater's comments on Goethe indicate that this fantasy encounter had real results. Because of his filial role, Goethe's "culture did not remain 'behind the veil': it ever emerged in the practical functions of art, in actual production" (230). It is for Goethe's sake, after all, that "criticism entertains consideration" of Winckelmann; but as Pater extols Goethe's achievement, it is clear that he is referring to a joint product. The union of Goethe and Winckelmann is, in fact, Pater's most explicit family romance, a genuine marriage:

> Goethe illustrates a union of the Romantic spirit, in its adventure, its variety, its profound subjectivity of soul, with Hellenism, in its transparency, its rationality, its desire of beauty —that marriage of Faust and Helena, of which the art of the nineteenth century is the child, the beautiful lad Euphorion, as Goethe conceives him, on the crags, in the "splendour of battle and in harness as for victory," his brows bound with light. Goethe illustrates, too, the preponderance in this marriage of the Hellenic element; and that element, in its true essence, was made known to him by Winckelmann. (226–227)

This child, "the beautiful lad Euphorion," mirrors the one to emerge unscathed from Winckelmann's murder scene; Pater even says that "Goethe conceives him." Despite that quality of his character which Pater describes as artlike, Winckelmann influences Goethe, in the language of the essay on Pico, as "one alive in the grave" (49), as if he never died at all. This is the central wish of all the fantasies Pater constructs around paternal images. "In Winckelmann, this type comes to him, not as in a book or a theory, but more importunately, because in a passionate life, in a personality" (228). He is, nevertheless, a "type," a "life" in the completed sense of a biography. Goethe's romance, as I have suggested, represents the romance of criticism and history, an affair with the past.

Paradoxically, much of Winckelmann's inspirational value for modern writers like Goethe and Pater derives from the impossible, archaic purity of his views. "His conception of art excludes that bolder type of it which deals confidently and serenely with life, conflict, evil. Living in a world of exquisite but abstract and colour-

214 Psychoanalysis and Literary Process

less form, he could hardly have conceived of the subtle and penetrative, yet somewhat grotesque art of the modern world" (223). Art
criticism, as I have suggested, takes Winckelmann to a "primeval,"
preheterosexual world; for the "conflict" he avoids is simply the
childish image of sex as battle, both "penetrative" and "grotesque."
Pater develops these metaphors, at the end of the essay, into language anticipating the terms of the more famous "Conclusion":

> For us, necessity is not, as of old, a sort of mythological per-
> sonage without us, with whom we can do warfare. It is rather
> a magic web woven through and through us, like that mag-
> netic system of which modern science speaks, penetrating us
> with a network, subtler than our subtlest nerves, yet bearing
> in it the central forces of the world. Can art represent men
> and women in these bewildering toils so as to give the spirit at
> least an equivalent for the sense of freedom? . . . Natural laws
> we shall never modify, embarrass us as they may; but there
> is still something in the nobler or less noble attitude with which
> we watch their fatal combinations. In those romances of
> Goethe and Victor Hugo, in some excellent work done *after*
> them, this entanglement, this network of law, becomes the
> tragic situation, in which certain groups of noble men and
> women work out for themselves a supreme *Dénouement*. Who,
> if he saw through all, would fret against the chain of circum-
> stance which endows one at the end with those great experi-
> ences? (231–232)

It is one of Pater's most magnificent passages, and absolutely central to the meaning of *The Renaissance*. Freedom here becomes a
function of vision; this, finally, is the chief application of criticism
to life.

Although the flowing, slipping, anal imagery of the "Conclusion" is
missing here, the same defense mechanism is operating. Retreat
from a "fatal," heterosexual world of "natural law" involves inter-
nalizing sexual forces to gain control of the "tragic situation."
Hence, in this passage, the "magic web" connecting men to the
dangerous external world is phallic; and the fretting against it,
even if consciously denied, implies the private pleasure of masturbation. As it has been throughout "Winckelmann," touch of this type
is focused in the act of seeing, so that the vision of a traumatic

scene represents a symbolic triumph over its threats. On a conscious level, Pater claims that understanding history, science, and fate keeps men from futile living. Psychologically, as in the "Conclusion," he insists that by focusing all erotic gratifications onto the vision of what we fear in the world, anxiety can be overcome.

As the reference to science in the last lines of the essay promised, Pater uses the "Conclusion" to try to advance some confidence in a relativistic view of the world. The fragment (once attached to an essay on William Morris) is one of his triumphs of allusiveness and compression. It is a psychological triumph as well, and its defensive strategy vis-à-vis science provides a crucial insight into the personal meanings of Pater's historicism. His modern aesthetic creed appropriates the imagery of science—biology particularly, and geology, in the crystalline beauty of the "hard, gemlike flame"— as an intellectual basis for impressionism. The success of this daring fusion is little more than a trick of mimicry, a tour de force of style. In the nineteenth century, science was the principal antagonist of feeling, of the sense of beauty, and of traditional religious faith. History also had contributed to the rising insecurity of the age, especially in Biblical criticism. Against this background, Pater asserts his delight in the disintegrating effect of the new knowledge, making it an object of beauty and fascination: "when reflexion begins to play upon . . . objects they are dissipated under its influence; the cohesive force seems suspended like some trick of magic . . ." (234–235). The entire "Conclusion," especially its opening paragraphs, is filled with instances of Pater's style celebrating uncertainty and decay. His modern "religion of beauty" deliberately identifies with the aggressor which had attacked prior religions so successfully. This is Pater's fundamental defense against the fatal, dissolving world described by science. Using the subjects, vocabularies, and rhythms of science—for Pater imitates random flux with lists and series of parallel clauses—he creates a passionate but fragile stoic language.

"Art for its own sake" (239), the famous phrase for this attitude, brings into play a full range of infantile erotic connotations by the time Pater introduces it. If a new type of psychic pleasure appears in the "Conclusion," it is on the anal level of the flux imagery: "While all melts under our feet, we may well grasp at any exquisite passion . . . With this sense of the splendour of our experience and of its awful brevity, gathering all we are into one desperate effort to see and touch, we shall hardly have time to make theories about the things we see and touch" (237). Here, however, Pater's anal-retentive "gathering" coexists with other levels of infantile pleasure. Indeed, the essay's pattern is to mass erotic images together into a rich display of polymorphous perversity. Pater's flamboyance in the "Conclusion," his exercise in the art of language for its own sake, amounts to a fusion of all levels of psychic response. This is clear in his equation of desires for "any stirring of the senses, strange dyes, strange colours, and curious odours, or work of the artist's hands, or the face of one's friend" (237). Pater's most famous image, burning with "a hard, gemlike flame," dovetails urethral, anal, and phallic pleasures; it incorporates all the psychic connotations of science, ritual, and, of course, art, which we have seen elsewhere in the book. In this sense, by defining art for art's sake, it embodies Pater's desire to "conclude" the book, to sum up *The Renaissance*.

Another phrase, less famous, serves the same function in a subtler way. It is the Latin caption to "Winckelmann," which Pater added when he adapted the essay for *The Renaissance*. When he removed the "Conclusion" from the second edition, the Latin heading seemed to stand as a caption for the entire volume: "Et ego in Arcadia fui." It draws together the conscious and unconscious themes of the book, but for this essay it has more specific relevance. Erwin Panofsky explains that its original Latin form, "Et in Arcadia ego," was defined by an "insular" English tradition well-known in literary circles.[37] Even George III understood Sir Joshua Reynolds' reference to it in a conventional portrait. "He saw it yesterday and said at once: 'Oh, there is a tombstone in the background: Ay, ay, death is even in Arcadia.'"[38] The phrase, then, is a *memento mori*. Pater would have known this connotation through Reynolds and the "insular" tradition, but also through his connection with a group revolting from established art and from Reynolds' influence, namely, the Pre-Raphaelite Brotherhood. One of the central sources of their knowledge of Italian primitive art was Pisa's Campo Santo, which contains a *memento mori* fresco on "The Three Quick and the Three Dead" by Guercino, whom Panofsky places at the focus of the sober, early-Renaissance treatment of this theme.[39]

37. "Et in Arcadia Ego: Poussin and the Elegiac Tradition," in *Meaning in the Visual Arts* (New York, 1955), pp. 310–311.
38. Panofsky, p. 295.
39. Panofsky, pp. 304–310.

The phrase is also used nostalgically, with Arcadia as the ideal past from which mankind originates: "I too have been there." Such a reading is familiar from Vergil, an explicit image of Winckelmann in the essay. Pater's treatment of Hellenic Greece and Renaissance history repeatedly invokes this longing. Particularly in "Winckelmann," he suggests that humanity has been cut off from roots in Paradise. I have quoted earlier Winckelmann's praise for the kissing contests held by the King of Arcadia, which Pater takes as a symbol of the Greek ideal. Arcadia, then, is for Pater an image of the world before repression.

After referring to Winckelmann's remark, Pater openly considers the value of his yearning for the past:

> A perfect world, if the gods could have seemed for ever only fleet and fair, white and red! Let us not regret that this unperplexed youth of humanity, satisfied with the vision of itself, passed, at the due moment, into a mournful maturity; for already the deep joy was in store for the spirit, of finding the ideal of that youth still red with life in the grave. (209)

Arcadia, here, becomes doubly valuable precisely because death has entered there. As a rediscovered Eden, it provides the modern consolation Pater values so highly. Pater defines this value with imagery combining suggestions of death and birth (a "youth still red with life"); and this blend, which we have observed elsewhere, indicates the final, psychological meaning to the "deep joy" of rescuing a lost past. Freud explains the constellation of fantasies involved in the wish to rescue in terms of the child's sense that birth itself is a traumatic event. His feeling that his mother has rescued him from its terrifying dangers leads to a reciprocal desire to rescue her, or both parents, in repayment.[40] Arcadia's implicit fusion of death and life thus becomes a symbol of the critic's task in *The Renaissance*.

Pater combines the two meanings of the Latin phrase in another way. His caption, in fact, is a quotation from Goethe referring to one of the most obvious similarities between himself and Winckelmann. Goethe is describing his Roman journey; like Winckelmann, he visited the Arcadia of art history. "I, too," he announces, "was

40. Freud, "Special Type," p. 173.

in the land of joy and beauty." [41] Pater stresses this implication of the caption and dramatizes its distinction from the English sense of its meaning by putting into Latin Goethe's mistranslation of the original phrase. "Et in Arcadia ego," meaning "Even in Arcady I hold sway," [42] becomes "Et ego in Arcadia fui," in other words, "I, too, was in Arcady." The double meaning gives the final definition to Pater's narration of Winckelmann's southern journey and return, indeed to the journey into the past implied by *The Renaissance* as a whole. The beauty of imaginative paradises is circumscribed. The transformation of a consciousness of fatality into a blissful vision is possible only in retrospect—hence, *fui*. Journey itself is artificial, limited, based on a fundamental denial. But it is also liberating, implying relaxation of repression and access to buried unconscious material. Through a brief return to the past a modern observer can give it shape and meaning. In psychological terms, history provides the occasion for a regression in the service of the ego. Pater's caption implies both possibilities, and combines them with an implied admission, as stoic as the tone of his "Conclusion": Even from Arcadia there must be a return.

41. Quoted by Panofsky, p. 319.
42. Panofsky, pp. 304–311.

SIX ~ BETWEEN FANTASY AND IMAGINATION

A *Psychological Exploration of* Cymbeline

MURRAY M. SCHWARTZ

*Virtutis est domare quae
cuncti pavent.*—SENECA

In his introduction to the Arden edition, J. M. Nosworthy observes
that "*Cymbeline* has evoked relatively little critical comment, and
no completely satisfactory account of the play's quality and significance can be said to exist."[1] Although this statement comes as no
surprise to students of this uneven and perplexing play, it does point
up the fact that *Cymbeline* reveals few obvious clues to those who
would derive its meaning from intrinsic relationships. Existing criticism simply leaves too much out of account in its attempts to find
a "way in" capable of coordinating the play's pervasive indirection,
its lack of coherent atmosphere, its manifold strategies for controlling and directing an audience's energies. Nosworthy's own introduction demonstrates the inadequacy of measuring the play against
traditional romance categories, since he is first forced to conclude
that *Cymbeline* will not conform to the mold and then ends up
evoking transcendental visions beyond the range of his measuring

1. London, 1955, p. xli.

rods. On the other hand, appeals to Shakespeare's apparent external interests in a new theater or in new public demands diminish the significance of *Cymbeline*'s frequently violent verse and its obsession with sexuality, chastity, and family bonds.[2]

Most critics (not content, as Johnson was, to dismiss the play as "unresisting imbecility"[3]) agree that the play experiments in some sense with conventional romance and tragicomic forms. But this approach often reduces *Cymbeline*'s specific preoccupations to Shakespeare's relations with available dramatic modes of communication and expression. The Jacobean theater was a public institution through which Shakespeare transformed intensely individual obsessions into culturally accessible modes of questioning and resolution. He never experiments for superficial or abstract reasons, and he always experiments *within* traditional forms, not only *with* them. A play as unevenly committed to the high evaluation of its central characters, as uneven in tone, and as structurally complex as *Cymbeline* calls for criticism psychologically sophisticated enough to disclose precise relationships among its parts and to account for the particularity of its imagery and metaphors. The nature of the experiment is inseparable from the play's manifest events and their unconscious as well as conscious significance.

What kinds of events does *Cymbeline* involve? Shakespeare activates a range of characteristic threats to sexual, familial, and national integrity in an attempt to resecure these corresponding orders. These levels of ordered relationships mirror one another, sexual and familial integrity being essential to British self-esteem in the play. The play releases dangers in order to pattern them; it self-consciously affirms the hierarchic boundaries designed to master threats which traditional roles generate.

At the end of Act II, scene i, after Iachimo has made his way into the court and Cloten has publicly displayed his licensed egotism, the anonymous Second Lord stands alone on the stage and shares this choral comment with the audience:

> Alas poor princess,
> Thou divine Imogen, what thou endur'st,
> Betwixt a father by thy step-dame govern'd,

---

2. Shakespeare's relation to a new theater is discussed by G. E. Bentley in "Shakespeare and the Blackfriars Theatre," *Shakespeare Survey*, I (1948), 38–50.
3. *General Observations on the Plays of Shakespeare* (1756).

A mother hourly coining plots, a wooer
More hateful than the foul expulsion is
Of thy dear husband, than that horrid act
Of the divorce, he'ld make. The heavens hold firm
The walls of thy dear honour, keep unshak'd
That temple, thy fair mind, that thou mayst stand,
T' enjoy thy banish'd lord and this great land! (II.i. 58–67) [4]

The speech moves from lament to prayer, from threats directed at Imogen's sacred virtue to the wish for secure defense against pervasive enemies. From the top of its hierarchic structure the court jeopardizes the sacramental status of Imogen's identity. The action of *Cymbeline* validates this microcosmic description. In this paranoiac world the Senecan (and Biblical) metaphor of the besieged temple crystallizes Imogen's symbolic position. *Cymbeline* is largely about a dissociated world brought back to rooted stability by the elimination of threatening forces.

The Second Lord's speech gives one sign of this dissociation, not only in its content but also in the fact that a minor character provides one of the play's few summary statements. No Enobarbus reflects normative response in *Cymbeline*. The play tends to resolve itself into its elements, like a dream in the process of what Freud called secondary elaboration. That is to say, we feel that latent ideas shape manifest events, but our sense of the relationship between manifest event and thematic continuity becomes hazy and precarious. It is as if we were perceiving the action through the ego of Leontes in the first acts of *The Winter's Tale*. *Cymbeline* projects a paranoiac vision of events almost completely *from within*, whereas *The Winter's Tale* recreates paranoia from within *and* from without by containing the disease almost completely in the character of Leontes. One thing which makes the play so difficult, if not impossible, to read coherently is that the preoccupations of the individual characters spread throughout the imagery without undergoing that transformation into meaningful statements that usually characterizes Shakespeare's iterative imagery. The play itself suffers from the dislocations it is about.

Cymbeline is structured by a web of confusions between inner and outer reality, as Shakespeare shuffles relationships to bring psychological and social defenses into traditional order. The most di-

---

4. Quotations from *Cymbeline* follow the Arden edition.

rectly corrosive threats to the moral continuity of the fragmented court and to Imogen's personal integrity emanate from the designs Cloten is permitted to fabricate. His role gathers to a head perverse insistence on individual right based on the power of birth and social standing. As a focal point of deranged values he can be seen as a touchstone for the play's sexual and social anxieties.

Cloten's first appearance signals his sacrificial role:

> *First Lord.* Sir, I would advise you to shift a shirt; the violence of action hath made you reek as a sacrifice . . . (I.iii. 1–2)

G. Wilson Knight says, "Cloten is a boastful fool: his name suggests clot-pole." [5] But Cloten is more than a conventional fool; he is also cast as a prince, granted access to courtly models of action, made to distort royal decorum to the shape of his special preoccupations in ways more inflatedly dangerous than those of previous Shakespearean fools. His wishes are violent: "Would there had been some hurt done!" (I.iii. 33). He represents in blunt and unabashed form the deepest hypocrisy, the bold and totally unexamined assertion of social privilege. Snobbish and boorish, he advertises moral vacuity and imaginative emptiness: "When a gentleman is dispos'd to swear, it is not for any standers-by to curtail his oaths" (II.i. 11–12). He attempts to solicit the cooperation of others on the assumption that they share his deep perversion.

"Separation of feeling from function," writes C. L. Barber, "is at the root of perversity and lust." [6] In Cloten we feel absolutely no residual reality: he *is* his roles. He provides the play with a parody of aristocratic decorum, a slashing critique of aristocratic degeneracy, a revelation of sexual rawness and narcissistic libido, a palpable sense of rottenness. He literally smells. He is unadulterable phallic aggression: ". . . I must go up and down like a cock, that nobody can match" (II.i. 23–24). The unconscious motives by which a degenerate aristocracy defines itself are brought to the surface in him: "it is fit I should commit offence to my inferiors" (II.i. 30–31). For him Imogen is pure acquisition, a thing to be possessed, an object for the release of phallic libido.

Cloten's imagery reduces sexuality to its bodily effects by lowering metaphors to their physical origins. The rhetorical technique is called *meiosis*, "whereby one makes a thing appear less than it is by putting

5. *The Crown of Life* (London, 1947), p. 132.
6. *Shakespeare's Festive Comedy* (Cleveland, 1963), p. 24.

a less thing for a greater."[7] In Act II, scene iii he is made deliberately disgusting, too crudely obvious to be comic. To the musi-
cians he says, "if you can penetrate her with your fingering, so: we'll
try with tongue too . . ." (14–15). Nor is this barely clothed sexual
drive confined to absurd attempts on Imogen's body; the same scene
announces the arrival of Caius Lucius, and III.i finds him using
the same sexual fixations to justify political circumscription and
defiance of Caesar's authority. "Britain's a world by itself, and we
will nothing pay for wearing our own noses" (III.i. 13–14). In
these two lines he brings together the play's dominant images of eco-
nomics and clothing. The nose obviously here assumes a phallic significance, displaced upward, and Cloten imagines it as detachable.[8]
It can display a reality independent of its current owner. In the
archaic logic of the unconscious, Cloten represents isolated, detached, and uncontrolled phallic wishes that seek their objects re-
lentlessly and without the least regard for otherness. These drives
toward sexual gratification resist any inhibition of their aims and
view the procedures of courtship merely as roadblocks on the way
to release. "I will pursue her," he says, "even to Augustus' throne"
(III.v. 101–102).

Cloten operates within a closed system of obsessional thinking;
his logic can never wrench free of the underlying aim he symbolizes.
Determined by the categories of quantitative loss and gain, he
becomes a grotesque parody of the courtly lover's *odi et amo*,
grotesque because of its excessive "rationality" and mechanical logic:

> I love, and hate her: for she's fair and royal,
> And that she hath all courtly parts more exquisite
> Than lady, ladies, woman, from every one
> The best she hath, and she of all compounded
> Outsells them all. I love her therefore, but
> Disdaining me, and throwing favours on
> The low Posthumus, slanders so her judgement
> That what's else rare is chok'd: and in that point
> I will conclude to hate her, nay indeed,
> To be reveng'd upon her. For, when fools
> Shall—   (III.v. 71–81)

7. Sister Miriam Joseph, *Rhetoric in Shakespeare's Time* (New York, 1947),
   p. 331.
8. See Eric Partridge, *Shakespeare's Bawdy* (New York, 1960), entries under
   "nose" and "nose-painting" for confirmation of this symbolism.

Imogen becomes a collection of attributes, "parts," a piece of merchandise which is either narcissistically had or paranoiacally rejected, possessed or contaminated. In this view Cloten presents us with the extreme of a condition present in Cymbeline, Posthumus, and even the lost sons. A central issue of the play crystallizes in Cloten: Who shall possess Imogen? To whom does she belong? For Cloten, love denied transmutes itself inexorably into the wish for revenge. Love becomes narcissism when gratification is assimilated to possession.

Cloten moves from "love" to revenge with a closed logic at once laughable and frightening, and only ceases because he is interrupted, cut off in mid-speech. Words themselves represent a manic form of potency for him. Shakespeare projects in Cloten the obsessional, mechanical, unidirectional aspect of sexual drives. Detached from a pattern of civilized defenses, they act like an automatic, autonomous being, gravitating to itself infantile notions of magic and omnipotence and projecting the sanction for its actions outside itself. Cloten appeals to the absolute authority of his mother (IV.i. 22–24) to justify his pursuit of Imogen and attempts to gain the support of Pisanio by assuming that the drive for power over others is universal and psychologically determined. He "thinks" on a level at which all responses are determined by undiluted instincts:

> How fit his garments serve me! Why should his mistress who was made by him that made the tailor, not be fit too? The rather (saving reverence of the word) for 'tis said a woman's fitness comes by fits. (IV.i. 2–7)

Bad puns, and Shakespeare knew it, but Shakespeare also knew that bad puns express a real psychology, as Leontes' jealousy proves. Bad puns form the free associations of the obsessional character; they are the capital in the economy of the lust-ridden demon. Cloten's language capitalizes on the power of words to clothe the confusion of wish and reality. He rides the pun down the stream of his associations to the center of his interest.

Four further aspects of Cloten's nature and function deserve our recognition. First, this "arrogant piece of flesh" (IV.ii. 127) is continually associated with dirt and excretory functions and with their sublimated counterpart, money. Words like "reek," "rot," "vent," "backside," "ass," "smell," "offense," "coining," "gold," "purse" surround him like flies or like the "south-fog" he wishes on the Romans. Gold, for Cloten, retains the magical powers of infantile feces: "what/Can it not do, and undo?" (II.iii. 73–74) [9] Anal aggression is here in the service of genital functions. Cloten embodies the belief that sexuality defiles its object and drags chastity through the mire. Shakespeare has concentrated in him the usually repressed aspects of the orderly, excessively rational, and clean personality. Second, his defensive stupidity perfectly complements his aggressive arrogance: he simply cannot comprehend any statement which accurately identifies his nature. When Imogen compares him to Posthumus' "mean'st garment" (II.iii. 134) he stands entranced by the suggestion, as if it were beyond imagination. We recall Lucio's reference in *Measure for Measure* to the "rebellion of a codpiece" (III.ii. 111), an appropriate description of Cloten.[10] Third, Cloten's intimate link with his mother's designs associates his perversions with dependence on a "bad" woman. The infant's feeling of absolute independence is based on the fact of absolute dependence. This psychoanalytic paradox accounts for the fact that Cloten and the Queen function as one unit in the play; with Cloten dead the Queen dies. The lurid connection receives marked emphasis in Guiderius' disposal of Cloten's head:

> I have sent Cloten's clotpoll down the stream,
> In embassy to his mother . . . (IV.ii. 184–185)

It is only after Cloten's power has been cut off that the Queen languishes in disease and the drama turns toward resolution of con-

9. See Otto Fenichel, *The Psychoanalytic Theory of Neurosis* (New York, 1945), pp. 281, 427–436, for a summary of psychoanalytic thought on this theme. See also Freud, "Character and Anal Erotism" (1908) in *The Standard Edition of the Complete Psychological Works of Sigmund Freud*, ed. James Strachey, *et al.* (hereafter abbreviated S.E.), 24 vols. (London, 1953–1966), IX, 169–175. Karl Abraham supplemented the connection between feces and money in "Contributions to the Theory of the Anal Character," in *Selected Papers on Psycho-Analysis* (New York, 1953). Doing and undoing is a characteristic defense in obsessional neurosis. See Anna Freud, *The Ego and the Mechanisms of Defense* (New York, 1966), p. 34. Fenichel (p. 155) remarks on "the fact that the mechanism of undoing is so often applied in conflicts around anal erotism." Cloten represents an example of what Freud called "regressive deteriorization of the genital function." "On Transformations of Instinct as Exemplified in Anal Erotism" (1917), S.E., XVII, 127–133.
10. I am indebted to Miss Margaret Darby for this suggestion.

flict and submission to authority, divine and human. Finally, this personification of infantile fixations stands at the right hand of the King, speaking for Cymbeline in defense of national honor and against the authority of Caesar. While the Queen and Cloten exist, the play is webbed with confusions of role and identity, and patriarchal family structure is rendered powerless to reform itself.

What is Cloten's significance in the play? The very fact that sexual drives are isolated and split off from a whole personality indicates that Shakespeare has embodied a deep-rooted ambivalence in *Cymbeline*. On the one hand we have the notion of chastity and married love and on the other we have the grim reality of unrestrained sexual energy. Under no circumstances must the "arrogant piece of flesh" be permitted to penetrate the temple of Imogen's chastity. Cloten acts out the problematical reality of sexual drives wherever they appear in unsublimated forms. The "arrogant piece of flesh" must literally be killed (symbolically castrated) before Imogen and Cloten's body in Posthumus' clothes can be brought together in the pastoral landscape of Wales. Shakespeare is not merely making use of a conventional Elizabethan version of ambivalence toward women in *Cymbeline;* he is making use of dramatic conventions to structure an ambivalence which ran deeper in him than in any other dramatist except Marston, who had little of Shakespeare's plastic ability to transform his obsessions into resilient forms.[11] The fool Cloten *contains* feared wishes, isolates one side of this personal and cultural ambivalence: "Sex is dirty. Man violates woman in the sex act. Therefore he must be punished by castration." As we shall see, this pattern of motives accounts for more than the fate of Cloten in the play.

The devil takes many shapes. Cloten's versions of violation sustain no concepts of beauty or dignity, but the same wishes that compel him can ramify into more engaging forms of perversion. In the character of Iachimo Shakespeare offers a professional violator as subtle as Cloten is crude. The difference between them is one of technique rather than intention. Compulsive intention to dis-

11. See Louis B. Wright, *Middle-Class Culture in Elizabethan England* (Chapel Hill, 1935), pp. 465–507, for a summary of material on "The Popular Controversy over Women." Evidence for this ambivalence is pervasive in Elizabethan and Jacobean drama. The other side of idealization is summarized by Vindice in Tourneur's *The Revenger's Tragedy:* "Wives are but made to go to bed and feed."

integrate binds them in the play's movement from negation to affirmation, but Iachimo broadens the circle of perverse possibilities. Since for both of them morality collapses into strategies for sexual possession, we can make our way through Iachimo to the character of Posthumus.

When we first encounter Iachimo he is talking about Posthumus. His first speech is worth noting for two reasons: he neatly separates Posthumus' personality from "the catalogue of his endowments . . . tabled by his side" (I.v. 5–6), separates the man from his moral qualities as if these virtues were but so many labels. He emphasizes the sense of sight: "But I could then have look'd on him without the help of admiration . . ." (I.v. 4). Before long we too will look on Posthumus without the help of admiration. Iachimo immediately focuses on the discrepancy between inner and outer, appearance and reality, so predominant in the play. Before Posthumus enters the Roman scene, Iachimo has already articulated his favorite metaphor in suggestive terms:

> Ay, and the approbation of those that weep this lamentable divorce under her colours are wonderfully to extend him; be it but to fortify her judgement, which else an easy battery might lay flat, for taking a beggar without less quality.
>
> (I.v. 19–23)

The metaphor of war is pregnant with prefigural meaning in both the national and wager plots. It is Iachimo who will "fortify her judgement" (and our judgment of Imogen) as he attempts to besiege and "lay flat" her sexual integrity. His metaphorical links between love and war feed on conventional associations to prepare us for the play's later displacement of aggression to military conflict, but they also work the other way, to libidinize heroic conflict. Iachimo's psyche (the psyche we fantasize when we hear him) is obsessed with sexual fantasy. His preoccupation with "the dearest bodily part" (I.v. 154–155) of women orbits his language around romantic imaginings of sexual encounters, providing an Elizabethan audience with vicarious participation in forbidden acts and wishes under the guise of Italianate evil and depravity.

Iachimo is Cloten in civilized dress. Driven by the logic of his fantasies to indulge erotic wishes, he sees the world's events *only* as occasions for the elaboration of tales. Verbal action replaces Cloten's physical reductive literalizations, so that through him Shakespeare projects sexual desire in a sublimated form. Instead of witnessing attempted actions, we are made to look through his eyes at a distorted and symbolic representation of sex. By projecting sexual fantasies in the character of Iachimo, Shakespeare provides a built-in set of defenses; the fantasies will be verbalized and not acted out, and the convention of Italianizing evil will provide moral distance and condemnation as it simultaneously provides distanced participation. Hence, Iachimo will be permitted to enter the bedchamber at which Cloten vainly knocks and will carry away with him a wealth of symbolic detail with which to weave the words of his deceptions on his overwilling victim.

Iachimo's imagery and metaphors employ the device of *auxesis*,[12] an amplification or hyperbolic enlargement of significance. He ritualizes and mythologizes sexual encounters. When he first faces Imogen, after a greeting of general as well as particular meaning, "Change you, madam," (I.vii. 11), he speaks at his characteristic level:

> [*Aside*] All of her that is out of door most rich!
>   If she be furnish'd with a mind so rare,
>   She is alone th' Arabian bird; and I
>   Have lost the wager. Boldness be my friend!
>   Arm me, Audacity, from head to foot,
>   Or like the Parthian I shall flying fight;
>   Rather, directly fly.   (I.vii. 15–21)

One need not remember the psychoanalytic discovery that flying in dreams represents sexual arousal to perceive Iachimo's erotic elation at merely looking at Imogen. He imagines his whole body erect and powerful, ready to engage in the supreme battle. The Arabian bird indicates to him a nature so purely sublimated that it no longer needs sex to reproduce itself, and therefore becomes his only imaginable obstacle. Mythological references cluster in the scenes of his presence; he calls up the world of Ovidian erotic poetry which the Elizabethans usually indulged under heavy moral trappings. Iachimo's Ovidian banquets of sense reflect the scoptophilia of a sensibility whose ambivalence toward the sense of touch seeks compensatory pleasure in the eroticization of the sense of sight.

12. Joseph, *Rhetoric*, p. 331.

Later in Act I, scene vii, Iachimo conjures up a vision of Posthumus' life in Rome calculated simultaneously to activate and to
condemn forbidden wishes. His speech is worth quoting in full,
because the form in which he tells a tale is as important as the tale
itself:

> Had I this cheek
> To bathe my lips upon: this hand, whose touch
> (Whose every touch) would force the feeler's soul
> To th' oath of loyalty: this object, which
> Takes prisoner the wild motion of mine eye,
> Firing it only here; should I (damn'd then)
> Slaver with lips as common as the stairs
> That mount the Capitol: join gripes, with hands
> Made hard with hourly falsehood (falsehood, as
> With labour): then by-peeping in an eye
> Base and illustrous as the smoky light
> That's fed with stinking tallow: it were fit
> That all the plagues of hell should at one time
> Encounter such revolt.   (I.vii. 99–112)

The speech breaks into two parts; first there is the attraction of
Imogen, then there is the degraded sex with common whores attributed to Posthumus. The first part fantasizes oral gratification
and erotic sight, the second changes "bathe" to "slaver" (with its
incorporated pun on "slave" corresponding to the previous use of
"prisoner"), substitutes mounting for looking, and makes feeding an
affair of disgust entailing all the punishments of hell. Iachimo's
narcissistic identification with each element of the fantasy ("Had I,"
"Should I") conjures a coherent structure of interpenetrating opposites; for every hallucinatory indulgence there is a more than
adequate punishment. Iachimo is a connoisseur of the repressed content of the overcivilized psyche which views direct genital expression as revolting and unconsciously cherishes the wish for oral fusion
above all others. Woman's labor becomes the labor of whores, the
hand that caresses becomes associated with erection and the interlocked genitals, genital sex becomes an exhibition surrounded by
dirt. The speech is a polymorphous confusion of pregenital sexuality.
Iachimo's ambiguous "damn'd then" can refer either to what came
before or what comes after. He allows us to view sexual scenes

through the distorting lens of the condemning conscience. In this, and in the contortions of syntax his vision involves, Iachimo presents in concentrated form what Shakespeare presents writ large in a number of *Cymbeline*'s scenes.

Iachimo's power, aside from the autistic gratification to which his unrepressed imagination gives rise (speeches like the above are literary masturbation fantasies), depends largely on the receptivity of his audience. His direct verbal assault succeeds only in shutting Imogen's ears, and he is forced to resort to the device of the trunk (which, incidentally, Shakespeare makes Imogen volunteer to place in her bedchamber in ironic accommodation of the convention). He succeeds in undermining the less fortified ego of Posthumus when the power to resist the encroachment of unconscious fantasies into consciousness breaks down, and repressed sexuality returns in horrifying forms. Before we turn to Posthumus, however, we should acknowledge the strange transformation Iachimo seems to undergo in the last act.

The besieger of Imogen's temple returns in Act V, scene ii, as a besieger of Britain and is disarmed by the penitent Posthumus in the dumbshow of battle. This gesture partially indicates the nature of his role in the play. Iachimo is an aspect or projection of Posthumus' psyche, that part of him which returns from its repressed status, enters Britain after his banishment, seduces Imogen *in fantasy*, and thereby gains dominant control of his personality at the expense of the restraints of conscience. This is not to say that Iachimo is not also an autonomous character in the play. *Cymbeline*, like all works of art, is overdetermined. Characters can function in many ways simultaneously, as allegorizations of ideas or attitudes (as do humor characters), or as fully rounded personalities (as Hamlet appears to an audience), or as both.

Because Iachimo's assault on Imogen is distanced by being enacted in words, he remains alive, unlike Cloten, whose unmediated aggression calls for the worst of punishments. In the final scene Iachimo is free to reimagine his obsessive dreams before the eyes of the King. ("I stand on fire. Come to the matter," says Cymbeline [V.v. 168–169].) Since the moral defenses against erotic wishes have by then been reinstituted, his story is longer and more obviously an elaborate fairy tale. "Upon a time . . . ," he begins, and spins a tale laden with vicarious gratification, until he is cut off by Posthumus. Just as Cloten could go on forever were he not

literally cut off, Iachimo descends so fully into his imaginative out-
pouring that the very characters seem to come alive. By isolating his
recapitulatory fantasy Shakespeare makes the larger fantasy which is
occurring on the stage seem all the more real by contrast. Iachimo's
retelling also functions within the defensive strategy of the final
reevaluation, because it allows him to edit the play's previous action
in the direction of diminishing Posthumus' responsibility. This re-
editing of the earlier action is the dramatic equivalent of negation.

For both Cloten and Iachimo chastity exists to be violated. They
represent two related obsessions of a Renaissance personality bur-
dened with the idealization and worship of women and seeking to
establish a stable relationship between platonic sublimation and
crude sexual expression. In the one we see a representation of unde-
ferred sexual drives imagined as a moral void, presocial and un-
educable; in the other Shakespeare projects a more complex, socially
viable manifestation of erotic conflict, combining displacement of
sexual drives to speaking and looking with expressions of negative
judgment. In Posthumus we witness a tense and precariously balanced combination of the two. Cloten and Iachimo indicate alternative modes of expression toward which Posthumus' character tends.
By following Posthumus carefully through the play, we can identify
the dreamlike logic which underlies its sometimes confusing, over-
sophisticated surface. The techniques of dreams—displacement, condensation, substitution, multiple symbolism—are also the play's dominant dramatic techniques.

The opening scene presents Posthumus' credentials for nobility
of spirit with open-ended ambiguity; phrases of unspecified reference generate curious suggestions of hidden malady. First we have
a contrast between Cloten and Posthumus:

> He that hath miss'd the princess is a thing
> Too bad for bad report: and he that hath her
> (I mean, that married her, alack good man,
> And therefore banish'd) is a creature such
> As, to seek through the regions of the earth
> For one his like; there would be something failing
> In him that should compare.   (I.i. 16–22)

The "thingness" of Cloten is balanced, not by direct expression of
nobility or virtue, but by the tortured expression of incomparability.

Posthumus is a "creature" who "hath her," and the immediate quali-
fication, "I mean, that married her," suggests that the marriage remains unconsummated. Words of intimacy and banishment or pain
enter the play's language as if linked by a special bond. The fourth
through seventh lines communicate two contradictory messages:
(1) no other man can measure up to Posthumus; (2) another man
comparable to Posthumus would have "something failing." Like so
much of the play's verse, the lines shun direct expression in favor
of elliptical hinting.

The Gentleman then extends the ambiguity in a deliberate gen-
eralization of the condition described:

> I do not think
> So fair an outward, and such stuff within
> Endows a man, but he. (I.i. 22–24)

The construction of the lines, the way they withhold specific reference until the last moment, marks a recurrent feature of *Cymbeline's*
verse. The contrast between appearance and reality, "fair outward"
and "stuff within," is prefaced by "I do not think," casting a further
oblique doubt on Posthumus' integrity. A few lines later we are told
that there is something inarticulable about Posthumus, again in unspecified terms: "I cannot delve him to the root" (I.i. 28). Delving to
the root is more than an agricultural image, once we remember
Elizabethan associations of plants and bodily parts, yet here its
erotic overtone serves no contextual purpose. The Gentleman simply
means to say that Posthumus' personality cannot be fully explicated.
A few lines before he said:

> I do extend him, sir, within himself,
> Crush him together, rather than unfold
> His measure duly. (I.i. 25–27)

This may be an unconscious image of erection followed by an unconscious punishment. The accumulation of phrases unanchored in
dramatic action tends to activate uncontrolled associations in the
minds of the audience, associations which may later find justification on the stage. As Robert Rogers has shown, such images can
profitably be studied as "microdramas," enactments in detail of the

play's larger unconscious concerns.[13] When successful, these micro-dramas fuse primary-process images (bodily associations) with the play's secondary process, discursive meaning. In *Cymbeline* the fusion is incomplete. The above lines activate unconscious images in a way that seems to baffle the conscious mind.

After these vague suggestions of disproportionate correspondence between inner and outer, Posthumus' lineage is presented. Sicilius, his father, had his martial power and nobility confirmed in the name "Leonatus," which Posthumus inherits. His two brothers died "with their swords in hand" (I.i. 36), indicating that their lives were devoted to the service of the state. Their father, "fond of issue" (I.i. 37),[14] died of grief. Posthumus' mother died as he was born. Deprived of parents and brothers, he finds a protector in the King, who has also lost two sons and a wife. The parallel is too clear to be overlooked. Sicilius and Cymbeline are identified by their pasts. Posthumus' relation to Cymbeline is that of son to parents, both parents, for Cymbeline "Breeds him, and makes him of his bed-chamber" (I.i. 42). It is a remarkable exercise in condensation, for the parallel between Cymbeline and Sicilius creates common parentage for Posthumus and Imogen without the charge of incest accompanying the marriage. In psychological terms, the absence of real parents corresponds to the shaky status of Posthumus' internal parents, the superego, and this in turn corresponds to the morally weak external father of the play, Cymbeline. Shakespeare takes great pains to restore the father-authorities, Caesar, Jupiter, Cymbeline, to active beneficent power at the end of the play. The restoration of external fathers accompanies the restoration of internal control of conscience in Posthumus.

Posthumus' virtue is not directly located within himself; his name and nobility are conferred by his past and by the fact that Imogen has chosen him. Like Antony's and Timon's, Posthumus' self-esteem depends on large doses of external confirmation. Deprived of external confirmation of their identities, all three succumb to regressive forces within.

13. The paper, entitled "The Psycho-Dynamics of Metaphor," is unpublished. It was delivered before the Group for the Psychological Study of Literature in Buffalo in the spring of 1968.
14. "Fond," meaning "foolish," seems to cast doubt on the father's integrity, as if Shakespeare were playing with his own reverence.

In the departure scene (I.ii) Posthumus reveals an inner assent to the forces of separation. His banishment objectifies a distance that is already manifest between him and Imogen, in spite of their exchange of symbolic gifts. His only gesture of physical intimacy is to place a bracelet on her arm. He is self-conscious about his manhood:

> My queen, my mistress:
> O lady, weep no more, lest I give cause
> To be suspected of more tenderness
> Than doth become a man.   (I.ii. 23–26)

"Tenderness" and manhood are placed in inverse relation to each other; as one increases the other becomes threatened. Renaissance identities were more sensitive than we are to degrees of social tact in close relationships. Imogen's tears soften Posthumus, and his response resists their power while admitting their potential for evoking sympathetic resonance in him. Yet in the eyes of the paranoiac King, Posthumus' tenderness has already far exceeded the limit, making his concern with the judgment of others sharply reflect an *inner* condition, a fear of physical intimacy. The juxtaposition of "queen" and "mistress" rings odd, since the Queen enters and exits throughout the scene, and she is not lovable.

Too close an identification of wife and mother can result in violent ambivalence toward sexuality.[15] On the one hand Posthumus needs to be reprimanded for his haste to depart *before* the gifts are exchanged, and on the other hand he expresses "loathness to depart" (I.ii. 39) at precisely the same moment. When he gives the bracelet, his words express more than conventional meaning:

> For my sake wear this,
> It is a manacle of love, I'll place it
> Upon this fairest prisoner.   (I.ii. 52–54)

The gift imposes an identity upon the giver as well as the receiver. His metaphor reveals an unconscious holding-on too tightly, an excessive dependence. Without her he is nothing, with her he is every-

15. See Freud, "On the Universal Tendency to Debasement in the Sphere of Love" (1912), *S.E.*, XI, 179–190.

thing. It is the relationship of child and mother (Imogen's ring belonged to her mother), not the relationship of mature love, and its roots lie in oral dependence:

> And with mine eyes I'll drink the words you send,
> Though ink be made of gall.   (I.ii. 31–32)

Drinking with eyes, which is what Iachimo does, for all its conventionality as a metaphor, here expresses the nature of a particular kind of love; it is the expression of an unconscious passivity experienced from an adult point of view. Hence the association of oral gratification and poisoning.

Posthumus' words contradict his actions because an unconscious need for total sustenance conflicts with the conscious expression of mutual love. What we witness in the departure scene is the first exposure of the confusion between queen and mistress, mother and wife. It is this confusion which will account, in psychological terms, for Posthumus' later behavior.

Before the scene ends, we get another significant instance of Posthumus' condition. Pisanio reports that Posthumus has been attacked by Cloten and violence only avoided because "my master rather play'd than fought" (I.ii. 93). Again, Posthumus takes the passive role, restraining his masculinity when threatened. Imogen responds with self-assured control:

> I would they were in Afric both together,
> Myself by with a needle, that I might prick
> The goer-back.   (I.ii. 98–100)

Posthumus will not actively use his sword until the last act, when he disarms Iachimo. Between the departure scene and that moment of self-possessed aggression, Shakespeare explores his complex motives with consistently revealing insight.

We have seen that Posthumus' actions in the departure scene indicate an inner prohibition against direct expression of physical intimacy. There is no middle ground between idolatry and Cloten's phallic aggression. This inner tyranny corresponds to the King's outer tyranny. Cymbeline too would "pen her up" (I.ii. 84). To Imogen's contrast of Posthumus and Cloten, "I chose an eagle,/And did avoid a puttock" (I.ii. 70–71), Cymbeline replies, "Thou took'st a beggar, wouldst have made my throne/A seat for baseness" (I.ii. 72–73). To keep the throne from contamination Imogen's purity must be isolated, fortified against the touch of defiling sexuality. With respect to Posthumus, Cymbeline represents the tyranny of the superego which, because sex is considered dirty, would split the psyche into diametric opposites, one part that worships and another that defiles.

It is precisely of this split that Imogen reminds us at the end of Act I. She tells us that the King's intervention, which, "like the tyrannous breathing of the north,/Shakes all our buds from growing" (I.iv. 36–37), has prevented three things from being done: (1) Posthumus has not been allowed to give assurances against betrayal of Imogen and "his honor" in Italy; (2) Imogen has not been allowed to charge him with the duty of worship; (3) the sensual expression of love, "that parting kiss," has been denied. The blind authority of the father breaks the delicate balance of love and sensuality, fragments the political world into opposing forces, and this fragmentation mirrors the internal struggle that will break out in Posthumus. Of course, repressed sexuality returns with greater violence. In banishing the alleged "baseness" of Posthumus, Cymbeline allies himself with Cloten and the Queen. Symbolically, he is split into Cloten and the Queen. The play's extremely complex overdetermination enacts the conflict between sexuality and purity over and over again. Just as Cymbeline's insistence on Imogen's purity entails his bonds with the evil pair, Posthumus' insistence on testing that purity activates his own unconscious wishes.

Defending the purity of his "fair, virtuous, wise, chaste, constant, qualified and less attemptable" (I.v. 61–62) mistress is not new to Posthumus. The Frenchman in Act I, scene v, tells us that he has done it before, "upon importance of so slight and trivial a nature" (I.v. 42–43). The effective cause of the "arbitrement of swords" (I.v. 50–51) remains unsettled; Posthumus tells us both that "my quarrel was not altogether slight" (I.v. 48–49) and that his judgment is "mended" (I.v. 47). Immediately after, his judgment is challenged by Iachimo, his alter ego ("we are familiar at first," says Posthumus [I.v. 105–106]). Iachimo says, "but I make my wager rather against your confidence than her reputation" (I.v. 114–115). After insisting on "convenants" (I.v. 148) with the Italianate fiend, Posthumus embraces these conditions more fully than he embraced Imogren:

I embrace these conditions, let us have articles betwixt us. Only, thus far you shall answer: if you make your voyage upon her, and give me directly to understand you have prevail'd, I am no further your enemy; she is not worth our debate. If she remain unseduc'd . . . you shall answer me with your sword. (I.v. 161–169)

Other men are his enemies only so long as she remains chaste; they cease to be his enemies if Imogen is seduced. It is quite clear that Posthumus is not defending Imogen. He is testing an *idea* upon which he is dependent for his own identity. The idea is that women, as the embodiment of chastity, transcend sexual impulses. "Where they love," said Freud of maternally fixated men, "they do not desire and where they desire they cannot love." [16] Once women are "voyaged upon," the debate ends; there is nothing left to fight for. Phallic aggression, answering with swords, exhausts its value and uses in defense of the idea, which is to say that the polarity of sublimated sexuality manifest in conflict and the maintenance of the idea of chastity is self-perpetuating. The instability of this psychological configuration exposes itself by its repeated need to be tested. When the test fails, the whole configuration collapses; the "stuff within" breaks its chains, violent ambivalence becomes conscious. The idea of desexualized purity has a vested interest in war.

The wager is a conventionalized form of altruistic surrender.[17] Iachimo will enact Posthumus' repressed wishes, and the consequences of his enactment will be embraced by Posthumus. As usual in such carefully stated mental bargains, the real reciprocity is unconscious. The covenant is the *occasion* for the release of unconscious wishes and the anxiety which infuses the possibility of their gratification.

The sequence of scenes from Act I, scene vii, to Act II, scene iv, is, with the exception of the final tour de force, the most sharply focused pattern of action in the play. Iachimo and Cloten alternate in attempts to penetrate Imogen's temple, with the end of the sequence being Posthumus' hysterical diatribe against women. As

16. *Ibid.*, p. 183.
17. The concept of "altruistic surrender" is discussed by Anna Freud, *Ego and Mechanisms,* pp. 122–134.

Cloten grows more absurd, Iachimo grows more successful. After this sequence Iachimo and Posthumus will be absent from the stage until Act V. As in *The Winter's Tale,* we are led to a point of maximum conflict at which our detachment threatens to fail, and the energy gathered in the form of anxiety is then free to be re-coordinated in a long pastoral sequence.

Shakespeare frames Act II, scene ii, by references to time, isolating it from the previous and subsequent action in a strategy of demarcation which serves to keep its symbolic contents controlled while permitting intensified verbal expression of Iachimo's stylized violations. Psychologically, every detail contributes to the fabric of highly defended erotic enactment. As Iachimo activates sexual fantasies, mythological allusion distances them; as he idealizes and depersonalizes his encounter with dazzling chastity, we participate vicariously in a ritualized symbolic rape. The entire encounter is not only distanced into words, but it becomes equivalent to the fabled reality of Imogen's book, a "story" the elements of which Iachimo reports as he records them.

Imogen's concern for external detail—she asks the time, marks her place in Ovid, requests that the taper remain, sets a time to be awakened, prays for divine protection—attunes us ironically to expect some threat to this careful preparation. Immediately after her prayer, we enter the timeless world of symbolic eroticism, the spell broken only by Iachimo's exit into the world of time ("One, two, three: time, time!" he says [II.ii. 51]). Iachimo "comes from the trunk" into the chamber, in what, from a psychoanalytic viewpoint, is a clear representation, by its opposite, of going in. As in dreams, the manifest act reverses its latent meaning. The trunk itself is too obvious a feminine symbol to need comment, and Imogen's bedchamber, given the play's frequent associations of contained or fortified spaces with taboo feminine parts, can be seen as a symbol of her body and its secret places. Iachimo's entrance thus represents an overdetermined act of penetration. Once inside, he turns to formalized descriptions of erotic detail colored by his scoptophilic interest. Twice he recalls mythological rapes:

> Our Tarquin thus
> Did softly press the rushes, ere he waken'd
> The chastity he wounded.   (II.ii. 12–14)

> She hath been reading late,
> The tale of Tereus, here the leaf's turn'd down
> Where Philomel gave up.   (II.ii. 44–46)

These allusions to sadistic primal scenes, however, define only one level of the scene's sexual engagement. Iachimo's sublimated presentation of Imogen's peerless body weighs idealized anal and visual excitement as heavily as the genital penetration his entry symbolizes.

> That I might touch!
> But kiss, one kiss! Rubies unparagon'd,
> How dearly they do't: 'tis her breathing that
> Perfumes the chamber thus: the flame o' th' taper
> Bows toward her, and would under-peep her lids,
> To see th' enclosed lights, now canopied
> Under these windows, white and azure lac'd
> With blue of heaven's own tinct. (II.ii. 16–23)

Moving from taboo touch to visual concentration characterizes Imogen's forbidden power as readily as it reemphasizes Iachimo's fixations. Imogen's perfumed breath and the intensity of response her veiled eyes evoke extend the range of Iachimo's vicarious gratification to include pregenital eroticism. Imogen becomes a cosmic image, magnified to proportions that shrink the participant by comparison. The taper displaces Iachimo's own excitement and visual response. We might almost call the description a sexual act performed by visual incorporation.

A few lines later Iachimo's fantasy marks the deepest level of oral gratification, the detail which will trigger Posthumus' hysteria:

> On her left breast
> A mole cinque-spotted: like the crimson drops
> I' th' bottom of a cowslip. Here's a voucher,
> Stronger than ever law could make; this secret
> Will force him think I have pick'd the lock, and ta'en
> The treasure of her honour.   (II.ii. 37–42)

The visually intense simile of the "crimson drops i' th' bottom of a cowslip," like Ariel's "in a cowslip's bell I lie" (*Tempest* V.i. 89), evokes a feeling of repose.[18] That this detail is associated with the breast and with the "pick'd lock" of sexual violation prepares us for the unconscious confusion of maternal and genital sexuality, with its incestuous potential, which will incite Posthumus' masochistic rage. The bedroom scene thus ritualizes the unconscious orientation repressed unstably in Posthumus, the view that adult sexuality inherently transgresses the law of the father because its object, purified into idealized chastity, promises the gratification attainable only from a mother.

In Act II, scene iv, Posthumus begins by expressing his passive relation to the King and ends in an ambivalent relation to action. To Philario's question, "What means do you make to him?" he replies,

> Not any: but abide the change of time,
> Quake in the present winter's state, and wish
> That warmer days would come: in these fear'd hopes,
> I barely gratify your love; they failing,
> I must die much your debtor.   (II.iv.4–8)

Only the Queen and Cymbeline share his faith in time's curative powers (cf. II.iii. 42–45), making his position an ironic defense of passive wilfulness. The oxymoronic "fear'd hopes" articulates a more complex motivation. The fear of the father, who is always associated in the first part of the play with barren winter, and the hope to be possessed by and possess the mother, who is warmth and fertility, result in stasis. Posthumus' feared hopes cancel active defiance as surely as they deny satisfaction of his wishes. A few lines later his metaphor of rooted exposure finds implicit contrast in his own praise of British "discipline" (II.iv. 23) in defiance of Ceasar's demand for subordination. Before Iachimo, returned from Britain,

18. Cf. Pastorella's birthmark, also on the breast, in *The Faerie Queene* VI.xii.vii:

> Vpon the little brest like christall bright,
> She mote perceive a little purple mold,
> That like a rose her silken leaues did faire vnfold.

Although this passage may be a "source" for Imogen's mole, notice how Shakespeare thinks in terms of enfolding while Spenser thinks in terms of opening out. In the other possible "source" for the image, *Frederyke of Jennen*, the mark is "a blacke warte" on "her lefte arme." Shakespeare accentuates the breast and with a tone characteristic of the play.

enters the scene, we have registered both Posthumus' ambivalence toward authority and his unconsciousness of that ambivalence.

Iachimo returns, but, ironically, the first erotic words come from Posthumus:

> The swiftest harts have posted you by land;
> And winds of all the corners kiss'd your sails,
> To make your vessel nimble.   (II.iv. 27–29)

Posthumus' consciousness is attuned to vicarious participation. Before succumbing to the evidence, however, he restates the terms of the contract. Unlike Faustus, he does not need to be reminded of his bargains:

> If you can make't apparent
> That you have tasted her in bed, my hand
> And ring is yours. If not, the foul opinion
> You had of her pure honour gains, or loses,
> Your sword, or mine, or masterless leave both
> To who shall find them.   (II.iv. 56–61)

Unconsciously, sex for Posthumus, as for so many Elizabethan and Jacobean characters and poetic personae, is oral gratification. In the economy of his psyche phallic action becomes relevant only insofar as "tasting in bed" does *not* occur. He defends the *thought* of "her pure honor" against "foul opinion" because otherwise the knowledge that sex is genital would stand up against the forces of repression, and the illusion of purity would be lost. In Posthumus' psyche the illusion of purity provides a strong counter-cathexis against the fact of genital sex, and this counter-cathexis enables the unconscious wish that sex be oral (infantile) to find metaphoric expression. This is why external conflict will be avoided if Iachimo can "make't apparent" that he has "tasted her in bed." A wish will have unconsciously been gratified, the wish to return to the oral stage *prior* to Oedipal conflict. Yet the very gratification is expensive to psychic integrity, because the confusion in his mind between oral and genital sexuality fails as a defense against Oedipal fears. Once the unconscious wish is granted to the receptive Posthumus, a violent conflict between the wish for purity and the wish for gratification erupts. Why? Because then the repressed truth that sex is genital forces its way into consciousness, and his rage is turned "against himself" (II.iv. 152).

The process by which Iachimo "induces" (cf. II.iv. 63) Posthumus to believe Imogen seduced begins with erotic descriptions of her chamber: that tapestry depicting the story of Antony and Cleopatra, "the chimney-piece,/Chaste Dian, bathing," "Her andirons" and "winking Cupids," the whole array of erotic ornamentation, which, like the Ovid at her bedside, rehearses the sexual life denied in reality but indulged in fantasy. Posthumus resists these suggestions easily; even the display of the bracelet is temporarily resisted at the rational advice of Philario, although we first have an extremely significant expression of its unconscious significance:

> It is a basilisk unto mine eye,
> Kills me to look on't. (II.iv. 107–108)

The bracelet betrays the gift's obligations because symbolically it presents the sight of the female genitals to Posthumus. The very bracelet he wished would be a "manacle" of chastity returns as an expression of sexuality. The sight of the female genitals "kills" because it is unconsciously interpreted as a castration of the male member. Women are men without penises: this is the unconscious message.[19]

Still, Posthumus is able to repress even this sight for a moment; he demands a "corporal sign" (II.ii. 119), but immediately succumbs at the mention of Jupiter:

> *Iach.* By Jupiter, I had it from her arm.
> *Post.* Hark you, he swears: by Jupiter he swears.
> 'Tis true, nay, keep the ring, 'tis true . . . (II.iv. 121–123)

Why should the mere mention of Jupiter cancel his ability to resist? Is it not because he *wants* to believe that "he hath enjoy'd her" (II.iv. 126) and finds in Jupiter an ultimate authority for his deception? His own repressed libido impresses the superego into its service, ignoring the rational persuasion of Philario. In a complete reversal, the most traumatic in a play full of reversals, he now

19. The bracelet's effect on Posthumus is precisely that of Medusa's head. See Freud, "Medusa's Head" (1940 [1922]), *S.E.*, XVIII, 273–274.

demands his own cuckolding, and Iachimo grants his most cherished unconscious wish:

> *Iach.*   If you seek
> For further satisfying, under her breast
> (Worthy her pressing) lies a mole, right proud
> Of that most delicate lodging. By my life,
> I kiss'd it, and it gave me present hunger
> To feed again, though full. You do remember
> This stain upon her?
> *Post.*   Ay, and it doth confirm
> Another stain, as big as hell can hold,
> Were there no more but it.   (II.iv. 133–141)

The gratification in fantasy of the oral wish to feed at the breast entails the recognition of the fact of genital sex: "it doth confirm another stain" the thought of which is absolutely revolting and leads to an image of violence. "O, that I had her here, to tear her limb-meal!" (II.iv. 147). The thought of that other stain and the horror of torn limbs are in the unconscious one and the same, the irrational fear that sex involves castration. This is the fear underlying Posthumus' insistent defense of chastity, his ambivalent relation to authority, and his unconscious confusion of wife and mother.

Posthumus' soliloquy at the end of Act II brings together all the strands of the conflict we have been discussing. In denouncing women, he attempts to negate his own sexual drives, to preserve the shreds of honor in the face of the facts of his own nature. He begins with a wish for self-sufficiency and an attempt to absolve his father:

> Is there no way for men to be, but women
> Must be half-workers? We are all bastards,
> And that most venerable man, which I
> Did call my father, was I know not where
> When I was stamp'd.   (II.iv. 153–157)

"Venerable" authority and sexual intercourse are irreconcilably opposed in his mind. Posthumus always insists on absolute authorization for his actions and thoughts, a determination which accords well with the play's total moral distinctions, but which forbids psychic compromises. The sexual father must be made anonymous, and the mother appears in the image of Diana, chaste huntress, woman with phallic power:

> Some coiner with his tools
> Made me a counterfeit: yet my mother seem'd
> The Dian of that time: so doth my wife
> The nonpareil of this.   (II.iv. 157–160)

Mother and wife are identified in purity, sexual taboo extending from one to the other. Birth and biological process diverge in the coin image in an attempt to deny genital reality.[20]

Then Posthumus reverses himself, claiming revenge for having been denied "lawful pleasures":

> O vengeance, vengeance!
> Me of my lawful pleasure she restrain'd,
> And pray'd me oft forbearance: did it with
> A pudency so rosy, the sweet view on't
> Might well have warm'd old Saturn; that I thought her
> As chaste as unsunn'd snow.   (II.iv. 160–165)

In this confluence of overdetermined images he manages first to project the source of restraint onto Imogen, and then to call up the very image which repels him. Earlier Imogen said:

> When he was here
> He did incline to sadness, and oft-times
> Not knowing why.   (I.vii. 61–63)

In other words, the sexual repression imposed by his own tyrannical conscience had already displayed its existence in unaccountable depressions. This view is consistent with the pattern of his actions.

20. The coining conception of birth derives from the child's equation of feces and child. See Freud, "On the Sexual Theories of Children" (1908), S.E., IX, 209–226. The defense against genital sex is thus a regression to this earlier conception of reproduction. It has the advantage of absolving the parents from sexual contact, and it makes generation a possibility for men alone. "If babies are born through the anus, then a man can give birth just as well as a woman" (pp. 219–220). In Act V this wish is symbolically fulfilled as Cymbeline becomes a "mother to the birth of three" (V.v. 370). Anality defends against incest.

In his present hysteria, Posthumus edits the past to externalize responsibility. The "pudency so rosy," the "sweet view" of which now enters his imagination, expresses opposites simultaneously; it is the blush of chastity and an image of sexual arousal. He is unconsciously entertaining the Iachimo part of himself which derives erotic pleasure in looking. And "old Saturn" projects an image of the father as lecher, in whose guise the looking can be permitted to enter consciousness. Next we get a vision of Iachimo as a boar, and sex becomes the primal scene, nothing but violence and violation:

> O, all the devils!
> This yellow Iachimo, in an hour, was't not?
> Or less; at first? Perchance he spoke not, but
> Like a full-acorn'd boar, a German one,
> Cried "O!" and mounted; found no opposition
> But what he look'd for should oppose and she
> Should from encounter guard. (II.iv. 165–171)

Yellow was the color of disease and jealousy; [21] "full-acorned" means full-testicled, and the word "German" may be a pun on "germen," the male seed. [22] The image of the boar is the greatest possible contrast to Iachimo's gorgeous description in the bedroom scene. It takes Posthumus two lines to say one word, "pudenda." Again we have emphasis on looking.

In the following lines another reversal occurs, as Posthumus projects the thought of hated sexuality onto women:

> Could I find out
> The woman's part in me—for there's no motion
> That tends to vice in man, but I affirm
> It is the woman's part: be it lying, note it,

21. See *The Winter's Tale* II.iii. 102–106, where Leontes wishes to banish yellow from the colors of the ordered mind. Yellow is there clearly associated with the jealous mind, and it is regularly associated with diseases like jaundice.

22. "German" also means "blood relation," which makes the boar a part of the family. Cf. *Othello* I.i. 112–113: "you'll have coursers for cousins, and gennets for germans." The boar is a traditional symbol of sexual aggression, as in *Venus and Adonis* and *Richard III*. This is true in the East as well as the West. "On the one hand it occurs as a symbol of intrepidness, and of irrational urge toward suicide. On the other hand it stands for licentiousness." J. E. Cirlot, *A Dictionary of Symbols* (London, 1962). Such ambivalence is appropriate in Posthumus' fantasy.

The woman's: flattering, hers; deceiving, hers:
Lust, and rank thoughts, hers, hers: revenges, hers . . .

(II.iv. 171–176)

In his search for the "woman's part" we have a clear example of affirmation by denial. By embodying an anthology of evils in women, Posthumus articulates his extensive terror at the possibility of female sexuality, his diseased relationship to genitality. The "part" against which he rages is exactly the part that Imogen has not played. Posthumus is trying to exorcise the image of the female genitals in himself ("the woman's part in me"). The pun, unconscious as it is, reveals the root of his disgust, as he simultaneously expresses and defends himself against his castration anxieties. The uneven, distracted movement of the verse corresponds to its ambivalent content.[23]

The speech ends with a final note of ambivalence over whether to write or not to write. After deciding to "write against them" (II.iv. 183), he decides that prayer, submission to a higher will, is the better alternative. Writing satire, an active way of coping with forbidden wishes through sublimated aggression and sadism, is judged inferior to dependence on God's authority. God will send devils to plague the sinners. In psychological terms, Posthumus' conflict centers ultimately on his relation to father-authority. The father demands the punishment of castration as the price of sexual desire. The fear of losing the vital organ in the sex act is converted into the fear of genital sex itself and this fear is then located wholly in woman. The obverse of chastity is castration fear, and castration fear is fear of the tyrannical father who possesses the mother (wife) for himself. In the test of Imogen, Posthumus ends up confronted with the unresolved Oedipal fears which the defense of purity was designed to preserve in a state of repression. We have observed his constant need to feel that ultimate authorities join the side of his wishes. But the wish to possess Imogen sexually conflicts with the dictates of conscience, in spite of Posthumus' attempt to claim the authority of Jupiter, and the conflict within him will hereafter cen-

---

23. It is worth noting that the speech keeps us at a distance from its fantasy content by the relative absence of images in its final fifteen lines. The absence of images and heavy reliance on general moral qualities may account for the "ungenuine" quality critics have sensed here. The speech does not permit the intensity of participation characteristic of, say, Othello or Leontes.

ter on the mollification of father-authorities at the expense of erotic gratification. It is no accident that the next scene begins with the line, "Now, say, what would Augustus Caesar with us?"

In Act III Shakespeare inaugurates the redeeming parts of the play's decomposed world. But *Cymbeline*'s solutions for its psychological conflicts are intertwined with the re-expression of the conflicts. The audience finds itself entangled in the same paranoiac web which grips Cymbeline. Illusions *in* the play merge with illusions *of* the play. Our powers of reality-testing strain to sort the multiplications of familial roles without relinquishing emotional participation, so that, as R. J. Kaufmann says, "The exact distribution invited for our sympathies is maddeningly difficult to establish with critical concision." [24] Before Posthumus reappears in Act V, scene i, the conflicts of the first two acts are transposed, with undisclosed purpose, into the new dimensions of politics and pastoral display. The effect of this transposition is to disperse our energies among discrete elements of the conflicts we have already witnessed. Characters come to represent isolated aspects of the play's central preoccupation with the consequences of ambivalent love, or they present to us examples of the rooted parental identifications which serve to protect against that ambivalence.

"Paranoia decomposes just as hysteria condenses," Freud wrote. "Or rather, paranoia resolves once more into their elements the products of the condensations and identifications which are effected in the unconscious." [25] As Otto Rank demonstrated, family romance plots are the mythological and literary counterparts of paranoiac fantasies.[26] The ambivalent attitude toward women finds expression in the Queen-Imogen opposition, and the faltering superego manifests itself in the multiplication of father-figures. Belarius, Cymbeline, Caesar, and Jupiter stage aspects of the father's familial, national, international, and supernatural power, or lack of it. Until the last act the antagonism of fathers coincides with the power of the anonymous evil mother, the "false" mother of the family romance. In the end she and her son become the scapegoats for everything divisive in the world.

24. "Puzzling Epiphanies," *Essays in Criticism,* XIII (October 1963), 397.
25. Psycho-Analytic Notes on an Autobiographical Account of a Case of Paranoia" (1911), S.E., XII, 9–82. The quotation is on p. 49.
26. *The Myth of the Birth of the Hero,* ed. Philip Freund (New York, 1959), pp. 64–96.

The Queen may be an attenuated version of Volumnia, but this should not blind us to the psychological implications of her presence in the play. The power attributed to her on the level of fantasy only flickers into dramatic reality, but she bears a weight of responsibility larger than her manifest role. Every deviation from patriarchal hierarchy is finally attributed to the Queen or to her instrument Cloten. In the Queen Shakespeare projects the fears associated with the sexual fantasies that emerge in Posthumus: fear of poison, fear of castration, or, more generally, fear of being rendered impotent before the demands of external reality.[27] As Coriolanus said,

> Not of a woman's tenderness to be,
> Requires nor child nor woman's face to see.
>   (V.iii. 129–130)

Cymbeline attributes immense determining influence to this figure of the "bad" mother, although her influence remains an underlying psychological *assumption* and is not dramatically validated by the audience's experience of the play. Her unrealized role makes the control attributed to her seem to diminish the stature of those within her web. Nevertheless, as Freud realized, what is apparently insignificant can mask what is latently most important. Once we see that the Queen projects one side of the ambivalence duplicated in Posthumus, the underlying link between Posthumus' actual response to Imogen's "betrayal" and the national plot becomes more available to analysis.

The Queen and Cloten defend Britain as an enisled and fortified ego. The challenge to Caesar can be seen as a displacement of the conflict projected in Posthumus. The wish for inner purity and autonomy imagined on a national scale directs aggressive wishes outside the sacred circle of familiar and traditional identities. The keynote of the Queen's famous description of Britain "As Neptune's park, ribb'd and pal'd in/With rocks unscaleable and roaring waters" (III.i. 20–21) is natural power and its past ability to beat Caesar twice and make "Britons strut with courage" (III.i. 34). Cloten is the only character imagined as strutting, so that even the description of British bravery bears his mark. Britain becomes in

---

27. G. Wilson Knight hints at this point when he says, "The Queen throughout personifies the ugly thing Posthumus suspects in Imogen." *Crown of Life,* p. 131.

her fantasy a *hortus exclusus* protected by engulfing forces, "sands that will not bear your enemies' boats,/But suck them up to th' topmast" (III.i. 22–23) and seas that crack ships "like egg-shells" (III.i. 29). These images of an overwhelming mother surrounding the nation correspond to the Queen's own wished-for role in the play. The island is not (*pace* G. Wilson Knight) that envisioned by Gaunt in *Richard II* ("This nurse, this teeming womb of royal kings" [II.i. 51]), but locus of self-engrossed exclusivity, a defensive place, not a creative one. In both the national plot and the wager a confusion of enemies within with enemies without determines the defensive position. Aggression seeks the wrong object, since what is pure and what is defiled are one and the same. Neptune's park exists only in the imagination; the play's reality has substituted the Queen and Cloten for the ordered generativity of Britain and its heroic, outer-directed defense.

Psychologically, the Queen and Cloten have usurped the defining qualities of British nobility, and until Act III, scene i, is half-over Cymbeline manages only two lines, one of which is immediately disobeyed by Cloten.[28] When he does speak, he acknowledges his loyalty to a lineage which antedates Caesar's conquests but also remembers that Caesar honored him as a youth. There is none of Cloten's frenetic defiance in his speeches, but neither is there any distrust of Cloten and the Queen. In his passivity he performs the same kind of altruistic surrender we observed in Posthumus. The Queen and Cloten, whose power renders the King impotent to determine British destiny, speak and act for him and with his reiterated assent. Without them he sags into perplexity:

> Now for the counsel of my son and queen,
> I am amaz'd with matter.   (IV.iii. 27–28)

The challenge to Caesar is quite clearly a pretext for structuring ambivalence, but an overdetermined one. It places us in the schizoid position of simultaneously recognizing mutually exclusive assumptions without having sufficient ground for choosing a stable emotional relation to those assumptions. On the one hand the challenge asserts the "natural" autonomy of British tradition and its renewed

---

28. Cymbeline says, "Son, let your mother end" (III.i. 40), but Cloten goes right on. Notice how Cloten is accepted here as the King's "son."

ability to ward off externalized sources of limitation. As Cymbeline says,

> Say then to Caesar,
> Our ancestor was that Mulmutius which
> Ordain'd our laws, whose use the sword of Caesar
> Hath too much mangled; whose repair, and franchise,
> Shall (by the power we hold) be our good deed,
> Though Rome be therefore angry.   (III.i. 55–60)

In this conception Caesar becomes a mutilating father, Cymbeline a son loyal to his ancestral heritage, ready to translate law into action even at the expense of angering the usurping father. But the danger to British integrity is standing before his eyes and ours, unrepudiated by him. Even a Jacobean audience with prior conviction of national greatness could not fail to see it. Cymbeline rages at Imogen, but seems more than a little reluctant to damage Caesar's stature:

> Thy Caesar knighted me; my youth I spent
> Much under him; of him I gather'd honour,
> Which he to seek of me again, perforce,
> Behoves me keep at utterance. (III.i. 71–74)

The second assumption is this: Britain achieved a noble identity by submission to the father Caesar; its integrity depends on acting in accordance with the father's example, and this involves defiance of the father.[29] The same father who conquered the warlike people authenticated Cymbeline's nobility. Here Cymbeline is represented as a son who reaped the benefits of service to a generous father, a relationship duplicated in Posthumus' brothers' and Cymbeline's own sons' relation to authority. Shakespeare is not merely structuring ambivalence toward the father in the national plot, he is ambivalent toward the very structuring process he has set in motion, and this leaves the audience in a position of uneasy ambiguity, especially since Caesar never appears, and his representative, Caius Lucius, will later become a "good" father to Imogen. The situation

---

29. The ambiguous phrase, "behoves me keep at utterance," may be illuminated if we remember that the superego frequently manifests itself in vocal forms.

here is similar to that in *Coriolanus*, in which the hero must repudiate his mother in order to be faithful to her past influence. In psychological terms, it is a double bind: we are asked to assent to contradictory emotional demands where no adequate choice is possible.

The only way out of a double bind, if it is not to end in tragic contradiction, is to introduce a rescuing force or person. In *Cymbeline* we have Belarius and Cymbeline's lost sons and, beyond them, the deus ex machina. But before we are transplanted to the idealized world of Wales another instance of British decomposition makes its way from Rome.

Posthumus instructs Pisanio to murder Imogen. Projected hatred of the sexual woman controls his response to his primal-scene fears; Imogen, no longer a goddess to be worshiped, becomes an object to be torn. (Pisanio says she bears herself in his absence "More goddess-like than wife-like" [III.ii. 8].) The letter Posthumus sends Imogen re-expresses the nature of his confusion:

> Justice, and your father's wrath (should he take me in his dominion) could not be so cruel to me, as you (O the dearest of creatures) would even renew me with your eyes. (III.ii. 40–43)

The sentence is one cumulative ambiguity, an acrobatics of evasion. Before the first parenthetical remark, we are set wondering what justice has to do with Cymbeline's wrath; in any case, Posthumus thinks of the father's wrath before Imogen. The first parenthesis turns on the ambiguity of "take me." Does it mean "take me (back) into" or "capture me"? Before we reach the second parenthesis, it seems as if Posthumus is comparing Cymbeline's wrath to Imogen's cruelty, which makes the second parenthesis either a bad pun on "dearest" (most expensive) or a contradiction. The last phrase refocuses on ocular identification, which defines one aspect of Posthumus' ambivalent love. His words are put into Imogen's mouth (a literalization of projection, but this time the projection is Shakespeare's): she voices his confusion. In more conventional terms, Imogen has become for Posthumus the objectification of inconstancy, which his guilt insists on murdering. The "stuff within" has become the driving force in the outer world.

The attempt to deny the existence of the sexual woman entails, paradoxically, the symbolic enactment of the crime Posthumus fears. Since genital sex is mutilation, Imogen must be mutilated. Again, denial generates the thing denied. Two scenes later Imogen articulates her willingness to die in speeches shot through with images of separation anxiety, sexual acts, castration, and self-sacrifice. For example:

> Speak, man, thy tongue
> May take off some extremity, which to read
> Would be even mortal to me. (III.iv. 16–18)

> I must be ripp'd:—to pieces with me! (53)

> Come, here's my heart,
> (Something's afore't,—soft, soft! we'll no defence)
> Obedient as the scabbard. (78–80)

> . . . and I grieve myself
> To think, when thou shalt be disedg'd by her
> That now thou tirest on . . . (93–95)

> The lamb entreats the butcher. (97)

If we have any doubt about the sadistic nature of the fantasized act, Posthumus' letter puts us straight:

> Thy mistress, Pisanio, hath played the strumpet in my bed: the testimonies whereof lie bleeding in me. (21–23)

The play juggles pronouns and family roles in accordance with the unconscious wishes of the moment. Here Imogen becomes "thy mistress" but the bed remains "mine." The boundaries between characters fluctuate in the interpenetration of subject and object; we are taken into the play's oral confusion, and only a strict distribution of roles, a precategorized map of reality, restores the distinction of "mine" and "thine." Even before this scene, the most anxiety-ridden in the play, Shakespeare has begun to erect defenses against this gruesome primal scene.

The world of Wales literally and psychologically distances the conflicts initiated in the court and displays with self-conscious didacticism the moral and psychological alternatives to the play's potentially tragic deviations. An all-male world presided over by a self-appointed surrogate for the gullible and paranoiac King, Wales is the vehicle for the retrieval of anchored defenses against the Queen-dominated subversion of British harmony. Within the structured life of cyclical pieties Shakespeare reenacts the play's controlling tensions, in a demonstration of familial identities designed to counter the threats Cloten and Posthumus in his deranged state represent. The pastoral world is a symbolic context, protected from the victory of desublimated sexuality by conventional agreement, a place where problematic experience is granted controlled release in order to be mastered and ordered. Isolation, apparent self-sufficiency, ritualized and idealized action, exemplary performance, hierarchic stability—all contribute to this world's symbolic reality. A reigning myth of this setting is that sublimation of basic drives can achieve an adequate and guiltless substitute for their original aims; but, as we shall see, Shakespearean sophistication expands this simplistic notion. In this arcadia there is a great deal of residual guilt and anxiety as well as the settled pattern of innocent identifications.

For Belarius, the world of banishment has become a moral dictionary advertising its difference from the court. In contrast to the court's phallic pride, his maternal environment engenders the daily adoration consequent on complete introjection of the "good" parents: [30]

> The gates of monarchs
> Are arch'd so high that giants may jet through
> And keep their impious turbans on, without
> Good morrow to the sun. Hail, thou fair heaven!
> We house i' th' rock, yet use thee not so hardly
> As prouder livers do.   (III.iii. 4–9)

The maternal symbols of the rock and the cave indicate the psychological locus of his life of basic sufficiencies. As Charles K. Hofling has noticed, the movement to Wales is a regression in the serv-

30. K. M. Abenheimer makes this point in "Shakespeare's 'Tempest': A Psychological Analysis," *Psychoanalytic Review*, XXXIII (1946), 399–415.

ice of the ego.[31] Life in Wales, as Belarius describes it, consists of
an elaborate generalized insistence that it is not like the world that
rejected him. The court's phallic impudence is explicitly in revolt
against religious order. Belarius' fantasy determines his images, which
correspond to the symbolic significance of the reality we have seen
on the stage.

Belarius' piety takes the anal form of a detailed, depersonalized
revenge, by perfect behavior, on his banisher Cymbeline. Like a
child whose attempts to please his father receive inexplicable rebuff, Belarius' response to rejection amplifies courtliness into unconscious parody, so that loyalty itself becomes a devious act of
aggression against the unfaithful father. The court is linked to un-
deserved moral reprimand, and Belarius directs at it a full range
of conventional accusations:

> O, this life
> Is nobler than attending for a check:
> Richer than doing nothing for a robe,
> Prouder than rustling in unpaid-for silk:
> Such gain the cap of him that makes him fine,
> Yet keeps his book uncross'd: no life to ours.
> (III.iii. 21–26)

That last metaphor of the tailor who ornaments others while neg-
lecting business detail distills Belarius' stiff sense of puritanical responsibility. His rhythms punctuate the egotism of opposition, but
keep him bound in tightly; as soon as he begins to run on (in line 25)
the phrase "no life to ours" puts a stop to this indulgence. Belarius
is a moral masturbator. In him Shakespeare projects a rigidly moralistic, legalistic reaction formation against courtly unreliability, a
schematic defense against violent abuses of chastity. Like that of a
salesman, his urgent insistence on the value of what he advertises
evokes skepticism rather than identification. As the Elizabethan
proverb says, "He praises who wishes to sell."

Belarius' rigidity argues an underlying guilt; and filial guilt in a
clearly Oedipal configuration shows through his actions in the past
and his uneasy response to events in Wales. In the past, Belarius,

---

31. "Notes on Shakespeare's *Cymbeline*," *Shakespeare Studies*, I (1965), 135.
Hofling's essay is biographical and provides guarded support for some of
the ideas I develop out of the play itself.

loved by Cymbeline for his military service, was "as a tree/Whose boughs did bend with fruit" (III.iii. 60–61). The image of the tree laden with fruit whose fertility is truncated by a wrathful father recalls Imogen's lines at I.iv. 35–37 and will recur in a more gratifying form in the last scene. Psychoanalytically, Belarius imagines a social relationship that reproduces the child's pre-Oedipal possession of and identification with the mother, before the son's rivalry with the father interrupted this primary relatedness. The child's subsequent antagonism toward the father is here displaced and represented anonymously as "two villains, whose false oaths prevail'd/Before my perfect honour," and who "swore to Cymbeline/ I was confederate with the Romans" (III.iii. 66–68). Following this false report (the only implication in the play of rivalry with Rome twenty years ago), Belarius is deprived of his "mellow hangings" (III.iii. 63) and left "bare to weather" (III.iii. 64), expressions both of symbolic castration and of removal from the social equivalent of maternal presence. As he sketches his response twenty years later the intention of symbolically castrating the father in return by depriving him of his lineage (an intention linking him with the Queen; cf. III.v. 65–66) emerges clearly:

> O Cymbeline, heaven and my conscience knows
> Thou didst unjustly banish me: whereon,
> At three and two years old, I stole these babes,
> Thinking to bar thee of succession as
> Thou refts me of my lands.   (III.iii. 99–103)

The opening scene points up the manifest absurdity of this strategy (I.i. 55–67), and conscious absurdity defends against unconscious significance. Belarius stole the sons not merely to vindicate his martial honor, which was ostensibly at stake, but to reciprocate the loss of his "lands," symbolically the mother. This detail, which seems unnecessary in the speech's manifest content, supports the Oedipal interpretation. The story of Belarius' banishment thus repeats the pattern of family romance motives operating in Posthumus' banishment. In both instances manifest purity of intention incurs an irrational father's wrath, and in both instances symbolic possession of maternal fullness is at issue. In Wales Belarius effectively replaces the son's parents, as Cymbeline did for Posthumus. Guilt is projected onto the King who is controlled by the dominating woman split off from her nourishing and sustaining counterpart. The difference is in the distancing of the first banishment; historically prior, it is psychologically tamed by time, enacted in words only.

The guilt, however, returns in Belarius' jittery reaction to Cloten's unannounced entry; beneath his moralisms the fear of paternal retribution shapes his stance:

> I fear some ambush:
> I saw him not these many years, and yet
> I know 'tis he: we are held as outlaws: hence!
> (IV.ii. 65–67)

After Cloten's death, Belarius is sure that "We are all undone" (IV.ii. 123) and that "this body hath a tail/More perilous than the head" (IV.ii. 144–145). His instructions to bury Cloten with the "reverence" (IV.ii. 247) due a queen's son bespeak the defensive nature of his piety, as if formal adherence to hierarchic value could automatically make reparation for his sense of transgression. Shakespeare is acutely aware in *Cymbeline* of the compensatory aspect of formalized adherence to social rules. When the sounds of approaching armies surround their cave, Belarius counsels retreat to maternal protection. On one level, he functions as a choral commentator and foil to the sons' "innate" nobility, but as an overdetermined projection of paternal and filial attitudes, the fear and guilt he embodies reinforce the play's pervasive emphasis on the ambiguous nature of family relationships.

Belarius' anxiety localizes the fear of punishment Cloten's death might generate and also enables Shakespeare to use his moral armor in a positive way. He can recognize Imogen as a pure "boy," an idealized perfection, visually distanced.

> Behold divineness
> No elder than a boy!   (III.vii. 16–17)

In psychoanalytic terms, Shakespeare presents us with a pattern of paranoia reversed. In relation to Imogen Belarius displays none of the anxiety of his response to approaching armies. Instead, the anal rigidity of his moralisms serves as a protection against the feared aspect of the mother, transforms her into a worshiped youth, the prototype of whom is the phallic mother of early infancy. Shakespeare makes tendering one's debts to heaven the psychological prerequisite for the ability to be tender to golden lads and girls.

In Wales ritualized action and the anxiety it exists to tame and structure coexist in uneven mixtures. Daily life is governed by earned distribution of domestic roles:

> You, Polydore, have prov'd best woodman, and
> Are master of the feast: Cadwal and I
> Will play the cook and servant . . . (III.vii. 1–3)

This diligent role-playing informs their lives in reverence to a matrix of limited social relationships. As Imogen later says, "the breach of custom is the breach of all" (IV.ii. 10–11). The hunt ritualizes aggression, and homage to a lost ideal mother-substitute fills out their daily ceremonial:

> Euriphile,
> Thou wast their nurse, they took thee for their mother,
> And every day do honour to her grave. (III.iii. 103–105)

Custom here compromises the sublimation into idealized forms of the child's cyclical reality. On one level, the collocation of exemplary poses that Wales presents revives the oral world of childhood, based as it is on parental guidance and what Erikson calls basic trust. The hunt, the feast, and the prayers to Euriphile constitute its three central facts. When Imogen enters famished, she finds food and recognition of her divinity. It is a "sweeter" (III.iii. 30) world, as opposed to the "sharper" (III.iii. 31) world of courtly experience.

Maternally oriented ordering of reality under the watchful eye of conscience (what G. Wilson Knight calls "this nature-fed existence"[32]) neatly escapes paranoiac divisiveness and shields Cymbeline's sons from all adult ambivalence. In Wales competitive reality consists of hunting tomorrow's feast and deciding who shall play master, cook, and servant. It doesn't take a psychologist to see how radically reductive this reinvestment of masculine energies is. But Shakespeare will not reject the alternative of pastoral retreat, since it provides a hypothetical context,[33] however restricting, for

32. *Crown of Life*, p. 158.
33. C. L. Barber recognizes this hypothetical aspect of pastoral in connection with *A Midsummer Night's Dream. Shakespeare's Festive Comedy*, p. 146.

mastering threats of sexual violation. Instead, he expands this context to include the active urge of Cymbeline's sons toward experience beyond their "pinching cave" (III.iii. 38).

Identification with the good mother inhibits more active forms of self-identification. The "quiet life" (III.iii. 30) feels like "A cell of ignorance, travelling a-bed,/A prison, or a debtor that not dares/ To stride a limit" (III.iii. 33–35). The prison and debtor metaphors reverse the honorific connotations of Belarius' conception, implying that his regressive ideas are themselves a form of punishment. The sons see their retreat as an accepted slavery:

> . . . our cage
> We make a quire, as doth the prison'd bird,
> And sing our bondage freely. (III.iii. 42–44)

They want to seize their own lives in heroic assertion, rather than merely use their situation as a way of paying "pious debts to heaven" (III.iii. 72). The overbearing superego which dictates the law of the talion to Belarius and keeps him submissive to heaven achieves a more resilient expression in their combination of idealized response to Imogen and guiltless disregard of restricting laws (cf. IV.ii. 124–129).

Pastoral retreat contradicts warlike action, but, as in dreams, the contradictory forms of action coincide: both reverence for their current life and the desire "to stride a limit" cohabit Wales. Shakespeare has it both ways; the sons exhibit automatic, asexual love for Imogen, include her in their "journal" (IV.ii. 10) life, and associate her in "death" with their lost mother (IV.ii. 190). Their unconscious recognition of familial bonds affirms defenses against the play's incestuous anxieties. In disguise, Imogen is assigned the desexualized role of "housewife" (IV.ii. 45) and her Platonic divinity is matched by her domestic skill (IV.ii. 48–51). In other words, combining sacred and profane, she becomes in fantasy everything the child wishes for in a mother, utter purity in an oral provider. The phallic or androgynous woman worshiped by Posthumus finds her symbolic home in this idealized childhood world. Ambivalence is structured by splitting the tenderness of pastoral care from the feared aggression of sexual contact. Her masculine disguise and playful reminder of its phallic appendage (III.vi. 25–26) restore her to the status of pre-Oedipal mother, a woman incompletely differentiated from masculine potentials.

In their love for Imogen the sons also project a potentially disruptive strain of decorous antagonism toward the father. As their maternal reality would lead us to expect, Imogen becomes not merely the equal of but an alternative to Belarius. Guiderius says:

> I love thee: I have spoke it,
> How much the quantity, the weight as much,
> As I do love my father.   (IV.ii. 16–18)

And Arviragus adds:

> If it be sin to say so, sir, I yoke me
> In my good brother's fault: I know not why
> I love this youth, and I have heard you say,
> Love's reason's without reason. The bier at door,
> And a demand who is't shall die, I'ld say
> "My father, not this youth."   (IV.ii. 19–24)

Shakespeare is repeating in modulated form the Oedipal wish for the father's death, here rendered innocuous by Arviragus' initial gestures and formal address. Still, the potential for rivalry remains, and a clear direction for aggressive wishes will soon be found as Cloten bungles his way into their world. Success in the play's search for legitimate paternal authority, a father who guarantees his children's wishes, requires that sexual rivalry find aim-inhibited, displaced channels of expression. Cloten's presence in Wales is not simply an intrusion, but a necessary part of the psychological configuration Shakespeare is establishing to cope with paranoiac and hysterical responses to Oedipal anxieties. If one side of this configuration is the restoration of religiously enacted domestic life, the other is sublimation of aggression in defense of parental values.

Shakespeare bifurcates threatening wish and virtuous defense in the particular characteristics of Cloten and the sons. Arviragus rejects Cloten's anality when Imogen offers payment for food. His lines link money to its desublimated source:

> All gold and silver rather turn to dirt,
> As 'tis no better reckon'd, but of those
> Who worship dirty gods.   (III.vii. 26–28)

As an expression of generosity these lines are particularly negative and defensive. Literal payment of debts contaminates divine order. The manifest intention of the lines spills over into Shakespeare's broader purpose of opposing purity and dirt, impulse and reaction, instinct and sublimation. Holding Cloten's head, Guiderius says, "This Cloten was a fool, an empty purse,/There was no money in't" (IV.ii. 113–114). The psychology of *Cymbeline* transforms the anal imagery association with Cloten into deliberate indications of moral purity and rarefied expressions of virtuous gratification. The sons' attitude toward money allies them with the play's other decontaminated derivatives of anality, the concern with the pure air of Britain (cf. V.ii. 3–4) and the oracular definition of Imogen as a "piece of tender air" (V.v. 447). The play manages differences dualistically and leaves no room for a sense of free interplay between opposites. The higher and lower forms of underlying impulses are set against one another and the victory of the higher is shown to us. It is the difference between reaction-formation and integration. The overall strategy of the pastoral sequences is one of undoing in its psychoanalytic meaning, magical reversal, and the resurrection of symmetrical defenses against sexual anxieties.[34]

Dualistic opposition peaks in Guiderius' killing of Cloten. Their confrontation reads like a parody of adolescent phallic narcissism:

Gui.   What's thy name?
Clo. Cloten, thou villain.
Gui. Cloten, thou double villain, be thy name,
   I cannot tremble at it, were it Toad, or Adder, Spider,
   'Twould move me sooner.   (IV.ii. 87–91)

As Guiderius explains after the symbolic castration, it was either Cloten's head or his. In the sons, phallic aggression in homoerotic contexts becomes a revelation of royalty, since the taboo against unregulated impulse has been restored. "Those that I reverence, those I fear," says Guiderius (IV.ii. 95), in a perfect definition of taboo. On one level, Shakespeare plays with the primitive aspect of the sons' princely narcissism, but the play is serious, ambivalently

34. Symmetry determines the one-to-one correspondences between perverse and noble attitudes, but the fact that there are two sons overbalances the scale away from anxiety and toward control, an appropriate comic technique.

serious. As Freud said, "'The opposite of play is not what is serious but what is real.'"[35] Cloten represents infantile, perverse forms of the sons' socialized potency.

As a form of active mastery, the verbal duel between Cloten and Guiderius opposes two forms of magical thinking: Cloten's magic of clothing and naming, with its schizophrenic identification of thing and representation, and Guiderius' magical princeliness, with its mystique of aristocratic potency, that "invisible instinct" (IV.ii. 177) Belarius praises to the audience. As a defense by exaggerated reversal, Guiderius' display of Cloten's head replaces castration fear by the wish-fulfilling image of phallic power based on mother identification, a pattern that will be repeated in Posthumus' regained military efficiency after his renewed identification with Imogen. Arviragus points up the psychological connection between love and war with ironic exactness:

> Poor sick Fidele!
> I'll willingly to him; to gain his colour
> I'ld let a parish of such Clotens blood
> And praise myself for charity. (IV.ii. 166–169)

The equivalence of narcissism and charity in these lines is conveniently overlooked by critics who like to see selfless devotion where there is platonic love. Shakespeare's intuition had little to learn from psychoanalysis on this point; after *Timon* he knew all he needed to know.

Act IV, scene iv, releases the sons from their prison into the pleasures of masculine conflict. Pleasure is Arviragus' word:

> What pleasure, sir, we find in life, to lock it
> From action and adventure. (IV.iv. 2–3)

War elevates the lower expressions of libido to the status of authorized satisfaction (IV.iv. 16). Instead of "coward hares, hot goats, and venison" (IV.iv. 37), Arviragus wants men. In the context of war, the erotic arousal expressed by flight and flying, Iachimo's sight-induced erectness, finds its proper direction:

---

35. "Creative Writers and Day-Dreaming" (1908 [1907]), S.E., IX, 143–153. The quotation is on p. 144.

The time seems long, their blood thinks scorn
Till it fly out and show them princes born.
                    (IV.iv. 53–54)

"Wedlock is the continuation of war by other means," writes Norman O. Brown.[36] In *Cymbeline* war is marriage carried on by other means:

Have with you, boys!
If in your country wars you chance to die,
That is my bed too, lads, and there I'll lie.
                    (IV.iv. 50–52)

The play's protection from incest is the vicarious incest of war. The true sons of Cymbeline make war, not love, and in making war restore their father's potency.

In Wales Cloten becomes the play's most overdetermined symbol. Frank Kermode and Robert Crams Hunter have recognized that Shakespeare created the dramatic equivalent of the equation Cloten = Posthumus deranged, but their intention of finding only ethical themes prevents them from seeing this equation's range of significance.[37] Of course, Posthumus has "lost his head" at the end of Act II, but it takes a certain literal-mindedness to reduce beheaded Cloten to a vague metaphor. Cloten is very clear for once: "Posthumus, thy head . . . shall within this hour be off" (IV.i 17–18).

The grounds for identifying Cloten and Posthumus go back to Act III, scene i, where Cloten is left to speak the direct challenge to Caius Lucius, in rhythms which remind us of Posthumus' wager:

Clo. His majesty bids you welcome. Make pastime with us a
    day or two, or longer: if you seek us afterwards in other terms,
    you shall find us in our salt-water girdle: if you beat us out of
    it, it is yours: if you fall in the adventure, our crows shall fare
    the better for you: and there's an end. (III.i. 79–85)

36. *Love's Body* (New York, 1966), p. 64.
37. Frank Kermode, *Shakespeare: The Final Plays* (London, 1963), p. 26;
    Robert Grams Hunter, *Shakespeare and the Comedy of Forgiveness* (New
    York, 1965), p. 158.

Only Cloten and Posthumus share this "if-then" mentality, and each presents a challenge to foreign threats (or threats imagined to be foreign). Cloten is thinking in terms of extensions to his body (the middle part), identifying his virility, as obsessional personalities do, with the possession of external signs of that virility. Cloten's challenge and Posthumus' wager run along parallel lines; each of them needs to project a personal intentionality as a socially valued form of defense.

This similarity in rhythm and intention may not be enough to identify Cloten and Posthumus, but the play's clothing imagery prepares us for a fuller response by building up associations between the human body and its coverings, and this accumulation of references results in a magical conflation of the two by the time Cloten, wearing "the same suit [Posthumus] wore when he took leave of [his] lady and mistress" (III.v. 127–129), compares himself to Posthumus: [38]

> the lines of my body are *as well* drawn as his; *no less* young, *more strong, not beneath* him in fortunes, *beyond* him in the advantage of the time, *above* him in birth, *alike* conversant in general services, and *more* remarkable in single oppositions; yet this imperseverent thing loves him in my despite (IV.i. 10–16; italics added).

The italicized comparatives arouse in the audience the opposite of their manifestly intended result; instead of differentiating Cloten from Posthumus, they confuse us in order to identify the two. In a tour de force of category-mixing Cloten jumps from the body to social evaluations with the agility of manic exhibitionism. To the contiguous magic of wearing Posthumus' clothes, the speech adds

38. J. C. Flügel, in *The Psychology of Clothes* (London, 1930), discusses the conflation of the body and its coverings from a psychoanalytic viewpoint. Angus Fletcher writes, in *Allegory: The Theory of a Symbolic Mode* (Ithaca, 1964), p. 195: "In poetry any two systems of images put in parallel, and kept in parallel, will appear to be magically joined—as readers of poetry we assume a primitive attitude and ask how two levels could fail to be united by occult affinity, if they are thus drawn together by formal correspondence." In *Cymbeline* clothing and animal images generate magical unions of this sort. For example, Guiderius says, "O sweetest, fairest lily:/My brother wears thee not the one half so well/As when thou grew'st thyself" (IV.ii. 201–203). The fusion is incomplete, however, and Posthumus never becomes a convincing eagle.

the ambiguity of the pronouns "my" and "his," reinforcing the visual identification by verbal confusions. By the time we get to the second "him"/"my" opposition the distinction has become a fluid area with doubtful boundaries. The speech draws us into Cloten's mental world by activating in us the same primary process illusions it reveals in him.

The regressive loss of boundaries is the play's alternative to Belarius' detailed differentiation of young and old, socially higher and lower, and to the emphasis on perspective (rational distancing) in the lines in which he teaches hierarchy:

> Consider,
> When you above perceive me like a crow,
> That it is place which lessens and sets off . . .
> (III.iii. 11–13)

Belarius teaches straight perception within a morally demarcated landscape. Cloten and Posthumus, however, are not clear perceivers but "imperceiverant things" enslaved to delusions that the play as a whole indulges and strives to contain.

As a symbol of instinctual drives uninformed by cultural capacity for guilt, Cloten embodies that part of Posthumus which struggles against conscience in a rage for gratification. As we have seen, Posthumus' ambivalence culminates in his revolted vision of a primal scene, and in the fear of castration associated with it. The decapitation of Cloten in Posthumus' clothes confirms that fear and also defends against it; Posthumus is punished vicariously for the forbidden wish to possess Imogen sexually, and Cloten is banished unequivocally from the play. After Cloten's head is displayed and disposed of, Shakespeare repeats the play's primal-scene preoccupation symbolically by bringing together the bodies of Cloten-Posthumus and Imogen. The conscious explanation for staging this double "burial" is Belarius' thin rationalization of Cloten's princeliness, which makes charity seem grotesque. (Guiderius' reply undercuts his father's puffed-up purity by immediately reminding us that the body is a body.) Shakespeare manipulates his characters in the interest of more pressing concerns than religious conformity; in those few seconds when Cloten-Posthumus and Imogen lie alone on the stage we witness the quietest primal scene in all literature. No wonder! It occurs between a castrated man and a phallic woman. It is a primal scene reversed, undone.

Since Shakespeare is attempting to master the fear of castration associated with Imogen as mother, what better strategy than to have *her* express the anxiety that fear arouses. This is precisely what he does, as she wakes to discover the mutilated corpse she mistakes for Posthumus:

> [*Seeing the body of Cloten*]
> These flowers are like the pleasures of the world;
> This bloody man, the care on't. I hope I dream:
> For so I thought I was a cave-keeper,
> And cook to honest creatures. But 'tis not so:
> 'Twas but a bolt of nothing, shot at nothing,
> Which the brain makes of fumes. Our very eyes
> Are sometimes like our judgements, blind.   (IV.ii. 296–302)

Her first sentence defends against the sight of the corpse by generalizing it into an emblem. In denying her cave life, however, she uses more highly cathected language: the "bolt of nothing, shot at nothing" [39] expresses and negates phallic aggression simultaneously and leads us, via the ambiguity of "which" (does it refer to "bolt" or to the "nothing," the illusion the brain makes?), to "fumes," an expression in terms of Elizabethan physiology of the anality the play associates with genital sex.[40] The next sentence, with its sight metaphor, ends in the thought of blindness, a frequent symbolization of castration. We can see how overdetermined these images and metaphors are if we try to paraphrase them. On a manifest level, the last three lines simply amplify the negation of her pastoral life: "But 'tis not so." But their latent content reveals the preoccupation of the play with the sexual drives directed *at* Imogen. Shakespeare has projected onto Imogen, as an expression of her distracted state, the unconscious associations which possess Posthumus and Cloten. The speech goes on for another thirty lines. Posthumus' myth-

39. The gender of "nothing" becomes clear in lines 367–368. Imogen says, "I am nothing; or if not,/Nothing to be were better." In the end the Queen becomes "naught" (V.v. 271).

40. Cf. the Arden edition note to *Macbeth* I.vii. 66–68: "The old anatomists divided the brain into three ventricles, in the hindmost of which, viz. the cerebellum, they placed the memory." It does not appear accidental that fumes originate in the hindmost region, displaced upward. Ernest Jones discovered elaborate and detailed relationships between anality and such physiological fantasies as this one. See his essay on "The Madonna's Conception Through the Ear" in *Essays in Applied Psycho-Analysis*, Vol. II (London, 1964), pp. 266–357.

ically heroic attributes—"His foot Mercurial: his Martial thigh:/The brawns of Hercules" (IV.ii. 310–311)—clash with the reality she imagines, the illusion before her eyes which is symbolically true. Her explanation of the sight confirms her powers of reality-testing and also mocks them, since the explanation results in paranoiac delusion. Within the limits of her knowledge she pieces together a logical theory of murder: Pisanio has "Conspir'd with that irregulous devil, Cloten" (IV.ii. 315) to strike "the main-top" "From this most bravest vessel of the world" (IV.ii. 319–320). "O 'tis pregnant, pregnant!" she says (IV.ii. 325), with hysterical, unconscious accuracy, for Shakespeare *has* made Pisanio a conspirator with Cloten in the mutilation of a symbolic Posthumus. But on another level pregnancy is precisely what the scene is designed to prevent. The speech itself mutilates the distinction between primary and secondary processes, making highly charged language serve an explanation which is rational, yet an illusion. Shakespeare forces Imogen to reenact regressive states we see in Cymbeline and Posthumus. She suffers for them. In this inverted primal scene Imogen is the "man" who "dies" at the sight of the castrated body; she has become a surrogate for Posthumus, who is "killed" by the sight of the female genitals. The scene works to deny the masculine fantasy by expressing it in an utterly inverted way. "It is not I, the man, who fear to be overwhelmed by a vision of my love mutilated. It is she, my mother-wife, who is filled with anxiety and overwhelmed with longing for a whole body." Shakespeare seems to be acting out the same kind of denial which led Posthumus to denounce women at the end of Act II, projecting a man's unconscious fears as a woman's barely mediated reality. The irony of the scene is felt *at Imogen's expense,* "and irony is a silent form of aggression, in which the ironist does nothing to his object except what his auditors do for him." [41]

Shakespeare is indirectly identifying with the aggressive side of Posthumus.[42] In a curious gesture of identification he has Imogen bloody her own face before falling on the body:

41. C. L. Barber, "'Perfection of the Work': The Use of the Drama for Shakespeare," *Sarah Lawrence Alumnae Magazine,* Fall 1965, p. 16.
42. Hofling, "Notes on *Cymbeline,*" p. 133, notes that "Shakespeare became parentless with the death of his mother at the beginning of the pivotal period which saw the writing of *Coriolanus* and *Cymbeline.*" Thus, the meager biographical facts support the identification of Shakespeare and Posthumus, whose name "clearly represents a conscious, deliberate effort to call to mind the parentless state of this protagonist."

O!
Give colour to my pale cheek with thy blood,
That we the horrider may seem to those
Which chance to find us. O, my lord! my lord!
(IV.ii. 329–332)

When Caius Lucius enters, hers is the "horrid" bloody head, the symbol of aggression's consequences.[43] Lucius, the "enemy" of Britain, rescues her from isolation. The enemy is more than a friend: "And rather father thee than master thee," he says (IV.ii. 395). Lucius becomes the "good" father, unfrightened by the "horrid" sight, who rescues the daughter from unchosen abandonment. He is the only important male character in the play who does not impose an identity on her. Lucius is a comforting father; he neither worships nor defiles:

Be cheerful; wipe thine eyes:
Some falls are means the happier to arise. (IV.ii. 402–403) [44]

In encountering Lucius, Imogen passively fulfills the wish she actively expressed before fleeing the court for her haven:

Go, bid my woman feign a sickness, say
She'll home to her father . . . (III.ii. 75–76)

Imogen will bury her "master" (IV.ii. 388) in a ceremony without the surface display Belarius and the sons exhibit. They announce every move as they make it, directing our attention to the form of the ritual and away from its mourning purpose. She describes a quieter mourning:

. . . when
With wild wood-leaves and weeds I ha' strew'd his grave
And on it said a century of prayers

---

43. C. L. Barber has suggested to me that this gesture may also represent a primitive way of accepting Posthumus' love, as if to say, "Even if it is violent I accept it as part of myself, I identify myself with it."

44. Shakespeare's obsession with reversal makes Imogen turn from Lucius to Posthumus in the last scene. She doesn't plead for Lucius' life. Shakespeare pays a high price for averting tragedy. The minor or representative characters in the play—Pisanio, Lucius, Cornelius, the Gaoler—are the only ones whose actions encourage our unambiguous identification with them.

(Such as I can) twice o'er, I'll weep and sigh,
And leaving so his service, follow you,
So please you entertain me.   (IV.ii. 389–394)

She is capable of going on in life. The irony, of course, is that Cloten becomes the best-mourned character in *Cymbeline*. Shakespeare does not relinquish him easily.

Lucius describes Imogen as someone on a bed, with Cloten as her "bloody pillow" (IV.ii. 363), an appropriate setting for the play's version of the primal scene. As soon as he saves her, the scene (in more than one sense) shifts to the court, where we are told of the Queen's fever "Upon a desperate bed" (IV.iii. 6). Psychologically, the Queen's power and Imogen's exposure to Cloten's aggression are equivalent facts; Cloten is the penis of that phallic woman. With Cloten dead and Imogen protected, the Queen's disease is determined.

The sequence of events acts out this determination on the level of plotting. To strengthen the role of the father in the play's romance psychology it is necessary to transfer the phallic woman (Queen) from a position of imagined dominance to a position of accepted and tender childhood, in which case she becames Imogen, the subordinate to Lucius, but also the gentle boy who "hath taught us manly duties" (IV.ii. 397). The Queen and Imogen emerge clearly in this sequence as radically opposed, yet identical figures, two versions of one unconscious imago. Imogen's fidelity transforms the overwhelming mother into the sustaining mother who is then in turn sustained by, "armed" (IV.ii. 400) by, the representative of the only untainted father of the play. Lucius' concerned tenderness, it seems to me, is Shakespeare's reparation for the "silent aggression" of the previous episode, as if he sensed the nature of his irony and then recalled his protective paternalism.

In Act V, scene i, Posthumus is alone again. His isolation is a psychological reality, since he wished Imogen killed in his paranoiac response to his primal-scene fantasy; it is a moral statement, since in the economy of his character moral failure is equivalent to the loss of generative relationships with others; and it is a dramatic statement, since it sets him apart as a spectacle for the audience to witness, as Cloten was set apart at the beginning of Act IV. He has become a veritable exemplum of the repentant husband, the "chaste linen" of Act II having become a "bloody cloth" (V.i. 1). Shakespeare turns Posthumus' hyperbolic paranoia into its opposite—hyperbolic, masochistic submission to the all-powerful otherness of God. The vast disillusionment of his previous soliloquy dwindles to calling Imogen's imagined betrayal "wrying but a little" (V.i. 5) and "little faults" (V.i. 12). Submission is distanced in its impact because he is presented as an almost allegorical image.[45] The wish for blood, conflated as it was with the ambivalent wish for sexual intercourse, had "Italianated" Posthumus, and now he comes down on the side of Italian aggression against the motherland.

The way out of this identification with his own enemy is to become a British "Christian." Repentance here means utter passivity before the gods:

> But alack,
> You snatch some hence for little faults; that's love,
> To have them fall no more: you some permit
> To second ills with ills, each elder worse,
> And make them dread it, to the doers' thrift.
> But Imogen is your own, do your best wills,
> And make me blest to obey.   (V.i. 11–17)

Imogen is the property of the father. As G. Wilson Knight says, "One feels the divine powers very near, he is *talking* to them." [46] Such intimacy is purchased at the price of independent masculine assertion. Notice how ironically paradoxical is Posthumus' submission, for even as he renounces Oedipal wishes, he makes the gods responsible for Imogen's "death," which he thinks a reality. This "thrift" is based on complete reciprocity. Since the gods are responsible for everything, his submission relieves him of a burden of guilt at the very moment he accepts the burden of their inscrutable wills. "The wish for punishment, then, has the following meaning,"

45. Allegorical distancing, displaying the characters in isolation to reveal discrete qualities or impulses, is a form of decontamination, the dramatic equivalent of obsessional categorization. The technique has a counterpart in reporting action, raising it to the level of mentation, speaking *instead* of acting, and has another aspect in the frequent sharp shifts of tone, as in the pastoral scenes, where we move from tenderness to anxiety to tenderness, from the funeral dirge to Imogen's sight of the body to Lucius' entry. Isolation by words, isolation of moods, isolation of characters—the play carries these to compulsive and unintegrated lengths.
46. *Crown of Life*, p. 182.

wrote Reich of the masochistic character, "to bring about the relaxation after all, by way of a detour, and to shift the responsibility to
the punishing person." [47] The will to suffer is the inverse of aggression against the father. According to the logic of Posthumus' statement he should have said "each younger worse," [48] but the old ambivalence toward the "elder" lingers even in his resolve to die for his
sin. The only course of action to which Posthumus commits himself
is based on the expectation of death. His essential passivity remains
unchanged, since his identification with "the strength o' th' Leonati"
(V.i. 31) is seen as a means to this passivity, and only secondarily
as a positive act in the service of Britain. In Posthumus the mother-
identification beneath the aggression of Renaissance heroes from
Marlowe to Chapman is so close to the surface that it shrinks his
stature throughout the play and needs to be supplemented by an
almost manic insistence on his noble origin and masculine potency.

The "Christian" nature of Posthumus' conversion has been emphasized by Robert Grams Hunter,[49] who places the play in a long
tradition of comedies of "forgiveness," but he does not propose a
psychology adequate to explain the relationship between Posthumus
sinning and Posthumus repentant. Ernest Jones defined the psychological core of the tradition in terms of passive homosexuality:

> Object-love for the Mother is replaced by a regression to the
> original identification with her, so that incest is avoided and
> the Father pacified; further the opportunity is given of win-

47. *Character Analysis* (New York, 1933), p. 243.
48. The note in the Arden edition tries unsuccessfully to wrangle out of this
    contradiction, but I take it as characteristic of the continuing confusion
    embodied in Posthumus. Earlier Arviragus spoke of "the stinking-elder,
    grief" (IV.ii. 59), referring to the tree, but the word "elder" had a
    derogatory sense for Shakespeare. Biographical and internal evidence indi-
    cates that Shakespeare is attempting to master his own unconscious
    incestuous desires in the last plays. It seems to me that in *Cymbeline* self-
    hatred is still too powerful for him to project an untainted father as a
    character on the stage. The only father we could identify with is Caesar,
    who isn't a character at all (another form of isolation). Shakespeare keeps
    apart the good and bad aspects of the father and then simply converts
    the King into a good father at the end. If Cymbeline were *only* a projec-
    tion of Posthumus' attitude toward the father, there would be no need to
    excuse the King at the end; he simply would *be* different, would change
    as in a dream. The failure of *Cymbeline* is a failure of secondary elabora-
    tion; it is a play with a broken ego.
49. *Shakespeare and the Comedy of Forgiveness*, p. 176.

ning the Father's love by the adoption of a feminine attitude towards him. Peace of mind is purchased by means of a change of heart in the direction of a change in sex.[50]

The test of Imogen's virtue was based on a fear of incest and a strong reaction-formation against that fear. Now Posthumus' repentance attempts to undo the crime committed in fantasy. His death wish is as obsessively self-negating as his earlier plan was a perversion of justice. He "pays his heart,/For what his eyes eat only" (*Antony and Cleopatra* II.ii. 225–226) His penance harbors the same regressive wish as the test of Imogen's chastity, the wish for total union with the maternal source of his identity: ". . . so I'll die/For thee, O Imogen, even for whom my life/Is, every breath, a death . . ." (V.i. 25–27).[51] Undoing the crime repeats its motive, once the motive has been isolated from the fear of castration. The play doesn't dramatize the overcoming of the wish for oral union, but fulfills the wish within the carefully controlled context of the final scene, after the vision has overcompensated for his weak defenses.

In his resolve to die for Imogen, Posthumus becomes a Briton once more. In terms of the play's magical thinking, this means that Iachimo, an embodiment of his sexual aggression, has been defeated within him. The next scene presents us with the correlative of this psychological fact:

Iach. The heaviness and guilt within my bosom
   Takes off my manhood: I have belied a lady,
   The princess of this country; and the air on't
   Revengingly enfeebles me, or could this carl,
   A very drudge of Nature's, have subdued me
   In my profession?   (V.ii. 1–6)

Posthumus' guilt having been magically displaced along with the castration fear, he can now join the lost sons in rescuing the father

50. "A Psycho-Analytic Study of the Holy Ghost Concept" (1922), *Essays in Applied Psycho-Analysis,* II, 366.
51. Shakespeare usually imagines one component of heroic action as a resistance to precisely this wish. Cf. *Hamlet* IV.iv. 33–35: "What is a man,/ If his chief good and market of his time/Be but to sleep and feed? A beast, no more."

from certain defeat. His aggression against the ideal woman has been converted into identification with her and aggression in her defense. Only then can the father be restored as a stable force within traditional social hieararchy. And only then are we ready to receive the vision of Jupiter. On the level of fantasy the situation of Acts I and II has been reversed, the defenses (literal and psychological) of British virtue restored by Shakespearean fiat. It is a technique which quartered hath three parts wish fulfillment and one part playful detachment.[52]

When the battle's lost and won, Posthumus finds himself reversed again, as constraint becomes the symbol of liberation. His initial gift of a "manacle of love" (I.ii. 53) is transformed into literal situation. The captive's chains ironically gratify the earlier wish to bind himself and Imogen beyond the vicissitudes of time. The father in him makes him a child and the child sees imprisonment as mercy:

> Is't enough I am sorry?
> So children temporal fathers do appease;
> Gods are more full of mercy.   (V.iv. 11–13)

The manacle (bracelet) appeared before as a symbol of genital betrayal, and now that its significance has been retransformed in a kind of visual pun into part of its sender's immediate reality, he can find withdrawn repose. Sleep will reunite him with the image of the good mother, beyond words. "O Imogen,/I'll speak to thee in silence" (V.iv. 28–29). Posthumus has become an infant, *infans*, speechless.

Solemn music, as always in Shakespeare, engenders a mood of relaxed and enraptured oral receptivity ("If music be the food of love, play on"). As in *Pericles,* it prepares us to retrieve lost identifications. We lose ourselves in the music to find the father whose

---

52. Posthumus' long speech at V.iii. 3–58 distances the battle into words in an attempt to monumentalize it (as a form of legendary history) and he emphasizes the complete reversal that also characterizes the description in Holinshed. Holinshed contains the "narrow lane" (line 52) and subscribes to the invincibility of Haie (Belarius). The idea that men "hurt behind" (12) are cowards goes back at least as far as Horace. Unconsciously, the speech describes a homosexual encounter in which Belarius and the sons, "having found the back-door open" (45), drive the Romans from the "narrow land." The emphasis on flight (24) and the repeated "Stand, stand" (28 and 31) indicate sexual arousal, and the anal aspect is symbolized by the strewn bodies of the dead, the "mortal bugs o' th' field" (51), and by Posthumus' line, "Will you rhyme upon't,/And vent it for a mock'ry?" (55–56). This is one of those "mortal accidents" Jupiter calls human history.

loss signified violent sexual release in a world saturated with confusions. The spectacular nature of the vision is consonant with its regressive and restorative aims, since it is literally a *spectacle,* something to be looked at intensely and introjected through the eye.[53]

The vision recapitulates the elements of Posthumus' family romance. Jupiter is first invoked by the denigration of humanity, but his "adulteries" are blamed for parental neglect:

> No more thou thunder-master, show
>   thy spite on mortal flies:
> With Mars fall out, with Juno chide,
>   that thy adulteries
> Rates and revenges.   (V.iv. 30–34)

The role of the father is to protect the child from "this earth-vexing smart" (V.iv. 42), his life, while all creative power is invested in "Great nature" (V.iv. 48). Since lineage defines essence, the dream presents Posthumus' past simply as a deviation from his true value. We are intended to forget the ambiguities which surrounded the initial presentation of his character, the ambivalent roots of what now becomes "needless jealousy" (V.iv. 66). His brothers identify Posthumus with themselves as servants of earthly fathers. The failure of trust is projected onto the god, as Jupiter is given the ultimatum of direct intervention or the loss of human love. In other words, the superego is threatened with the superego's own weapons. Posthumus' family projects onto the paternal figure the very deviations Posthumus attempted unsuccessfully to defend himself against before his repentance, the adultery he feared, the trust that failed. The heavenly father seems tainted, not the son.[54]

53. In one of the more orthodox passages of *Love's Body,* Norman O. Brown writes: "Identification with the representative person whom we 'look up to' takes place through the eye. In psychoanalytic jargon, the super-ego is based on 'incorporation through the eye' or 'ocular introjection'; it is the sight of a parental figure that becomes a permanent part of us; and that now supervises, watches us" (p. 122).

54. This antagonism toward the father supports Ludwig Jekels' view that "the feeling of guilt which, in tragedy, rests upon the son, appears in comedy displaced on the father; it is the father who is guilty" ("On the Psychology of Comedy," reprinted in *Comedy: Meaning and Form,* ed. Robert W. Corrigan [San Francisco, 1965], p. 264). In *Cymbeline,* as in *Measure for Measure* and *All's Well That Ends Well,* the "problematic" aspect of the comedy derives from the fact that the father is finally absolved from guilt.

Jupiter descends in all his phallic power, "sitting upon an eagle." The vision is a kratophany, a revelation of the father's unmitigated power, expressing in its crucial lines a teleological assurance of patriarchal stability:

> Be not with mortal accidents opprest,
>   No care of yours it is, you know 'tis ours.
> Whom best I love I cross; to make my gift,
>   The more delay'd, delighted. (V.iv. 99–102)

The vision restores the nucleus of Posthumus' superego in a god who minimizes the significance of human suffering in order to bind the fulfillment of wishes to a sense of the ego's dependence. Jupiter is a god designed to keep humanity in a state of infantile expectation of external rewards, precisely the god appropriate to the conflicts Shakespeare imagines in Posthumus. His "gifts" imply the need for self-sacrifice, and he withholds gratification in order to intensify human responses. *Cymbeline* is a regression in the service of Jupiter as superego, a god who takes care of humanity because it cannot take care of itself. The sheer power of such an internalized father would make homosexual submission and mother-identification almost inevitable.

Jupiter's sublimated anality reverses Cymbeline's paranoia. While Cymbeline would "pen her up" (I.ii. 84), Jupiter gives Imogen as a gift. Cymbeline withholds out of fear of baseness, Jupiter withholds in order to delight. ("Delight" incorporates a homonymic pun on "light" and a projection of visual interest onto its object. The gift, rather than the receiver, is imagined as delighted.) Yet for both Imogen is a possession, for Cymbeline a "thing" and for Jupiter a "piece of tender air" (a curious image which expresses substantiality and insubstantiality at the same time).[55] Jupiter is a con-

55. Of course, air is a "higher" element in Renaissance philosophy, cosmology, and physiology, but this doesn't explain the effect or meaning of the conception. Imogen becomes a pervasive *presence*, literally sustaining, yet ungraspable and impersonal. That the father gives the "tender air" as a gift implies an unconscious anal conception of birth and masculine sexual sufficiency. The notion of woman as man's possession is the other side of Renaissance idealization. In III.vii. 43, Guiderius says, "I bid for you as I do buy." Fenichel writes that "a society whose ideology makes one marriage partner appear as the property of the other, for this reason increases the psycho-economic usefulness of jealousy" ("A Contribution to the Psychology of Jealousy," in *The Collected Papers of Otto Fenichel, First*

trolled and elevated version of the King, a father who grants the son's Oedipal wish in exchange for the ability to withhold gratification and idealize erotic interest. Jupiter does for Posthumus what Shakespeare does for the audience, for Shakespeare also withholds gratification until the last dazzling scene, carrying a conventional comic form to an unprecedented degree of complication before offering us the gift of total reconciliation.

Shakespeare seems to sense how reductively escapist the vision is—it patches over all of Posthumus' violence in wish and act—since he instills it with comically humanized tension between the ghosts and the god. On one level he is playing with the idea of awe-inspiring deity. Jupiter "throws a thunderbolt," tells the ghosts to "hush!," exhibits the impatience of a father taken from more immediate pleasures to perform parental functions, and ascends with his eagle preening its feathers in self-satisfaction. Insofar as the deus ex machina is a deus, he has been humanized; insofar as he comes ex machina, he is divorced from the fluctuations of the human world. The sheer mechanics of the vision, together with the use of fourteeners and alexandrines (those old, repetitive, and "crudely" familiar rhythms providing a sense of tradition together with a sense of detached superiority in a Jacobean audience) come together to displace our energies away from the awe-inspiring and toward control. Formalization provided, and still provides, a way of coping with what otherwise might be an anxiety-releasing situation. The vision thus suits Shakespeare's felt need to bring his audience into contact with paternal authority from a child's point of view without engendering the sense of abject submission Posthumus contains.[56]

On the other hand, the formal defenses of the vision are improvised for the occasion. They do not fit into a recurrent pattern, and therefore evaporate with the ghosts. Posthumus wakes to remember

---

Series [New York, 1954], p. 351). For documentation of the notion of woman as property see Louis B. Wright, *Middle-Class Culture*, pp. 465–507.

56. The spectacular nature of the vision has obvious connections with the masque, but it seems to me that a critic who only notes masque conventions—surface display, stage machinery, the equivalence of character and function, magical power—misses the point of the vision. The important fact is not that the vision has affinities with the masque form, or that Shakespeare might have been "influenced" by his courtly audience at Blackfriars, but that he found in the convention a way of embodying the kind of experience I am discussing.

his family but makes no mention of the god. But at least he restores generative potency to his depression:

> Sleep, thou hast been a grandsire, and begot
> A father to me: and thou hast created
> A mother, and two brothers . . .   (V.iv. 123–125)

The powers of generation now reside completely in a masculine figure, a grandsire. The ambiguity of "begot . . . to me" contains the implication that Posthumus is the passive partner in the relationship. A few lines later, however, he is back to distrust of earthly fathers, and we are wondering how Shakespeare will conflate or at least structure split paternity. Before Posthumus' speech ends, we are smiling half out of indulgence, half to contain irritation. He reads the oracular tablet and then says,

> 'Tis still a dream: or else such stuff as madmen
> Tongue, and brain not: either both, or nothing,
> Or senseless speaking, or a speaking such
> As sense cannot untie. Be what it is,
> The action of my life is like it . . .   ,
>   (V.iv. 146–150)

Compulsive doubt about the action of his life *does* define all his relationships, with the exception of the mother-imago he worships. Given that confusion, the only unequivocal act left to him is self-sacrifice. He relishes the possibility of sacrificing his life to become a source of gratification:

> *First Gaol.* Come, sir, are you ready for death?
> *Post.* Over-roasted rather: ready long ago.
> *First Gaol.* Hanging is the word, sir: if you be ready for that, you are well cook'd.
> *Post.* So, if I prove a good repast to the spectators, the dish pays the shot. (V.iv. 152–157) [57]

The feeling we have is that Posthumus is to be hanged "on the expectation of plenty" (*Macbeth* III.iii), only it is *we* who are expect-

---

57. In *Erogeneity and Libido* (New York, 1957), Robert Fliess notes the cannibalistic conception of execution contained in these lines.

ing the sacrificial feast, he who is conscious of providing it. There could hardly be a better way of transforming his mother-identification into a comic gratification.[58] As the dialogue moves along, we get metaphors from the Gaoler for payment of debts (as drained vitality), ego-loss in drinking, death as release from castration fear ("he that sleeps feels not the toothache" [V.iv. 175–176]) and finally a series of "eye" images which also defend against castration fears by distancing them into structured prose. The Gaoler's line, "Unless a man would marry a gallows . . . I never saw one so prone" (V.iv. 204–205), repeats as humor the associations of marriage and mutilation so prevalent in the earlier manifestations of Posthumus' condition. Posthumus is imagined to share an unproblematic exchange with another person for the first time in the play, which shows how essential his passivity is to the characteristic responses Shakespeare projects in him.

The prison scene reinforces Posthumus' earlier regression and expands his purified mother-identification to include the restoration of the traditional family matrix and, in the theophany, a revelation of the ego-ideal which authenticates human roles. From a psychoanalytic point of view, Jupiter is no arbitrary deity. In an analogy to the fragmented personality, Freud wrote: "If we throw a crystal to the floor, it breaks; but not into haphazard pieces. It comes apart along its lines of cleavage into fragments whose boundaries, though they were invisible, were predetermined by the crystal's structure." [59] The vision of Jupiter is the final stage in a regressive process which reveals the structural center of Posthumus' conflicts while it recovers the therapeutic efficacy of his omnipotent paternal superego. Posthumus moves in his psychic disintegration and partial reintegration from reaction-formation (which fails) to violent ambivalence (which releases the wish for the death of the sexual mother-wife) to mother-identification (which restores original purity and denies castration fears by assuming a castrated position) and finally to the

58. Freud writes in "Humour" (1927), *S.E.*, XXI, 162: "There is no doubt that the essence of humour is that one spares oneself the affects to which the situation would naturally give rise and dismisses the possibility of such expressions of emotion with a jest." Freud cites the humour of a man about to be executed. In Posthumus' last appearance before the reunion Shakespeare allows us a modicum of identification with his weak hero.

59. "New Introductory Lectures on Psycho-Analysis" (1933 [1932]), *S.E.*, XXII, 59.

restoration of the father's care for his impotent child. The child's potency is representative of paternal values; it only operates effectively as aggression in the service of the mother country. *Cymbeline* reinstitutes a participatory hierarchy; the moral and military restoration of the child depends, psychologically, on identification with the aggressor after homosexual submission.[60] It would be more accurate to say that Posthumus *is moved* through the stages of this process, since Shakespeare's strategy is to display him to us at critical stages along his psychological journey.

Only in the last scene does Posthumus find oral union without castration. He strikes Imogen in a moment of rage against the futility of possessing her:

> O Imogen!
> My queen, my life, my wife, O Imogen,
> Imogen, Imogen!
> *Imo.*   Peace my lord, hear, hear—
> *Post.* Shall's have a play of this? Thou scornful page,
> There lie thy part. *[Striking her: she falls]*
> (V.v. 225–229)

"There lie thy part." Aggressive compulsion to subdue the "woman's part," which was a projection of his fear for his masculinity, is recapitulated in a sudden blow. Then there is a separation of thirty lines, and the final reunion. Posthumus speaks the most beautiful line in the play:

> Hang there like fruit, my soul,
> Till the tree die.   (V.v. 263–264)

The line is a magnificent condensation of fantasy and meaning. At once oral and phallic, it grants his deepest wish and platonically de-

---

60. We thus have a double identification: (1) identification with the mother-wife, passive and receptive; and (2) identification with the father, the aggressor feared because of aggressive and incestuous wishes. The two identifications are expressed simultaneously by condensing the parents into a phallic mother or androgynous father, as Shakespeare does at the end of the play. On the "hermaphroditic ideal offered to the world by Christianity" see Ernest Jones, "Holy Ghost Concept," pp. 367–369. The quoted phrase is on p. 368.

sexualizes it.[61] Symbiotic reunion with the nourishing mother creates an image of merger in absolute dependence. Read one way, the line says that Posthumus himself becomes the fruit-bearing tree, Imogen the sublimated fruit. But Posthumus can also be seen as the fruit sustained by Imogen as the tree. The distinction between subject and object has been removed. (Even the movements of the mouth involved in speaking the line parallel its meaning. The lips only touch once, gently on the sound of "my," every other word open-mouthed in receptivity, and "tree die" leaves Posthumus' mouth opening.) [62]

Phallic restoration and oral merger recur in the oracular tablet and the Soothsayer's vision. The reunion of Cymbeline and his sons re-members the familial body of the King and of Britain:

> The lofty cedar, royal Cymbeline,
> Personates thee: and thy lopp'd branches point
> Thy two sons forth . . .   (V.v. 454–456)

Even the Soothsayer's verb ("point . . . forth") emphasizes the phallic nature of the act of reconstruction. The King's body made whole, Cymbeline can submit to Caesar without fear of mangled laws. The rationalization of his previous defiance is forgotten as he invests all responsibility in the castrating Queen:

> Although the victor, we submit to Caesar,
> And to the Roman empire; promising
> To pay our wonted tribute, from the which
> We were dissuaded by our wicked queen.
>   (V.v. 461–464)

The play's escapist way out of the ambivalence it embodies grants the wish for bodily and political integrity at the price of polarizing

61. As if to emphasize the sublimity of Posthumus' line, Cymbeline next says, "How now, my flesh, my child?" Imogen thus embodies heaven and earth, as before she embodied sacred and profane. This is not her literal nature, however, but a wishful idealization in the interest of reconciling opposites.

62. Although sound-interpretations can be used to "prove" anything, this is one instance where the sound of a line merges completely with its unconscious "oral" meaning, fusing poetry with character and situation.

guilt and innocence. Shakespeare reverses Cymbeline's responsibility because, psychologically, submission to the father Caesar is a safeguard against the evil mother's feared powers. With the Queen dead, Cymbeline has again become the composite parent who bred Posthumus:

> O, what am I?
> A mother to the birth of three?
> (V.v. 369–370)

Cloten becomes "her son" (V.v. 272) alone. Behind these lines we can see the fulfillment of Posthumus' wish that men be without the aid of women.

Submission to Caesar is the play's final act of fusion:

> For the Roman eagle,
> From south to west on wing soaring aloft,
> Lessen'd herself and in the beams o' the sun
> So vanish'd; which foreshow'd our princely eagle,
> Th' imperial Caesar, should again unite
> His favour with the radiant Cymbeline,
> Which shines here in the west.   (V.v. 471–477)

For the purposes of this recapitulatory fantasy, Caesar becomes a female eagle, an androgynous prince, yet the active force in the reunion. The suggestion of submission in "Lessen'd herself" reverses the true situation, and Cymbeline becomes stationary, "radiant," receptive in his power. Oral fusion of equally potent powers transcends the sense of submission, as does Cymbeline's order to "let/A Roman, and a British ensign wave/Friendly together" (V.v. 480–482). Political antagonism was an unpaid debt to the father, just as Posthumus' enraged paranoia was an attempt to absolve the father of sexual responsibility, and in the final harmony both earthly fathers are elevated to the level of sublimely potent nobility, bisexual, active and submissive at once.

The eagle flies from south to west, from Rome, the scene of sexual betrayal, to Milford Haven, the "heaven" of harmony. In his earlier telling the Soothsayer said:

> I saw Jove's bird, the Roman eagle, wing'd
> From the spongy south to this part of the west,
> There vanish'd in the sunbeams . . . (IV.ii. 348–350)

The "spongy south" suggests the softness of the lower regions, sexual as well as geographical. The play's other uses of the word "south" link it to Imogen's chamber ("The chimney/Is south the chamber," says Iachimo [II.iv. 80–81]) and to Cloten's anality ("The south-fog rot him!" [II.iii. 132]). In the jargon of psychoanalysis, the eagle's flight summarizes the flight in the play from genital and anal eroticism to sublimated oral fusion which guarantees masculine virility. Caesar, Cymbeline, Posthumus (in his identification with the fruitful tree) all become symbols of a deeply rooted identification with the omnipotent mother the child imagines in infancy. In Shakespeare's world the good father includes the maternal within himself. The King is both parents combined, and thus a model for the son to follow if he would avoid the potential for self-destruction involved in seeking external sexual gratification. Shakespeare's re-mythologized world defends against anxiety and disillusioned fantasies by the regressive restoration of preambivalent parental figures.[63] The sense of wonderful and mysterious harmony so many critics find in the final scene derives from the convergence of ego-ideals with the characters' actual situation. The tension between wish and reality dissolves in the sense of interdependent relationships identical with their ideal images. But not completely, because we are aware of how compensatory this final fantasy is.

Shakespeare replaces the paranoiac Cymbeline, the one who raged against Imogen, by a new Cymbeline, one who thinks in terms of trust, without any transition from one conception to its wish-fulfilling substitute. The new Cymbeline says,

> Mine eyes
> Were not in fault, for she was beautiful:
> Mine ears that heard her flattery, not my heart
> That thought her like her seeming. It had been vicious
> To have mistrusted her . . . (V.v. 62–66)

63. By preambivalent I mean prior to sexual differentiation.

This is an example of compulsive thinking. As Simon O. Lesser points out, "Compulsives . . . develop alternative explanations of events to express their ambivalence and to avoid decisions; their thinking is a mechanism of defense." [64] Shakespeare is apologizing for Cymbeline's past, succumbing to magical denial in the interest of purifying the final reunions. The elation of the final scene contains an admixture of manic defense against the play's potentially catastrophic illusions. Shakespeare is patching over a deep split in his ego (and the dominant ego of his age) which leads to violent conceptions of genital sex and radically polarized images of sexual identity. The final scene edits the past to conform to present wishes. As Norman Rabkin, following a suggestion of Granville-Barker's, has acknowledged, at the center of the play's conscious strategy of plot complication and its rationally absurd disclosures lies a wish fulfillment. "If everything comes out happily, we must be aware in the end that it does so because the playwright has made it do so by tricks which he has made us acknowledge as tricks even while we believe them." [65] An accurate analogy here is not to religious experience of total harmony, but to the evasion of ambivalence which caricatures religious atonement.[66] The dialectical relationship between sin and repentance freezes into a duality; the trick lies in Shakespeare's ability to *substitute* happiness for guilt while temporarily seducing us into a sense of *felix culpa*.

Cymbeline presents us in its final tour de force of restorations with a compensatory fantasy beneath which the original fears still lurk. Posthumus becomes merely the innocent victim of Iachimo's subtlety. The Queen, without whom Cymbeline was helpless, becomes "naught" (V.v. 271). Even Belarius' responsibility is partially siphoned off to Euriphile (we are told that she actually stole the sons at his instigation). The other side of this negating process is the idealization of familial and aristocratic roles. Cymbeline is ready

64. "The Source of Guilt and the Sense of Guilt: Kafka's 'The Trial,'" reprinted in *Psychoanalysis and Literature*, ed. Hendrik M. Ruitenbeek (New York, 1964), p. 193. E. C. Pettet has recognized the absence of transformation in Cymbeline: "We do not feel that the king overcomes his evil instincts (if he ever had any), and he certainly does not impress us as a figure of regeneration" (*Shakespeare and the Romance Tradition* [New York, 1949], p. 192).
65. *Shakespeare and the Common Understanding* (New York, 1967), p. 210.
66. Such evasion of ambivalence is discussed in Charles Rycroft's "On Idealization, Illusion, and Catastrophic Disillusion," in *Imagination and Reality* (London, 1968), pp. 29–41.

to put Guiderius to death for murdering a "prince" (V.v. 291) who by that point has been drained of his princely blood ten times over, and Shakespeare, as throughout, achieves his irony at the father's expense. Legalistic compliance in the myth of noble birth, the automatic assumption of hierarchic value, allegorically reductive and romantically useful, becomes in *Cymbeline* a device for more problematic restorations. We have no sense that Cymbeline has overcome his past deviations from the proprieties of his role. Shakespeare is playing god, and while his grace may be good theology, it makes unsatisfying drama. The final scene, as R. J. Kaufmann has observed,[67] restores roles rather than persons, each role being slipped into place with jigsaw precision. This may be enough for the illusion of harmony but it sacrifices the intensity of felt psychic conflict for the depersonalized establishment of defenses. Shakespeare fences off what threatens the coherent expression of love, but pays the price of diminishing his characters to their familial functions. The final scene retells the story of the play, not as it was, but as it might have been.

Shakespeare has not yet found the psychic courage to admit that the fears and aggressions he evokes in *Cymbeline* reside in a father, and that their object is an unconsciously harbored mother-imago. In order to save the King, Shakespeare splits the mother into Imogen and the Queen and thus perpetuates the illusion of external responsibility. In *The Winter's Tale* Leontes will become the focus of paranoiac illusion and there will be no apology for the violence of his regression and no need to keep him from direct acceptance of maternal love.

Perhaps Shakespeare knew the truth beneath the illusion. In the final line, in a final parenthesis, we seem to have a last ironic hint of his intuition that the purification has not occurred:

> Never was a war did cease
> (Ere bloody hands were wash'd) with such a peace.
> (V. v. 485–486)

67. "Puzzling Epiphanies," p. 398.

ᐳBIBLIOGRAPHICAL GUIDE

These suggestions are meant to provide a barely minimal course of reading that covers the outlines of psychoanalytic theory, places psychoanalysis in historical and scientific perspective, introduces the theory and practice of psychoanalytic criticism, and shows where reference information can be found. No attempt is made to cover rival theories and therapies, however meritorious, and many important works within the Freudian tradition are not mentioned.

For works available in paperback editions, publishers' names are given; hardbound books show only the place and date of publication. Subtitles have been omitted except where necessary for clarity.

I. PSYCHOANALYTIC THEORY

A clear and succinct theoretical summary is:

CHARLES BRENNER, *An Elementary Textbook of Psychoanalysis.* Anchor.

All three of FREUD's introductions of psychoanalytic theory for the layman are of interest, though none is satisfactory by itself. Of these three, the first takes greatest account of possible objections:

A General Introduction to Psychoanalysis. Washington Square Press.

New Introductory Lectures on Psychoanalysis. Norton.

An Outline of Psychoanalysis. Norton.

The importance of reading Freud would be difficult to exaggerate. Very few of his *Collected Papers* (10 vols., Collier) are unenlightening; promiscuous and repeated reading among them is probably the best way of deepening one's acquaintance with psychoanalytic thought. Because papers that seem incomprehensible when first encountered often begin to make sense in the light of other papers, and because individual reactions vary greatly, no sequential list of papers can be given. Volume 10 of the Collier series (*Studies in Parapsychology*), however, may be safely ignored. Some of Freud's papers pertaining especially to art are collected in his:

On Creativity and the Unconscious. Harper.

Among Freud's books, of paramount importance is:

The Interpretation of Dreams (especially chapters 6 and 7). Avon.

A helpful book for readers who question the reality of unconscious causation is:

The Psychopathology of Everyday Life. Norton.

Other important books of Freud's include:

The Ego and the Id. Norton.
Jokes and Their Relation to the Unconscious. Norton.
Leonardo da Vinci and a Memory of His Childhood. Norton.
The Problem of Anxiety. Norton.

Some of Freud's best known books are less useful for basic theoretical understanding than are his clinical papers. Works such as *Beyond the Pleasure Principle* (Bantam), *Civilization and Its Discontents* (Norton), *The Future of an Illusion* (Anchor), *Group Psychology and the Analysis of the Ego* (Bantam), *Moses and Monotheism* (Vintage), and *Totem and Taboo* (Norton) attempt, with varying success, to extend psychoanalytic theory speculatively; they should not be mistaken for the underpinnings of Freud's system.

A readable and important book extending Freud's developmental theory is:

ERIK H. ERIKSON, *Childhood and Society.* Norton.

The same author has written one of the most challenging books that attempt a psychoanalytic understanding of historical problems:

Young Man Luther. Norton.

Important books for a grasp of ego psychology include Erikson's *Childhood and Society* and the following:

ANNA FREUD, *The Ego and the Mechanisms of Defense.* Revised edition. New York, 1966.

HEINZ HARTMANN, *Ego Psychology and the Problem of Adaptation.* New York, 1958.

DAVID RAPAPORT, *The Structure of Psychoanalytic Theory.* International Universities Press.

Useful attempts to clarify obscure points of theory are:

MERTON M. GILL, *Topography and Systems in Psychoanalytic Theory.* International Universities Press.

PETER MADISON, *Freud's Concept of Repression and Defense.* Minneapolis, 1961.

The most important reference work, indispensable for any detailed use of psychoanalytic concepts, is:

OTTO FENICHEL, *The Psychoanalytic Theory of Neurosis.* New York, 1945.

In addition to Fenichel's excellent but dated bibliography, specialized studies can be located in:

ALEXANDER GRINSTEIN, *Index of Psychoanalytic Writings.* New York, 1956–

II. PERSPECTIVES ON THE PSYCHOANALYTIC MOVEMENT

A concise survey of Freud's concepts and those of rival schools is:

J. A. C. BROWN, *Freud and the Post-Freudians.* Pelican.

A more detailed study is:

RUTH L. MUNROE, *Schools of Psychoanalytic Thought.* New York, 1955.

The relation of Jung's psychology to Freud's is explored by:

FREUD, *On the History of the Psychoanalytic Movement.* Collier.

EDWARD GLOVER, *Freud or Jung.* Meridian.

Valuable information about the scientific origins of psychoanalysis and the history of its development is contained in:

ERNEST JONES, *The Life and Work of Sigmund Freud.* 3 vols. New York, 1953–1957; or 1 vol. abridged. Anchor.

Books exploring the background and influence of Freudian thought include:

FREDERICK J. HOFFMAN, *Freudianism and the Literary Mind.* Louisiana State University Press.

BENJAMIN NELSON, ed., *Freud and the Twentieth Century.* Meridian.

PHILIP RIEFF, *Freud: The Mind of the Moralist.* Anchor.

PAUL ROAZEN, *Freud: Political and Social Thought.* New York, 1968.

GEORGE F. WILBUR and WARNER MUENSTERBERGER, eds., *Psychoanalysis and Culture.* Science Editions.

Considerations of psychoanalytic methodology and its empirical grounding are:

NORMAN S. GREENFIELD and WILLIAM C. LEWIS, eds., *Psychoanalysis and Current Biological Thought.* Madison and Milwaukee, 1965.

E. PUMPIAN-MINDLIN, ed., *Psychoanalysis As Science.* Stanford, 1952.

MICHAEL SHERWOOD, *The Logic of Explanation in Psychoanalysis.* New York and London, 1969.

III. PSYCHOANALYTIC THEORY OF LITERATURE

A helpful argument in favor of applying Freudian concepts to criticism is:

SIMON O. LESSER, *Fiction and the Unconscious*. Vintage.

A more technical and miscellaneous work, especially useful for its bibliography, is:

ERNST KRIS, *Psychoanalytic Explorations in Art*. Schocken.

The most ambitious model of reader psychology, applied to a wide spectrum of literary and nonliterary forms, is:

NORMAN N. HOLLAND, *The Dynamics of Literary Response*. New York, 1968.

An early but still striking demonstration of the applicability of psychoanalysis to the study of myths is:

OTTO RANK, *The Myth of the Birth of the Hero*. Vintage.

A suggestive adaptation of psychoanalytic theory to the problem of definining a genre can be found in:

ANGUS FLETCHER, *Allegory*. Ithaca, 1964.

A brief survey, containing some bibliographical suggestions, is:

FREDERICK CREWS, "Literature and Psychology," in *Relations of Literary Study*, ed. James Thorpe. Modern Language Association.

A more extensive bibliography, not very dependable, is:

NORMAN KIELL, *Psychoanalysis, Psychology, and Literature*. Madison, 1963.

IV. PSYCHOANALYTIC CRITICISM

Excellent anthologies, showing the range of possible applications of psychoanalysis to criticism, are:

LEONARD and ELEANOR MANHEIM, eds., *Hidden Patterns*. New York, 1966.

WILLIAM PHILLIPS, ed., *Art and Psychoanalysis*. Meridian.

Studies representing various critical and biographical uses of psychoanalysis are:

FREDERICK CREWS, *The Sins of the Fathers: Hawthorne's Psychological Themes.* Oxford.

KURT EISSLER, *Goethe: A Psychoanalytic Study, 1775-1786.* 2 vols. Detroit, 1963.

PHYLLIS GREENACRE, *Swift and Carroll.* New York, 1955.

NORMAN N. HOLLAND, *Psychoanalysis and Shakespeare.* New York, Toronto, London, 1966.

ERNEST JONES, *Hamlet and Oedipus.* Anchor.

BERNARD C. MEYER, *Joseph Conrad: A Psychoanalytic Biography.* Princeton University Press.

DANIEL A. WEISS, *Oedipus in Nottingham: D. H. Lawrence.* Seattle, 1962.

ᔉ CONTRIBUTORS

Sheldon R. Brivic was born in Newark, N.J., in 1943. He became interested in Joyce while studying with Professor Marvin Magalaner at the City College of New York, and he received his doctorate from the University of California at Berkeley in 1969. His work on Joyce includes two articles in *James Joyce Quarterly*. He is now assistant professor of English at Temple University.

Frederick Crews was born in Philadelphia in 1933. Educated at Yale and Princeton, he is now professor of English at the University of California, Berkeley. His books include *E. M. Forster: The Perils of Humanism, The Sins of the Fathers: Hawthorne's Psychological Themes, The Pooh Perplex,* and *The Patch Commission.*

Albert D. Hutter was born in New York City in 1941. He holds an A.B. from Antioch College and an M.A. from Cambridge and is currently finishing his Berkeley dissertation on Dickens. He has been appointed assistant professor of English at UCLA.

David Leverenz was born in Orange, N.J., in 1942, and grew up in Princeton. He holds an A.B. from Harvard and a Ph.D. (1969) from the University of California, Berkeley. His dissertation was a psychoanalytic overview of American literature. He taught briefly at Mills College and is now assistant professor of English at Livingston College, Rutgers University.

Murray M. Schwartz was born in New York City in 1942. At the University of Rochester he studied literature and psychoanalysis under the influence of Norman O. Brown and R. J. Kaufmann. His Berkeley dissertation will be a psychoanalytic study of Shakespeare's last plays. He is now assistant professor of English at the State University of New York at Buffalo.

Richard L. Stein was born in Los Angeles in 1943. He holds degrees from Amherst College and the University of California, Berkeley, and is currently preparing a study of the role of the arts in Ruskin, Rossetti, and Pater. Beginning in 1970, he will be assistant professor of English at Harvard.

INDEX

Budgen, F., 155n., 162n.
Butt, J., 35–36

Caricature, 60–62
Carlyle, T., 52
Castration, 30–31, 33, 38–39, 44–48, 50, 53, 71, 82, 87, 94, 100–103, 111–112, 124–126, 128–132, 135, 137, 143, 146–150, 154, 157, 161, 173, 198, 226, 242, 243, 248, 252, 255, 260–261, 264–267, 277–278
Chase, R., 113
Chomsky, N., 15n.
Cirlot, J., 245n.
Cohn, N., 13n.
Collins, P., 52n.
Comfort, A., 12n.
Compulsion. *See* Obsession
Condensation, 233, 247
Conflict. *See* Ambivalence, Oedipus complex
Corrigan, R., 273n.
Crews, F., 288, 289
Criticism, theory of, 1–23 (passim), 138–139, 207–208
Crompton, L., 25n.

Darby, M., 225n.
Denial, 173, 184, 187, 198, 231, 252, 264, 266, 282
Dependency. *See* Passivity
Dickens, C., 25–65
Distancing, 191, 195, 228, 238, 246n., 256, 264, 269n., 272n., 277

Edwards, J., 93
Eissler, K., 289
Eliot, G., 64n.
Eliot, T., 16
Ellmann, R., 124n., 127n., 142n., 154n., 204 and n., 212
Emerson, R., 84
Erikson, E., 13n., 257, 286
Evans, L., 165n., 166n., 179n.

Family romance, 63–64, 213, 247
Farrell, B., 200n.
Father-conflict. *See* Ambivalence, Oedipus complex
Feidelson, C., 114
Fenichel, O., 22n., 41n., 125, 127n., 129n., 130n., 137n., 142n., 157, 160, 200, 225n., 274n., 286

Fetishism, 127, 130, 133, 137, 148, 151–152, 154–155, 157–158, 161–162
Finkelstein, D., 91n.
Flanagan, T., 137n.
Fletcher, A., 263n., 288
Fliess, R., 276n.
Flügel, J., 263n.
Fodor, J., 15n.
Ford, G., 47n., 53n.
Forster, J., 26n., 54n.
Franklin, H., 91n., 114n.
Freud, A., 225n., 237n., 286
Freud, S., 4, 5, 8n., 12, 14n., 15n., 16n., 17, 19, 33, 34n., 41n., 46n., 48n., 51n., 57n., 125, 127, 129n., 130, 134, 136, 140n., 148, 149 and n., 151n., 157n., 170n., 188–189, 195, 197, 198, 199, 200, 212n., 217, 225n., 234n., 237n., 242n., 244n., 247, 261, 277 and n., 285, 286, 287
Freund, P., 247n.
Frye, N., 2–7, 9, 10 and n., 19n., 162n.

Gilbert, S., 155n.
Gill, M., 286
Glover, E., 8–9, 287
Gluck, C., 117
Goldberg, S., 118–119, 120
Goldman, A., 120–121
Gottschalk, L., 16n.
Greenacre, P., 289
Greenfield, N., 17n., 287
Grinstein, A., 286
Grossman, A., 10n.
Guetti, J., 114 and n.
Guilt. *See* Oedipus complex

Hagan, J., 41n.
d'Hangest, G., 183n., 185n.
Hardy, T., 64n.
Hartmann, H., 286
Hayford, H., 67n.
Healey, G., 136n.
Hemingway, E., 22
Hendry, I., 134n.
Hoffman, F., 287
Hofling, C., 254 and n., 266n.
Holinshed, R., 272n.
Holland, N., 16n., 18–20, 288, 289
Homosexuality, 34–35, 48n., 75, 82–83, 99, 108, 109n., 111, 113, 126, 129–131, 148, 158, 175–179, 186, 193–